The
EXODUS

ALSO BY
RICHARD ELLIOTT FRIEDMAN

The Exile and Biblical Narrative

Who Wrote the Bible?

The Disappearance of God

The Hidden Book in the Bible

Commentary on the Torah

The Bible with Sources Revealed

The Bible Now, with Shawna Dolansky

The
EXODUS

RICHARD ELLIOTT
FRIEDMAN

HarperOne
An Imprint of HarperCollinsPublishers

HarperOne

The author is grateful for permission to include the following previously copyrighted material:

> Excerpts from "Love Your Neighbor—Only Israelites or Everyone?" *Biblical Archaeology Review* (September/October 2014): 48–52.

> Excerpts from "The Exodus Is Not Fiction" (published as an interview), *Reform Judaism* (Spring 2014): 6–8, 60.

> Excerpts from "Parashat Beshalach: 'The Historical Exodus: The Evidence for the Levites Leaving Egypt and the Introduction of YHWH into Israel,'" TheTorah.com (January 2015), http://thetorah.com/the-historical-exodus.

> Excerpts from "Parashat Qedoshim: 'The Exodus, the Alien, and the Neighbor,'" TheTorah.com (May 2017), http://thetorah.com/the-exodus-the -alien-and-the-neighbor.

> Excerpts from "Does Israel Have No Roots There in History?" *Huffington Post,* October 13, 2012.

All Bible translations from the Hebrew are by the author.

FIRST HARPERCOLLINS PAPERBACK EDITION PUBLISHED IN 2018

Designed by SBI Book Arts, LLC

Library of Congress Cataloging-in-Publication Data is available upon request.

ISBN 978-0-06-256525-9

HB 06.23.2023

For my wife, Janet, with love

CONTENTS

❦◀ ACKNOWLEDGMENTS ▶❦

In past books I expressed my good fortune to have had teachers and friends who were among the greats. I was touched and taught by more wise and learned souls than a person has a right to have in a lifetime. Now their entire generation has passed, and the first part of my acknowledgments has become an *In Memoriam*. They are:

Ernst Pinhas Blumenthal, wise educator

Frank Moore Cross, biblical scholar

Mary Douglas, anthropologist

John Emerton, biblical scholar

Louis Finkelstein, scholar and Chancellor of the Jewish Theological Seminary

David Noel Freedman, biblical scholar

Sir Martin Gilbert, historian

Nahum Glatzer, philosopher

Moshe Goshen–Gottstein, philologian

Moshe Greenberg, biblical scholar

Menahem Haran, biblical scholar

Thorkild Jacobsen, Assyriologist

Mordecai Kaplan, scholar of Judaism

Jerome and Miriam Katzin, who endowed my chair at the University of California and taught me much about life along the way

Walter Kohn, physicist, Nobel Laureate

Abraham Malamat, historian

Arnaldo Momigliano, historian

William Moran, Assyriologist

Yochanan Muffs, biblical scholar

Frank Nelson, debate teacher and coach

Jacob Neusner, scholar of Judaism

Yigal Shiloh, archaeologist

Melford Spiro, anthropologist

Hayim Tadmor, historian

Shemaryahu Talmon, biblical scholar

Geza Vermes, historian of religion

Moshe Weinfeld, biblical scholar

G. Ernest Wright, archaeologist and biblical scholar

All are gone now, as is my wife Randy Linda Sturman, law-yer, anthropologist, teacher, my *basherte,* whose influence was the deepest and most pervasive of all.

—∞∞∞—

The second half of my acknowledgments is to the living. What a strange feeling it is that I share with some of my colleagues, that we are the old guys now. I wish them: to 120. And I am grateful to:

Ike Williams, of Kneerim and Williams, my new literary agent whose skills amaze me.

Mickey Maudlin, my superb editor at HarperOne, and the smart, professional team at HarperOne.

The University of Georgia, my students, and my welcoming colleagues in the Department of Religion, who gave me a new home and a new energy for teaching and research for ten years after my retiring from the University of California.

Ann and Jay Davis, who endowed my professorship at the University of Georgia.

Baruch Halpern, still the unsurpassed historian in our field.

Ronald Hendel, who read and commented on the entire manuscript.

Thomas Lambdin, a teacher from my days as a graduate student whose generosity, wisdom, and wit stay with me.

Paul Wolpe, who amiably and collegially set me on the trail of the genetic evidence concerning the Levites.

Alice Hoffman, on whose novel the *Dovekeepers* I had the pleasure of consulting.

John Buffalo Mailer, my professional partner and invigorating friend in television and books.

My blessed children Jesse and Alexa, and Jesse's loving husband Nick.

My partner in life, my wife Janet. We came together after we each had a terrible loss of a beloved spouse, and she has brought me comfort, partnership, love, and a tremendous new community of family and friends.

I had the opportunity to test and refine these ideas in lectures at Harvard University, the University of North Carolina at Chapel Hill, the University of California, San Diego, Wright State University, Southern Methodist University, Mercer University, the University of Haifa, the University of Georgia, at Limmud conferences at the University of Warwick, England, and at Ramah Darom in Georgia, at the Biblical Archaeology Society, at the Society of Biblical Literature, and at the Rabbinical Assembly at their annual convention. I am grateful to these institutions for their kind hospitality.

The
EXODUS

INTRODUCTION

History's a thing not easily captured
And once deceased not easily exhumed.

—R. E. Friedman's misquotation
of Dan Fogelberg

Three questions: Is the exodus from Egypt a story—or history? How did monotheism, the idea of there being only one God, come about? What person or events gave us the idea that we should love others as ourselves? Three mysteries. Or one.

It is 1956, I am ten years old, and I am standing in line to see the opening of the movie *The Ten Commandments*. My passion with the exodus must have kicked in even before that day because I already knew the story by the time I saw the film, and that passion has not ended. As for the film, it was a wonder to the ten-year-old. I was short and had big eyes and was overwhelmed like everyone else looking up at the scene of the Red Sea splitting. About forty years later (a biblical number), when I had become a biblical scholar, I was a consultant on another movie about the exodus, *The Prince of Egypt*. Jeffrey Katzenberg at Dreamworks graciously allowed me to bring my daughter to one of the sessions at the studio. She was about the age that I had been when I had seen *The Ten Commandments,* so I met the story again through a child's eyes.

There has been a surge of interest in the exodus lately: live movies, animated movies, books, cover stories in magazines, archaeological surveys and excavations, conferences, lectures, sermons, debates, documentaries, online videos. And the quantity of interest means a quantity of different treatments at a quantity of different levels. You can find everything from nutty "theories" to serious, respectable scholarship. People blow small items out of proportion. People focus on items of evidence without taking into account other evidence that challenges or outweighs those points. People deny that it happened. People insist that it happened. People say that it happened but not the way the Bible tells it.

The exodus is the story of the birth of a nation—and the birth of some cornerstone ideas. Practically everything that follows it in the Bible flows from it: the greatest concentration of miracles in the Bible, the first statement of the Ten Commandments ("I am the Lord your God who brought you out of the land of Egypt"), the introduction of Moses as well as Aaron and Miriam, the early great prophets, and the first priests. William Propp, possibly the preeminent scholar of the biblical book of Exodus, says it simply in his two-volume commentary: "The story of Israel's flight from Egypt is the most important in the Hebrew Bible."[1] Scholars have written thousands of articles and books about it. Biblical scholars, Egyptologists, archaeologists, linguists, historians, literary scholars, geologists, anthropologists: people from practically every background have been drawn to it. Millions of people tell it and retell it and celebrate it and teach it to their children. And we do not even know if it really *happened.*

This is truly frustrating. Until very recently we had the same situation with the Bible's King David. David is, after all, the only figure in the Hebrew Bible who compares to Moses, both in the sheer amount of the texts about him and in the degree of development of his life and character. Some said that there was no such person, no such kingdom, no royal house of David. But then we found two references to kings of the House of David in ancient texts,[2] and also our work in the City of David Project archaeological excavations of Jerusalem—in which my students and I joined the virtuoso archaeologist Yigal Shiloh—along with subsequent excavations, uncovered monumental architecture from David's period.[3] So now there have been a host of books about David, so many that one can hardly choose which to read.[4] Archaeology and skilled historical detective work have accomplished a great deal toward solving the David problem. But the exodus problem has remained.

The Bible's story of the exodus was always on the menu in my introductory courses on the Hebrew Bible, and I wrote in detail about that story in my *Commentary on the Torah:* the meaning, the artistry, the character of Moses, the connection with other parts of the Bible. But I had little to say as a scholar about the exodus itself, the real exodus, the historical event, whatever that was, behind the Bible's story. I knew that many of my colleagues in Bible studies and most of my colleagues in archaeology doubt, or even deny, that it happened. That never felt right to me.

The event figures centrally in the very earliest texts of prose, poetry, and law in the Bible. And those texts seem to refer to something with which their audiences are already familiar. And beyond this, a scholar, like a detective, has to rely to some extent on his or her instincts. My great teacher, Frank Moore Cross, the Hancock Professor of Hebrew at Harvard, was a model for his students of an intuitive scholar. Sometimes while he was still working on a problem he could make the leap to a solution. As he went on to test the solution, in some cases his intuition proved to be right. In some cases it turned out to be wrong. In some cases he left it to his students to work out the evidence that would prove it right or wrong. But we learned to respect and admire his intuitive scholarship, and we learned how much or how little each of us was able to trust our own intuition as we worked on our own challenges.

My intuition was always that there was something histori-cal behind the exodus story. Probably this intuition came partly from that kid in line back in 1956, who renewed his attraction to the exodus through his own kid's eyes decades later. And it came partly from a sense that there was something in all the different bodies of facts that would eventually come together. That kid still thinks that something really happened in Egypt around thirty-three hundred years ago. Together with some superb fellow detectives, scholars from many countries, in dif-ferent fields, it took forty years of studies (still a biblical number) to work it out sufficiently to formulate it in writing. Studies of literature and history, archaeology, art, architecture, genet-ics, linguistics, cultural anthropology, and, not to leave out the obvious, religion—all of these separate kinds of evidence came together in just the last few years for us all to see.

Let me ask you a question. Before you set out on this sea of evidence, what is your intuition? If you are a person of faith, this is not a question about what your faith tells you. If you are a person of facts and reason, this is not a question about what your intellect tells you. This is not a question about opinion. This is a question about what your gut tells you. What does your in-tuition say: that something happened in Egypt, or that nothing happened? And if your answer was "Why should I care?" then the objective of this book has to be to show you what probably happened and also to show you why it matters.

This book is a work of detective nonfiction. But I am going to give away where it is headed. I believe we can get at what probably took place in Egypt over three millennia ago. That would be a lot. But we have much more. We have evidence that without the historical anchor of the exodus, we would not have had the rise of the idea of monotheism. And without the experience of that returning group from Egypt, we might not have had the ethic of caring for the stranger. Monotheism and loving others as ourselves—two radical developments, *major* developments, in human consciousness became embodied in the heart of Western religion.

Whether one is a monotheist, a polytheist, an atheist, an agnostic, or an observer from another planet, one can recognize the significance of monotheism as a stage in the human adventure here on earth. And whether one is an ethicist, a politician, a minister, a rabbi, or just any decent human being, one can estimate the value of humans' arrival at the idea of loving others as ourselves. Without the exodus we might have arrived at these ideas much later, or in a much different form, or not at all. Those are the stakes here: a story, history, and immense consequences.

CHAPTER ONE

HISTORY RECAPTURED

FIRST: THE STORY

It is a fabulous story, one of the best we have. A kingdom over-powers a community of aliens in their country. The kingdom enslaves the aliens, and they kill their male children. But one baby survives, a princess takes him in as her own, and he grows up in royalty. As an adult, he kills a man who is assaulting one of his people, and when his manslaughter becomes known he flees to another land. There he rescues a priest's daughters, and he stays in that land, marries one of the daughters, has sons, and lives tending flocks. And then he encounters God.

Miracles occur. A mountain of God. A miraculous fire. An angel. The man's staff becomes a snake, then turns back as it was. The man's hand becomes leprous, then turns back as it was. And during all this, God speaks, telling the man that God will free the enslaved people and that the man must be the one to carry it out. He must go back. And God reveals His name to him: Yahweh.

He returns. He faces the king. The king declines to let the people leave. The man initiates divinely ordered miracles: signs and wonders, ten plagues on the kingdom, on land and water and even blacking out the sun, suffering for humans and animals and plants, and, finally, death, but only to firstborn humans and animals. The king yields. The freed people leave the kingdom. The king has a change of heart, and he and his army pursue them to the sea. But the sea splits, they pass through it, and it closes on the pursuing army. The people then trust in God and in the man, and they sing.

More stories will follow. The people will go to the mountain of God and will all encounter God. More miracles. More struggles. Covenant with God. Laws. A journey to their ancestors' homeland. Then the man will die, and a new man will lead them there. But all of these stories depend on and flow out of what happened with the man, Moses, and the departure, the exodus, from that kingdom, Egypt.

SECOND: THE HISTORY

Is any of this true? Is it subject to evidence and reasoning, or is it strictly a matter of each person's religious conviction? In the last couple of decades an array of scholars, archaeologists, and clergy have seriously questioned whether this happened. This is not a tiny little academic spat. This is about two million people. The text says 603,550 adult male Israelites, plus the women and children, leave Egypt.[1] If the Bible has this wrong, how did it get it *this* wrong? These scholars, clergy, and laypersons were right to question the Bible. Questioning is a healthy thing to do. But were they in fact correct in this case? Was there really no exodus?

Some will say: It does not matter if it is historical or not. What matters is what it has meant, the exodus' meaning to religion over the centuries. That is a lovely thought. I used to say it sometimes myself. But nowadays I find myself saying: Whom are we kidding? We want to know if it happened, or if what people have been believing for millennia is an illusion, an invention. It matters plenty to people whether it happened or not. There is an anti-historical wind blowing lately. People claim that we cannot really recover what happened in the past: we do not have history. But something happened. We can recover some of it from real evidence and reasoning. There are other parts of it that we cannot exhume. We also happen to have some great stories about it, a fabulous narrative. We have both, and we can study both: history and narrative. They are both great enterprises—as long as you tell people which you are doing at the time. And let us say that we investigate the history, and we find that 20 percent of it is true, or 10 percent of it is true, or that none of it is true. Then how did we get these stories? They are not like Cinderella. They are not merely entertainments. The authors wrote the exodus account as part of their nation's history, and millions of people have taken it as history for thousands of years. What was happening in their world that made them tell the story this way?

This is the process of literary-historical method. We can read a story that we think is fiction, or even know to be fiction, and still extract historical information from it. At a meeting on the exodus in San Diego (see below), the American biblical historian Baruch Halpern stirred things up saying that the Bible's story of the exodus should be read as a fairy tale. My wife's reaction was precisely to look at a fairy tale: Cinderella. It has mice become horses, a pumpkin become a coach, and a poor oppressed girl become a princess because a glass shoe fits only her. The story is fiction. It is not history. But the element of the shoe at least reflects that shoes were a real thing in the culture that produced that story. Everyone who heard the story understood it. So eliminate much of the biblical story from the category of history if you wish. The ten plagues may be a fairy tale. The staff that becomes a snake may be a fairy tale. But we shall see that the exodus itself is not the fairy tale. It is the shoes.

And here is the pot of gold at the end of this particular historical rainbow: we do not have to choose between recapturing the history and caring about the values we might derive from the exodus. Once we exhume the history, we shall find, more intensely, more vividly, more *really* than before, the meanings that people can derive, the fruits that those events bequeathed for all the centuries that followed since then.

It is ironic—no?—that at the same time that an upsurge of exodus movies and books were coming out, the doubts about the whole thing were rising. But those doubts have led to new research and new findings.

How did we get to this point? First we had to arrive at a mindset at which we were ready to address this. Discoveries concerning evolution in biology, discoveries about the age of the earth in geology, about the origin of the universe in astronomy and cosmology, and about the background of the Bible itself in critical biblical scholarship and archaeology: all of these unlatched the gates so people could question the history behind the Bible's stories—the patriarchs, the exodus, the kings, the priests, the miracles.

ENTER ARCHAEOLOGY

When biblical archaeology came along, at first it appeared to be an antidote to the doubts that these questions had raised. Starting with excavations in the nineteenth century, it flourished by the 1920s and onward to the present minute. Especially in the work of the father of this field in America, William Foxwell

Albright, and his student and successor George Ernest Wright, who was my teacher, people were getting a message that archaeology was confirming much of the Bible.[2] This made people in the Christian and Jewish communities trust archaeology rather than see it as a threat. But then, in more recent years, archaeology started to reveal things about both sides, sometimes confirming and often seriously challenging people's beliefs about the Bible's reports. By then, though, conservative religious communities had proudly praised archaeology's results, so now they were bound to argue its findings, both positive and negative, in its own terms.

And then, in fairly quick succession, a series of things happened.

A new generation of archaeologists and biblical scholars disputed Albright's and others' approach and conclusions as an insufficiently critical acceptance of evidence that did not actually confirm the Bible's story.[3] And then this spilled over into the popular realm.

A distinguished Egyptologist, Donald Redford, wrote in a 1992 book that, instead of having ever made an exodus from Egypt, the Israelites had made the story up out of Canaanite folklore. He wrote:

> The Exodus was part and parcel of an array of "origin" stories to which the Hebrews fell heir upon their settlement of the land, and which, lacking traditions of their own, they appropriated from the earlier culture they were copying.[4]

A Bible professor at a Reform rabbinical seminary, David Sperling, taught his students—future rabbis—for years that the exodus did not happen, and he made his case in a 1998 book.[5] He wrote:

The evidence from archaeology has been decisive. The traditions of servitude in Egypt, the tales of wandering in the desert, and the stories of the conquest of the promised land appear to be fictitious.

A Conservative rabbi in Los Angeles, David Wolpe, said in a sermon in 2001, on *Passover!*:

The truth is that virtually every modern archaeologist who has investigated the story of the Exodus, with very few exceptions, agrees that the way the Bible describes the Exodus is not the way it happened, if it happened at all.

This was not a shock to anybody in the field, not to scholars or to lots of clergy. But it was news to the wider community and to the media, who were intrigued by it. And those last words, "if it happened at all," especially put an exclamation mark on it even though he did not actually say that it did not happen.

That same year a historian and archaeologist, who also was a rabbi, Lee Levine, wrote an essay that was included in a new volume that was to be in the pews of practically every Conservative synagogue in America.[6] After noting some points of evidence that fit with the possible milieu of the exodus, Levine concluded:

These few indirect pieces of evidence are far from adequate to corroborate the historicity of the biblical account, but they do suggest a contextual background for the Egyptian servitude (of at least some of the people who later became Israelites) and the appearance

of a new population in Canaan. Nevertheless, it also
has been maintained that here too, as in the patriarchal era, later writers used earlier material to present
an account of what in reality was a folk tradition with
little or no historical basis.

This too stirred a strong reaction and treatment in the media.

Also in that same year the archaeologist Israel Finkelstein and
the writer/archaeologist Neil Silberman wrote a book for laypersons, *The Bible Unearthed,*[7] which asked, "Was a Mass Exodus
even possible in the time of Ramesses II?"[8] And they concluded,
"One can hardly accept the idea of a flight of a large group of
slaves from Egypt."[9]

Also in 2001 the American archaeologist William Dever
wrote a series of books for laypersons, starting with *What Did
the Biblical Writers Know and When Did They Know It?* Dever and
Finkelstein were famously on opposite sides on a lot of things.
But they were not far apart on the exodus. Dever wrote:

> Archaeological investigation of Moses and the Exo-
> dus has been discarded as a fruitless pursuit. Indeed,
> the overwhelming archaeological evidence today of
> largely indigenous origins for early Israel leaves no
> room for an exodus from Egypt or a 40-year pilgrim-
> age through the Sinai wilderness. A Moses-like figure
> may have existed. . . . But archaeology can do nothing
> to confirm such a figure as a historical personage.[10]

No exodus, no evidence, probably no Moses.

How did this happen? How did we shift from "archaeology
proves the Bible" to "archaeology disproves the exodus" in just

a few decades? What changed? We can say that it was partly the natural pattern that we see in archaeology. A new discovery gets attention and headlines. Then things slow down, and we examine the discovery and what it implies more slowly and critically. This process can lead us to refine, reaffirm, or reverse what we thought at first. And another part of this shift was just the politics of the field. Those who leaned toward archaeology got tired of seeing themselves in the service of those who leaned toward the Bible. The very phrase "Biblical Archaeology" became unwelcome. Now it was "Syro-Palestinian Archaeology" (which is not accurate since the term Syria did not come into use in place of Aram, and Palestine did not come into use in place of Israel and Judah, until the Roman period[11]) or "Archaeology of the Levant" (but most people had no idea what the Levant was) or whatever. As one who had a foot in both text and archaeology, I was sympathetic to my archaeological colleagues for wanting to carve out something of their own. But the result, in this particular case, was that archaeologists were making judgments without awareness of the evidence that we could derive scientifically from biblical research. And, ironically, Bible scholars like Sperling and rabbis like Wolpe and others, to whom the archaeology sounded persuasive, sincerely accepted what the archaeologists were claiming.

THE WAY IT IS TOLD IN THE BIBLE

Now, while these books and sermons and other examples were in the news and in the pews, making it seem to the public like we had obviously rejected the exodus as historical, many scholars in the field still went about their work, with the evidence still persuading them that the exodus was indeed real. The Israeli biblical historian Abraham Malamat concluded in a paper presented at Brown University in 1992 that, in the light of texts showing Egyptian analogies, the biblical event was likely.[12] A Dutch scholar, Johannes de Moor, independently came to the same conclusion based on the same texts.[13] And more conservative scholars, like Bible scholar James Hoffmeier in the United States and Egyptologist K. A. Kitchen in England, argued the case for a historical exodus as well.[14] Some archaeologists had said, "We've combed the Sinai and didn't find anything." But an Israeli archaeologist laughed at that claim and told me, "It was five jeeps." It was a survey, not an excavation of the whole Sinai Peninsula. Moreover, even if we *had* excavated the whole Sinai, what could we find that people traveling from Egypt to Israel around thirty-three hundred years ago would have left that we would dig up now? A piece of petrified wood with "Moses loves Zipporah" carved in it? An Israeli archaeologist told me that a vehicle that was lost in Sinai in the 1973 war was found recently under sixteen meters of sand. Sixteen meters down in forty years (a biblical number)! Finding objects thirty-three hundred years down presents a rather harder challenge. And, above all, our archaeological work did not turn up evidence to show that an exodus did not happen. What it turned up was *nothing,* an absence of evidence. And some archaeologists then interpreted this nothing to be proof that the event did not happen. On the other side, people who challenged such interpretations were fond of quoting the old principle: "Absence of evidence is not evidence of absence."

While the publicized brouhaha was going on, academic books and articles and conferences were treating the subject as well. When the University of California, San Diego, held a major conference on the exodus in 2013, the impressive list of forty-five participants included men and women from several continents and all kinds of backgrounds: biblical scholars, archaeologists, Egyptologists, geologists, oceanographers.[15] Questioning the exodus had gone global. (Listening to forty-five papers in three days! Mothers, don't let your children grow up to be scholars.) Most sober of all the scholarship was William Propp's thorough treatment of the historical, archaeological, and textual evidence in his masterful two-volume commentary on the book of Exodus for the Anchor Bible series in 1998 and 2006.[16] It was remarkable as an even-handed treatment of the arguments and evidence on many sides, academically sound while written in language that both scholars and the general public can appreciate.

I was drawn in as well. I had been doing research and writing on the Bible's sources and their authors for about forty years (a biblical number).[17] I thought that I had moved on from biblical source criticism to other things, but, like Michael Corleone in *Godfather III,* just when I think I'm out, they pull me back in! First, UCSD invited me back for that conference. I had spent thirty years there in San Diego until the University of Georgia made me an offer I couldn't refuse. But I would never reject an invitation back to that Garden of Eden in Southern California. You can check out any time you like, but you can never leave.

And then Harvard invited me to give a seminar back in Cambridge, Massachusetts. It had been thirty-eight years since I had left my doctoral program there and moved to San Diego for my first job. After thirty-eight years of waiting to be invited back, I could hardly decline. So I went and gave a paper on the exodus as a trial run before the San Diego forty-five.

And then, the clincher: In 2013, *Reform Judaism* magazine came out with the heading "We Were Not Slaves in Egypt" on the cover. It contained excerpts from Sperling's and Wolpe's publications. But it came out just before Passover. I, for one, was troubled that this was informing an audience of about a million Reform Jews that the exodus was not real just before they sat down with their children on Passover eve to celebrate the holiday. I expressed my concern, and the magazine's editors kindly let me write something as well. So one year later, just before the next Passover, *Reform Judaism* magazine appeared with my article. This time the heading on the cover was "The Exodus Is Not Fiction." The next thing I knew, I was invited to debate with Sperling at Temple Emanu-El in New York. I could not say no. It is the biggest synagogue in the western hemisphere.

I had no quarrel with Sperling or Wolpe about any research or discoveries of theirs. I just felt that they had too readily accepted the authority of some archaeologists. (Wolpe cautiously said that the archaeologists agree that the exodus did not happen "the way the Bible describes" it. Sperling went the whole way and said the exodus is "fictitious.")

The question to both the archaeologists and those who followed them is: are they saying that the Bible's multi-miracle, multi-million-people, multi-year story did not happen as written? Or are they saying that *nothing* happened?

If they mean the former, that "it did not happen *the way it is told in the Bible*," well what do they mean by that? In the Bible, staffs turn to reptiles, the sun goes dark for three days, a destroyer mysteriously kills only firstborn animals and humans in Egypt, and it halts at the homes of people who smear blood on their doorposts. And then there is the matter of the Red (not Reed[18]) Sea splitting into walls of water. Whether one believes these things or not, archaeology has nothing to do with it. Archaeology has not proven any of the miracles of the Bible's exodus story to be true or false.

The archaeologist Eric Cline summed this up well and succinctly:

> We do not have a single shred of evidence to date. There is nothing [available] archaeologically to attest to anything from the biblical story. No plagues, no parting of the Red Sea, no manna from heaven, no wandering for 40 years. However, I should add that there is also no archaeological evidence that proves it did not take place. So at this point in time, *the archaeological record can neither be used to confirm nor deny the existence of the Exodus.*[19]
>
> (emphasis added)

So what are the discoveries that made writers think that we now had proof that it did not happen *the way it is told in the Bible*? In a way, this is a variation on people who account for a biblical miracle by saying it happened, only differently:

"The Red Sea did not split into two walls of water; it was the tides." Actually, there are no tides on the Red Sea. Tides (of significant size) are only on the oceans.

"The darkening of the sun was an eclipse." Eclipses do not last for three days. Now one might say that maybe they exaggerated a normal solar eclipse and claimed that it was three days. But how does that solve anything? Solar eclipses occur in every year. Taking a normal event and turning it into something miraculous is, in effect, no different than just making up the miraculous event altogether.

"The firstborn had the richest diet, so they got illnesses and died." Outside of the fact that this argument is just plain ridiculous on the face of it, the firstborn *animals* die in the story as well.

And it all happens in one night. And firstborn people with blood on the doorposts do not die.

Some tried to account for the huge number of 603,550 males (hence two million) by asserting that the Hebrew word for "thousand" (*'eleph*) actually means "clan."[20] But in over 250 occurrences in the Hebrew Bible the word *'eleph* regularly means thousands and is joined alongside the word for hundreds in giving total numbers. And the number of *firstborn* Israelite males in the biblical census is 22,273 (Numbers 3:43). Since firstborn sons as a group do not constitute clans, this confirms that those who take the word for "thousand" in the census to mean "clan" are mistaken. Those who try to understand this term as "clan" do this presumably because they are troubled by the high numbers of Israelites in the census in Numbers. But we cannot escape the problem by redefining a term.[21]

Some move the chronology of the Pharaohs up or down by centuries to find a coordination between the exodus and various other events and references. But, as we shall see below, such recalculations are unnecessary to account for the timing of the exodus.

And then there are the Thera theories. (It has great alliteration if nothing else.) A tremendous volcanic eruption occurred at Thera on what is now the island of Santorini in around the seventeenth or sixteenth century BCE. Some have suggested that its plume of smoke could have inspired the Bible's account of a column of cloud and fire that led the Israelites from Egypt to the promised land. Some have suggested that the smoke is connected to the Bible's account of the darkening of the sun. Some have suggested that the eruption caused a tsunami that affected the Red Sea. But we could ask: where is there more proof that any of these possibilities happened than the biblical stories anyway?

Mark Harris, of the University of Edinburgh, made this point with regard to the various Thera theories. He wrote:

> One thing is clear: the Thera theories are following a trajectory towards increasingly complex naturalistic scenarios while the historical, theological and textual questions raised by critical scholarship are largely overlooked.[22]

That is, they connect possible big natural events to splitting seas and darkening skies and plagues without taking account of how those stories are composite (i.e., with no awareness of who wrote the Bible and its sources[23]), or that there is a nonmiraculous portion to those sources that is more believable than the Thera stretches of imagination. And that is not to mention that the Thera eruption, coming in the seventeenth or sixteenth century BCE, was way too early to have had anything to do with the exodus. Harris puts it mildly when he says,

> Serious difficulties are identified with the Thera theories.[24]

There is not much point in saying that *something* happened but that it was different from how the Bible tells it, unless we can figure out what that something was. So it still comes down to this: What happened? And what is the connection between what happened and the way that the Bible's authors wrote the story? That is where the historical study and the literary study of the Bible come together. And that is what has gradually been mounting up, especially in recent decades. For too long our field was made up of Bible scholars who were not trained in archaeology or historical method. And then for too long we leaned on archaeologists who were not trained in biblical texts, their history, language, and authorship. Albright's ideal was that eventually the two would work together. My teacher George Ernest Wright was Albright's student and successor and was the leading American biblical archaeologist of his day. The interesting thing is that he was also the leading American Old Testament theologian at the same time.[25] He never saw the two—archaeology and theology—as unrelated or in competition. I think that is how I learned that both text and archaeology can go together. The two separated for a while, but their inevitable reunion has begun to happen. We can read a story closely, excavate the earth carefully, and figure out what happened that led to that story. And one of the first fruits of this high-yield merger of literary study, historical study, and archaeology is a grasp of what happened in Egypt all those years ago, the story behind the story.

The investigation of this mystery is a time machine. We can look back and see what happened some thirty-three hundred years ago. Then we can move through time and watch the story evolve. And in the end, I think we shall stand in awe at how it still informs us and has willed to us some of our most precious values. The event and the story are thousands of years old, but they can still enrich and preserve us in our precarious times.

CHAPTER TWO

THE MYSTERY OF EGYPT

*How Do Two Million
People Disappear?*

A SMALLER EXODUS?

The principal points that people generally bring up in doubting the exodus are mostly about numbers: We have found no remnant of the two million people in the Sinai region. We have found no widespread material culture of Egypt in early Israel: no Egyptian style pottery or architecture. We have found no records in Egypt of a huge mass of Israelite slaves or of a huge exodus.

True. But none of this is evidence about whether the exodus happened or not. It is evidence only of whether it was big or not. For heaven's sake, did we need archaeological work to confirm that an exodus of two million people was, shall we say, problematic? It had already been calculated long ago that if the people were marching, say, eight across, then when the first ones got to Mount Sinai, half of the people were still in Egypt. And I think it was Bishop Colenso who calculated around 150 years ago the amount of, let us say delicately, residue that that many people would have deposited in the Sinai over a period of forty years, and he figured that the Sinai wilderness should be fertile! Did we really need archaeologists combing the Sinai and not finding anything to prove what we knew anyway? The absence of exodus and wilderness artifacts questions only whether there was a massive exodus.

Part of being a scholar-detective is learning what questions to ask. If there were two million people, how did they disappear? If the answer is that they could not just disappear, then the question is why and when would somebody make them up? If numbers figure so much in the argument, then the question is not just why would someone make up the exodus, but why would someone make it an exodus of two million persons?

Would it be a wild and crazy idea if we consider the possibility that the exodus happened but that it was not big?

One thing that came out at the San Diego conference and in published articles and books in our field was: we nearly all recognize that there were Western Asiatic people in Egypt.[1] Call them Asiatics, Semites, Canaanites, Levantine peoples. But whatever we call them, these aliens were there, for hundreds of years. The literature on this is voluminous. They were everything from lower class and slaves (called variously Shasu, 'Apiru, Habiru) to a dynasty of Pharaohs (the Hyksos, the Fifteenth Dynasty). And they were coming and going all along, just not in millions at a time.[2] We could say: there were many *"exoditos."* The idea that our exodus was one of these is well within reason. The archaeologist Avi Faust put that line about the exodus not happening the way the Bible tells it into this context, writing:

> While there is a consensus among scholars that the Exodus did not take place in the manner described in the Bible, surprisingly *most scholars agree that the narrative has a historical core, and that some of the highland settlers came, one way or another, from Egypt.*

Faust cites twenty such scholars.[3]

Even Finkelstein and Silberman, who had done so much to raise doubts about a *massive* exodus,[4] still wrote:

> One thing is certain. The basic situation described in the Exodus saga—the phenomenon of immigrants coming down to Egypt from Canaan and settling in the eastern border regions of the delta—is abundantly verified in the archaeological finds and the historical texts.[5]

Lee Levine, too, in the passage I quoted above, referred to the possible cultural background for

> the Egyptian servitude (of at least some of the people who later became Israelites).[6]

Wolpe followed the scholars on this as well:

> The probability is, given the traditions, that there were some enslaved Israelites who left Egypt and joined up with their brethren in Canaan. This seems the likeliest scenario.[7]

And James Hoffmeier, in his survey of responses from twenty-five Egyptologists from eleven countries, wrote:

> Those who offered additional thoughts indicated that given the regularity of Asiatics, to use the Egyptian term, entering Egypt during the days of famine or drought in the Levant it was likely that the biblical Hebrews were one such group.[8]

Verified immigrants from Canaan in Egypt, "the regularity of Asiatics . . . entering Egypt," "*some* of the . . . settlers," "at least *some* of the people," "*some* enslaved Israelites," "one such group." Alright, then, maybe we are looking for one particular group among the many immigrants from and back to Asia. But who could this "one such group" have been? Back in 1987 in *Who Wrote the Bible?* I included the possibility that it was just the Levites.[9] The Levites were the group who later became the priests of Israel and some of the main authors of the Bible. The Bible identifies them as the group that was connected with Moses and his family. The story says that both his mother and his father were Levites.[10] What if it was just the Levites who made the flight from Egypt? I wrote there that this idea about the Levites was "in the realm of hypothesis, and we must be very cautious about it." That was to convey the caution with which I always urge my readers to examine new hypotheses. But it has now been thirty years (not a biblical number) that we have had to think, research, and consult with colleagues, and there is new evidence to take into account, and so I am vastly more confident of the situation now. My field has come a long way since 1987. It is very exciting. I hope that the evidence, when it is fully assembled here together with the other works that I cite, will tantalize many readers as it has tantalized me. I recall that Professor Baruch Halpern, now my colleague at the University of Georgia, wrote a book on *The Emergence of Israel in Canaan* in which he said:

> Biblical scholarship is no more methodologically equipped to reconstruct the exodus than is America's National Aeronautics and Space Administration technologically equipped to send video probes to the

Alpha Centauri system. The period of the judges, like Pluto or Uranus, presents a more realistic, if still elusive, target.[11]

He thus explained why he chose to focus his work a little later, on the period of the judges (the twelfth and eleventh centuries BCE), rather than to go as far back as the exodus. He wrote this in 1983. In 1986 the Voyager 2 spacecraft flew by Uranus. In 2015 the New Horizons spacecraft flew by Pluto. And in 2013 the Hubble telescope sent back photographs of the Alpha Centauri system. I am sure that Halpern would be delighted with these developments. My point is how quickly the rate of new developments has accelerated in recent decades. All of us in this generation have seen it in hundreds of ways, in all areas of knowledge and research. That goes for the Bible and archaeology too. We have new tools, new findings, and new answers.

THE LEVITES AND THE EXODUS

Archaeological findings alone did not do it. What is it that we biblical scholars bring to enrich what we have found through archaeology? Answer: the text. What evidence can we derive from the text about who were the ones who made the exodus from Egypt? I mean real textual evidence, not just reading the Bible and taking its word for it that sticks became snakes and seas split. And how does this textual evidence connect with the archaeological evidence? And I mean real archaeological evidence— findings, artifacts, material culture, *stuff*—not just surveys that did not turn up anything. What evidence shows that the group that left Egypt over three thousand years ago were the Levites?

1. *What's in a Name?*

Only Levites have Egyptian names. Hophni, Hur, two men named Phinehas, Merari, Mushi, Pashhur, and, above all, Moses are Egyptian names.[12] But *all* of these biblical persons are Levites, and not one person from any of the rest of Israel has an Egyptian name. We in North America, lands of immigrants, especially are aware of the significance of what names tell about a person's background. Friedman: probably a Jewish American whose family came from the Austro-Hungarian empire. Shaughnessy: probably not a Jewish American from the Austro-Hungarian empire. Now there are exceptions in North American names. Not every Friedman is Jewish, and not every Shaughnessy is Irish. But we have no exceptions in biblical Israel. Moses, Phinehas, and the rest of the eight persons with Egyptian names are all from the Levite/priestly group. And no one else, from all the names mentioned in the Bible from all of Israel's tribes, has an Egyptian name.[13]

Now we must ask if perhaps the Bible's authors invented these Egyptian names precisely to help make the story of Egypt and the exodus look believable. But (a) this still begs the question of why all the named figures are Levites; no one invented a single Egyptian name for anybody else in the story. (b) The Egyptian names appear in texts from at least twenty different authors and editors, spread out over five hundred years.[14] These authors and editors did not all work together to invent this. People say that the Bible is the only book ever successfully written by a committee, but we also note that this is probably because the committee never held a meeting. And we cannot attribute all the Egyptian names to an editor (usually referred to as a redactor) who threw them in when he assembled the text. We know this because no single person edited all of these texts. The Pentateuch (Genesis to Deuteronomy), the Deuteronomistic history (Deuteronomy to 2 Kings), the Psalms, the prophets, and the Chronicler's history (1 and 2 Chronicles, Ezra, and Nehemiah) were all edited at different times by different people. (c) We can know for a fact that it cannot be that the authors deliberately gave characters Egyptian names in order to fool us. How? Because we can see where the authors themselves did not know that the names were Egyptian. This is apparent in one of the most famous stories in the Bible: the baby in the basket.

It is the story of Moses' birth. The Pharaoh has decreed the death of the slaves' newborn males. A Levite woman places her baby son in an ark of bulrushes sealed with bitumen.

> And she put the boy in it and put it in the reeds by the bank of the Nile. And his sister stood still at a distance to know what would be done to him. And the Pharaoh's daughter went down to bathe at the Nile, and her girls were going alongside the Nile, and she saw the ark among the reeds and sent her maid, and she took it. And she opened it and saw him, the child: and here was a boy crying, and she had compassion on him, and she said, "This is one of the Hebrews' children."
>
> And his sister said to Pharaoh's daughter, "Shall I go and call a nursing woman from the Hebrews for you, and she'll nurse the child for you?"
>
> And Pharaoh's daughter said to her, "Go."
>
> And the girl went and called the child's mother. And Pharaoh's daughter said to her, "Take this child

and nurse him for me, and I'll give your pay." And the woman took the boy and nursed him. And the boy grew older, and she brought him to Pharaoh's daughter, and he became her son. And she called his name Moses, and she said, "Because I drew him from the water."

(Exodus 2:3b–10)

Now that is very logical. She called his name Moses—Hebrew *mosheh*—because she drew—Hebrew root *mashah*—him from the water. I have always told my students that the translation of his name in English should be Drew. So it would be that she says, "I'll call his name *Drew,* because I *drew* him from the water." Puns do not usually translate. But this is a really good exception.

But the point is that the author of this story is treating the name Moses as *Hebrew.* The author is manifestly *not* trying to give the hero an Egyptian name. The author rather gives the princess a flair for language. She knows Hebrew exquisitely enough to make Hebrew etymologies when naming a boy. The author either did not know that the name was Egyptian, not Hebrew; or else deliberately was hiding the fact that it was Egyptian, not Hebrew. Either way, we cannot read this story and think that the authors were falsely making up Egyptian names. The Egyptian names are real, native to the text, and they belong only to Levites.

2. Our Earliest Evidence: The Song of the Sea and the Song of Deborah

Which did humans compose first: poetry or prose? I think that most people would be surprised, maybe even incredulous, to learn that we wrote poetry and songs for thousands of years before we wrote any long works of prose (at least any that have survived). That may possibly be because poetry and songs are easier to remember, and this mattered in an age when writing was more difficult and literacy was perhaps less common (though not as uncommon as people sometimes claim). I think I can sing all the words of the Beatles' songbook and maybe a thousand other songs from memory, but I could never learn to recite *The Brothers Karamazov,* which is probably about as long, from memory. Poems, and especially songs, are easier to retain.

And that goes for the Bible as well. Two of the many eminent students whom Albright produced at Johns Hopkins University were Frank Moore Cross and David Noel Freedman. Cross became the Hancock Professor of Hebrew at Harvard. Freedman had chairs at both the University of Michigan and the University of California and became the General Editor of the Anchor Bible, the most successful series of commentaries on the Bible (over three million volumes sold). Cross produced over a hundred PhD students. Freedman produced (wrote or edited) over three hundred books. Now when Frank and Noel were still students at Hopkins, Albright put them together to write two joint PhD dissertations instead of one each. Both dissertations became classics, but one is particularly relevant for our present probe. It was titled *Studies in Ancient Yahwistic Poetry.*[15] Cross and Freedman argued (this was back in the 1940s) that the oldest parts of the Bible were a group of songs. They based this early dating on spelling (orthography), contents, setting, language, and new knowledge from inscriptions that had been discovered (epigraphy). Meanwhile, as they were writing in 1947–1948, a goat made the greatest archaeological discovery of the twentieth century: the Dead Sea Scrolls. Evidence from the scrolls further convinced

Cross and Freedman of their conclusions. I have been listening to challenges to those conclusions since my very first session at my first international conference thirty-five years ago, but Cross and Freedman and others have defended their work, and I think that it has held up.[16] David Noel Freedman wrote in 1997:

> I am as firmly convinced today as I was forty-five years ago that early poems really are early. While it is true that many, perhaps most, serious scholars date this poetry across the whole spectrum of Israelite history, from premonarchic to postexilic, I believe that the whole corpus belongs to the earliest period of Israel's national existence, and that the poems were composed between the twelfth and tenth–ninth centuries BCE. I have encountered neither compelling evidence nor convincing argument to the contrary, or to make me think otherwise.[17]

I do not mean to redo the entire history of this scholarship here. But its relevance to our present questions will be visible and will show that their work on the early poetry and the work on the evidence for the exodus are mutually supporting. Two of the group of old songs are the Song of the Sea (also known as the Song of Miriam) and the Song of Deborah. Noel identified them as the two oldest things in the Bible. They were composed close to the time of the events that they portray. They are written in an early form of Hebrew, and other datable texts use them as sources.[18] Though I mean to make another point, I also cannot help but note that the two earliest texts in the Bible are both associated with women: Miriam and Deborah. Even in our age of interest in matters of gender, this fact continues to go insufficiently appreciated.[19]

What do the songs say? The first, the Song of Miriam, or Song of the Sea, is the earliest reaction we have by an ancient writer to the culmination of the exodus story: the Red Sea calamity. If Cross and Freedman and their successors are right, people sang it within maybe a hundred years, maybe a year, of the event. (Or the alleged event. We have not yet determined whether it was historical.) Here is my translation, as literal as possible while still trying to capture the poetry.

> Let me sing to Yahweh, for He *triumphed!*
> Horse and its rider He cast in the sea.
> My strength and song are Yah,
> and He became a salvation for me.
>
> This is my God, and I'll praise Him,
> my father's God, and I'll hail Him.
> Yahweh is a warrior.
> Yahweh is His name.
>
> Pharaoh's chariots and his army He plunged in the sea
> and the choice of his troops drowned in the Red Sea.
> The deeps covered them.
> They sank in the depths like a stone.
>
> Your right hand, Yahweh, awesome in power,
> your right hand, Yahweh, crushed the foe.
> And in your triumph's greatness you threw down
>   your adversaries.
> You let go your fury: it consumed them like straw.
>
> And by wind from your nostrils water was massed,
> surf piled up like a heap,
> the deeps congealed in the heart of the sea.

The enemy said, "I'll pursue!
I'll catch up!
I'll divide spoil!
My soul will be sated!
I'll unsheathe my sword!
My hand will deprive them!"

You blew with your wind. Sea covered them.
They sank like lead in the awesome water.

Who is like you among the gods, Yahweh!
Who is like you:
awesome in holiness!
fearsome with splendors!
making miracles!

You reached your right hand: earth swallowed them.
You led, in your kindness, the people you saved;
you ushered, in your strength, to your holy abode.

Peoples heard—they shuddered.
Shaking seized Philistia's residents.
Then Edom's chiefs were terrified.
Moab's chieftains: trembling seized them.
All Canaan's residents melted.
Terror and fear came over them.
At the power of your arm they hushed like a stone.

'Til your people passed, Yahweh,
'til the people you created passed.

You'll bring them, and you'll plant them in your
    legacy's mountain,

your throne's platform, that you made, Yahweh;
a sanctuary, Lord, that your hands built.

Yahweh will reign forever and ever!

(Exodus 15:1b–18)

The first thing to notice is that the text never gives any numbers. Our original source for the event never even hints at whether the group that made it to the Red Sea was large or small. It also never says that they passed through walls of water. What happened to the people is not clear. What is clear, though, is that some catastrophe at the sea happened to the Egyptian force that was pursuing them.

But the more surprising thing to notice is that the word "Israel" does not occur in the Song of the Sea. The text never speaks of the whole nation of Israel. It just refers to a people (in Hebrew, an *'am*) leaving Egypt. David Noel Freedman wrote: "The group that was the object of divine intervention, who were rescued from the pursuing chariots, is known only as the people of Yahweh. Although they have been redeemed by him, even created by him, they are not called Israel."[20] And God does not lead this *'am* to the entire land. It says that

He leads them to His "holy abode,"
He plants them in His "legacy's mountain,"
at the Lord's "sanctuary" (Hebrew *miqdash*),
where His "throne's platform" is.

That last phrase occurs only here in the Song of the Sea and in reference to the Temple.[21] The term *miqdash* ("sanctuary, temple, holy place") likewise commonly refers to a temple or the Tabernacle in the Hebrew Bible (fifty-two times).[22] This arrival only

at the Temple, not at the whole land, makes sense if we are reading about Levites, who became the Temple priests. It does not
apply to all of Israel. In the past, scholars have proposed a variety
of possible locations to which these words might refer. They
have identified the holy abode, mountain, sanctuary, and throne
platform as Mount Sinai, Gilgal, possibly Shiloh, or Canaan.[23]
The first three are all possible as sanctuaries. The last (Canaan)
really does not correspond well to the words of the song, which
uses those four different terms or phrases that imply a sanctuary.
So if a group left Egypt in an exodus, they were a people, an
'am, who ended up in some priestly status, in service of the God
named Yahweh, in a location belonging to Yahweh.

Now what does the Song of Deborah have to do with this? It
has no reference to the exodus. It appears in the book of Judges,
which is set back in Israel. Composed in the twelfth or eleventh
century BCE, it celebrates the battle in which the tribes of Israel united and triumphed over the Canaanite army led by the
powerful king of Hazor and his general Sisera. This was likely
the battle that first established Israelite hegemony as a country.
It hails Deborah, who musters the tribes with her commander
Barak. The song lists the ten tribes of Israel whom Deborah
summoned to battle.[24] It calls each tribe by name. But one is
missing. It does not mention Levi. Why? Either (a) the Levites
were not there yet. They were in Egypt (or on the road). Or
(b) the Levites were not a tribe of Israel going into battle; they
were a priestly group, dispersed among the tribes.[25] Actually the
answer involves both. But first let us appreciate this most basic
fact about our two earliest sources: The Song of Deborah, set in
Israel, does not mention the Levites; and the Song of Miriam, set
in Egypt, does not mention Israel. It was David Noel Freedman
who especially emphasized this crucial fact.

And just to add another ancient piece to that ancient evidence, Freedman pointed to another of the songs that he and Cross had identified as the oldest texts in the Bible: the Blessing of Moses, found in Deuteronomy 33. It contains oracles about many of the tribes of Israel and Judah, and it includes Levi among them. But Freedman emphasized this about the oracle of Levi (Deuteronomy 33:8–11):

> This is the only tribal oracle with an explicit and necessary association with the wilderness wanderings. If the oracle may be trusted as authentic and ancient, then we have here the transference of tribal status to a group which participated in the Exodus and Wanderings, without, however, a comparable territorial allocation.[26]

This fits with the other evidence we have tallied here. The Levites came to be accepted and counted as one of the tribes of Israel. But, unlike the rest of the tribes in the song, they are the only ones who are connected in any way with the journey from Egypt to Israel. Their role in that journey is explicit. No other Israelite group has any role at all. Thus in all of our earliest sources, only the Levites have any connection with the exodus.

3. Who Wrote the Exodus Story?

Examining those poetic texts, our oldest sources, produced some useful information. That information is intriguing as pieces of the puzzle. If we examine the old prose sources embedded in the Bible, we can learn a good deal more. Figuring out how the Bible came to be composed—who wrote the parts, who put the parts together—has been a central question of Bible scholarship for the last two centuries. It has yielded phenomenal information about the Bible's sources.[27] When we put that information together with our archaeological information, that is when the puzzle starts to come together into a picture. Our mistake until now, as I have been stressing, is that we have looked almost solely at archaeology. We left out our biggest source, the Bible itself, because that was the thing that we were testing. We were trying to see if its stories were reliable as history or not. But our research on the Bible for over two hundred years has been much more sophisticated than merely reading stories and rating them as true or false. We have used the stories and poetry and laws as source material to study in order to see what history we can recover behind them. That is comparable to what we do in archaeology, studying sites and artifacts to see what history we can recover behind them. The methods are sometimes the same, sometimes different. But the goal and the end results are the same: to see what these two kinds of evidence can reveal. And best of all: to see what we can bring to light when we combine the two. Some years ago, at a united meeting of archaeologists and Bible scholars, I proposed as a thought experiment: what if we had had the archaeological work first, and then someone discovered the Bible? What would be our reaction? Front page *New York Times*! Headline news! Blogs going crazy with discussion of all kinds. From archaeology we would have had two inscriptions that referred to a king of the House of David,[28] but we would have had no idea to whom or what that referred. But now, in this newly discovered Bible, we would have had long, detailed accounts of King David and his descendants on the throne of Judah in the books of 1 and 2 Samuel, 1 and 2 Kings, and 1 and 2 Chronicles. From archaeology we would have had an inscribed prism from the Assyrian emperor Sennacherib claiming that he besieged a King

Hezekiah the Judean in Jerusalem, his royal city. And now, in this new book, we would have the Judean report of the same event from their perspective inside the city in the Bible's books of 2 Kings and Isaiah.[29] These texts would confirm much of what the Sennacherib prism claimed, and they would challenge parts of it.

What would be the reaction to this find? Some would say that this newly discovered book was a forgery. But it would in fact be the greatest literary, archaeological, historical, religious discovery of all time. To the religious it would be a revelation. To the secular it would be the stuff dissertations are made of. To *Reader's Digest* it would cry out for an abridgment.

Just as we see and hear excitement over a new archaeological find that sheds light on the Bible, we would get excitement over this new long text that sheds light on our excavated artifacts. In fact, this latter excitement would be greater. This book would put flesh on the archaeological bones. Most of all, this book would give us connections, continuity, chronology. In other words: it would help to give us history.

We have been collecting evidence of the actual history that we can derive from the Bible, rather than just accepting or rejecting its stories, for about two centuries. Why would we not use two hundred years of research and learning on the exodus question? We needed to reach a point in both this textual research and archaeological research where we could be able to put the two together meaningfully. We are now at that point.

The best-known, most compelling explanation of all of our textual evidence is called the documentary hypothesis. A lot of people will tell you that this hypothesis about who wrote the Bible has a smaller consensus than it used to. That is true. Others will tell you that it has been disproved. That is false. The part about consensus, I must admit, reflects a rather strange breeze blowing through the field of Bible scholarship in recent years. The situation is not that the documentary hypothesis does not have a clear consensus of Bible scholars. It is that no hypothesis has a clear consensus of Bible scholars. The documentary hypothesis is just what it says: the Hebrew Bible is made up of documents, of source texts that editors (redactors) put together in several stages. That is the central idea, and nearly all scholars known to me outside of orthodox or fundamentalist communities are persuaded by that idea. (And even the orthodox and fundamentalist communities are beginning to come to terms with it just in the last few years.[30]) The point about consensus is that we are now getting a profusion of variations of this central idea. There are supplementary hypotheses, meaning that authors wrote some of the documents and then other authors wrote more pieces around those documents as supplements. There are hypotheses of many very small documents that were expanded and connected to each other. There are hypotheses that date the documents later and later in Israel's history. Some hypotheses propose a different order in which the source documents were written. There are hypotheses that deny that one or another of the documents ever existed.[31] In all of these variations, the scholar remains critical: not automatically accepting or rejecting the Bible's reports, but rather identifying the Bible's sources and their history to see what trustworthy information they can yield.[32]

There is a classic story, some two thousand years old, of a teacher (Hillel) who is challenged to teach the entire biblical instruction while someone stands on one foot. He answers:

> What is bad to you, don't do to someone else. Now
> go and learn.

Brilliant (though a lot of people leave out that second sentence when they quote this story). So, in the name of brevity, I shall make this summary of the hypothesis by that one-foot standard of timing:

> First: The Bible's first five books are Genesis, Exodus, Leviticus, Numbers, and Deuteronomy. We call them the Pentateuch, the Torah, or the Five Books of Moses.
>
> Second: They are composed of four main documents. There are also some smaller ones.[33]
>
> Third: Brilliant editors (usually called redactors) used these documents as sources, which they combined in stages exquisitely to form the five book work.

We can read each of these sources individually. If you wish to do so, there are now several books and online treatments. I have translated them and printed them in distinct colors and fonts so you can read them either individually or in any combination you choose.[34] There are other works that distinguish the sources in various graphic ways.[35] And the text is available online in the original Hebrew with the sources in distinct colors.[36] I have provided an example in Appendix A of how this works with a story from Exodus. I gave another example, the story of Noah and the flood from Genesis, in *Who Wrote the Bible?*[37] Thousands, perhaps millions, of people have now been able to read the individual sources. The reaction of amazement at how smoothly and consistently each source reads when separated from the others is common. It would be as if we could find four originally separate works, by four different authors, that someone combined to make *The Brothers Karamazov,* and each work flowed as a whole continuous story with hardly a gap, each had its own very specific language and names of persons, and each had parallel stories in the other texts.

We name the sources by letters:

J It is called that because Yahweh's name in it (spelled Jahwe in early German studies) is known by humans from the very beginning of the story at creation.

E It is called that because Yahweh's name in it is not known until the time of Moses. Before that Yahweh is called El or is just called generically "God," which in Hebrew is Elohim. Hence the E.

P It is a Priestly source.

D It is exclusively in the book of Deuteronomy. It takes up almost the entire book.

One more point turns out to be huge for our exodus investigation. The last three sources (E, P, and D) were written by Levites. J was not.[38] This need not be controversial. The priesthood of ancient Israel came from the Levite group, and the concerns of Levite priests are all over those three sources. They contain long bodies of religious rules and laws. The other source, J, does not. Their stories have polemic between the various Levite priestly groups, reflecting their ancient competitions.[39] The J stories do not develop this. The three Levite sources have more text on the period starting with Moses and the establishment of the Levite priesthood. The J text has more on the period before this, the period of the patriarchs Abraham, Isaac, and Jacob. The J text reflects more familiarity and interest in the royal court than in the priesthood. It is so non-priestly that I raised the possibility that it could have been written by a woman, as opposed to the three Levite sources, which come from a priesthood that did not include women.[40]

To be helpful, there is a chart showing what each of the main sources contains in Appendix B. The intriguing story of how we discovered the existence of the sources and separated them from one another is told in *Who Wrote the Bible?* and now in many other books. For now, I just wanted to give enough of a basic picture so that any reader will be able to understand what follows: we shall see how this basic model in biblical scholarship joins the other evidence about the Levites and the exodus.

GOD'S NAME

Probably the single most famous clue of the hypothesis is the point about God's name. People who challenge the hypothesis often refer to this as a problem of "the names of God." They think it means that God has one name in one of the sources and a different name in another source. But that is not correct. The distinction is not that God has different names in different sources. God's name is Yahweh in all the sources. The distinction rather is that the sources give different pictures of when God revealed His name, Yahweh, to humans. In the Levite source E and in another Levite source P, they call God Elohim, which, as I said above, is not a name. It is just a generic word for a god. Or they call God El, which may be both a name and also a generic word for a god. They use El or Elohim consistently until God reveals to Moses that His name is Yahweh. After that He is referred to by this name as well as by Elohim. But in J, people know the name Yahweh from the beginning. It is already used by the first woman, Eve.[41] In the J source, the story's narrator never once refers to the deity as Elohim. Persons in the story use the term; but the narrator does not. The narrator always says Yahweh, without a single exception.

People made the mistake of thinking that it was a matter of different names in different sources because the original work was done by a French physician, Jean Astruc, who worked only through the first book of the Bible, Genesis, and people still usually work through Genesis first. It is only in the second book of the Bible, Exodus, that we find out what the name thing has been all about: it is about when God first reveals to Moses that His name is Yahweh.[42] In the Levite source E, God reveals it to Moses at a bush on the Mountain of God, where they first meet. Moses says that when he tells the people that their fathers' God sent him they will ask, "What is His name?" They do not know it. The E text has not given the name up to this point. God answers:

> Yahweh, your fathers' God, Abraham's God, Isaac's God, and Jacob's God has sent me to you. This is my name forever, and this is how I am to be remembered for generation after generation.
>
> (Exodus 3:15)

And in the Levite Priestly source P, God reveals the name to Moses in Egypt. God says:

> I am Yahweh. And I appeared to Abraham, to Isaac, and to Jacob as El Shadday. And I was not known to them by my name, Yahweh.
>
> (Exodus 6:3)

It has been 260 years since Astruc, the text could hardly be more explicit, and at least some of us have read the Bible as far as Exodus, so we should regard this matter of the divine name as settled now.

Just how carefully, consistently, is this distinction in the revelation of God's name developed? The words El, Elohim, and Yahweh occur two thousand times in the Torah, and there are just three exceptions out of the two thousand. Three out of two thousand is amazing in a text that was copied by hand for its first two thousand years. There are differences in the Greek version, the Septuagint, which is no surprise since a translator from Hebrew to Greek can easily slip and substitute *kurios* (LORD) or *theos* (God) in Greek for the Hebrew Yahweh or Elohim and vice versa. But now we also have the Dead Sea Scrolls, which are Hebrew texts. They are a thousand years older than the oldest Hebrew texts we had until that goat found the Scrolls in 1947. In the Dead Sea Scrolls the picture is the same as in those existing Hebrew texts, known as the Masoretic Text. The scrolls and the Masoretic Text are equally consistent with regard to the deity's name. Only two verses have Elohim in the Dead Sea Scrolls where it is Yahweh in the Masoretic Text, and, as it happens, those are verses that do not contradict the hypothesis in any case.[43]

The significance of this source distinction concerning the doctrine that God's name was not revealed until Moses remains unrefuted and, I want to emphasize, underappreciated. It was a first clue that led us on a trail of working out who wrote the Bible. If it had done just that and nothing more, that would have been a tremendous contribution. But the reason I reviewed it here is to go further now. The question now is: what might be the reason for this?

EL IS YAHWEH

What is the shoe behind this story? What made it necessary for two of the Bible's greatest writers to develop an idea that God did not reveal His name until the time of Moses and the exodus? Following the other evidence that it may have been just the Levites who made the exodus from Egypt, this makes sense. The *'am* who left Egypt are connected to the worship of the God Yahweh. In our oldest source, the Song of the Sea, their God is mentioned nine times, and in all nine the name is Yahweh. Where did they get the worship of Yahweh? We do not know. (We shall look at possibilities in Chapter 4.) But we do know that back in Israel the people worshipped the God called El. The very name Israel is Hebrew *yiśrā-'ēl*. That has been taken to mean everything from "El Persists" to "Struggles with El."[44] The first part, "*yiśrā*," is uncertain. But there is no doubt of the second part: El. The Israelites and the Canaanites worshipped the chief god El.[45] So when the Levites arrive with their God Yahweh, and they meet up with the resident Israelites with their God El, what do they do?

I quoted the distinguished archaeologist William Dever above, where he wrote that there is "overwhelming archaeological evidence today of largely indigenous origins for early Israel." Israel was indigenous. They did not come from Egypt or anywhere else. They were just there as far back as we can trace them. Dever meant this as evidence against the exodus. But, as I have been saying, it is evidence only against an exodus of all of Israel. The Israelite tribes had "largely indigenous origins." Most of them were in Israel all along. That fits fine with the evidence that just the Levites came from Egypt. Then the Levites united with those Israelite tribes. Why? Either because (1) they felt kinship with each other, or (2) these Levites had originally come from Israel (probably called Canaan at that point) themselves, so their uniting was actually a re-uniting with their old brethren, or (3) those Israelite tribes had defeated the Canaanites (as the

Song of Deborah reports), so the Levites naturally allied with them as the new strong force in the land. Maybe it was a mixture of all three. We do not doubt that this union of Levites and the Israelite tribes took place, though, because the Levites have been counted among the people of Israel from biblical times until the present day.

But what about the God of this united confederation? Were they going to worship El or Yahweh? Israel had choices. They could have chosen to worship only El. They could have chosen to worship only Yahweh. They could have chosen to worship both. They could have said that El is Yahweh's father, or his son. But they chose none of these. They said: El *is* Yahweh. He was always Yahweh, but the Israelites in the land had not known this name because He did not reveal it until the time that these Levites were to come from Egypt to Israel.[46] He revealed it to His greatest prophet, their leader, Moses. The Levites' sources E and P retained this story as a crucial development in the people's history.[47] But the author of the J source, living in this same period, long after the acceptance of Yahweh as the proper name of God, and who was not a Levite priest, could not have cared less about when it started, and so he or she just told the story without including that transition.[48] And that would explain how we came to have the crucial name of God distinction that helped us to separate the Bible's sources to this day. That story is important itself, but it reflects something vastly more important. Yahweh and El are one. Scott Noegel of the University of Washington wrote:

> The Late Bronze Age . . . was a formative and flexible period in the history of Israelite religion as it also saw the gradual fusion of the Canaanite god El with Yahweh.[49]

Frank Cross wrote of how biblical Israel made no distinction between El and Yahweh:

> 'El is rarely if ever used in the Bible as the proper name of a non-Israelite Canaanite deity in the full consciousness of a distinction between 'El and Yahweh, god of Israel. This is a most extraordinary datum.[50]

And Professor Mark Smith of Princeton University explained this datum thus:

> At an early point, Israelite tradition identified El with Yahweh or presupposed this equation. It is for this reason that the Hebrew Bible so rarely distinguishes between El and Yahweh.[51]

We shall definitely return to this fusion of El and Yahweh because its implications are potentially tremendous. For now, our concern is that it is one more piece that fits with the picture of the Levite exodus from Egypt and subsequent union with Israel.[52]

The premium of this body of evidence from the sources behind the Bible is that it explains so much. It harmonizes with the other evidence about the Levites and the exodus. It provides the reason for the accounts of the revelation of God's name in the Bible. That was, as I said at the beginning, the first and most famous clue in the investigation into who wrote the Bible, but the reason behind this clue always eluded us. Now we have a reason, and it connects the hypothesis about the Bible's authors to a real-life historical course of events in ancient Israel, a course of events that other evidence supports. In the early days of modern Bible scholarship, people would attribute a passage in the Bible to one source or another, to J or E or P, because it used a particular word or told a story a particular way. But now, as we uncover logical connections between the source texts and the historical events that produced each of them, this tapestry of connections in turn gives the hypothesis more strength, more appeal, than ever. In scientific terms, it is a more elegant theory. In everyday terms, it is more likely that the theory is correct. This is not circular reasoning. It is convergence of evidence in mutual support. I said that there is currently a plethora of models competing for consensus. No other model known to me coincides so consistently with what we know of history and archaeology. Indeed, we commonly find books, lectures, and courses that introduce the subject with a discussion of "the names of God" without even raising the question of why this prominent thing exists. And the trail of archaeology and history continues through all the evidence below.

4. The Tabernacle and the Battle Tent of Rameses

What about the claims that we have found no widespread material culture of Egypt in early Israel? Those claims, like the ones about not finding two million people, are true only if we are still thinking of all of Israel making the exodus from Egypt. The whole country of Israel does not have such cultural connections back to Egypt. But the Levites, and only the Levites, do have the cultural connections. We have already seen that they have Egyptian names. And there is much more. The Levite priests' description of their Tabernacle, the sacred Tent of Meeting, is long and detailed. It obviously was extremely important to them. There is in fact more about the Tabernacle than about anything else in the Five Books of Moses. Now, my former student, Professor Michael Homan of Xavier University of Louisiana, in a wonderful combination of Bible and archaeology, showed that the Tabernacle has architectural parallels with the battle tent of Pharaoh Rameses II.[53] Its size, shape, proportions, surrounding courtyard, golden winged accoutrements, Eastern orientation, and arrangement of outer and inner rooms are a match. My own calculations of the Tabernacle's construction differ in some ways from Homan's, but still I acknowledge enough of a match that the connection is visible.[54] The Levite sources of the Torah mention the Tabernacle, or Tent of Meeting, over two hundred times. And how many times does the non-Levite source J refer to it? Zero.

5. The Ark and the Bark

While Professor Homan focused on the Tabernacle, Professor Noegel, in another combination of Bible and archaeology, showed parallels between the Levite priests' description of their Ark of the Covenant and Egyptian barks. Though barks are boats, these barks were rarely set in water. They were rather carried in processions. They were sacred ritual objects. Like the ark that the Levites carry in Israel, the barks were sometimes gold-plated, many were decorated with winged cherubs or birds, they were carried on poles by priests, and they served as a throne and footstool. Noegel concluded that "the bark served as a model, which the Israelites adapted for their own needs."[55]

6. Circumcision

Also, it is the texts written by Levites that give the requirement to practice circumcision. Circumcision was a known practice in Egypt. The biblical texts required circumcision in the Levite Priestly covenant between God and Abraham in Genesis and in the Levite Priestly law in Leviticus.[56] Levite authors, and only Levite authors, used the metaphor of circumcision of the heart, which is found both in Leviticus (26:41) and in Deuteronomy (10:16; 30:6). This metaphor of circumcision of one's heart also appears in two prophets: Jeremiah (4:4; 9:25) and Ezekiel (44:7, 9), and it happens that both of these two famous prophets, Jeremiah and Ezekiel, were Levite priests.[57] The Levite Priestly writer in Exodus also uses the metaphor of Moses' uncircumcised lips (6:12, 20); and Jeremiah adds the metaphor of uncircumcised ears (6:10). All eleven of these references to circumcision appear only in these Levite sources.

The non-Levite source J, meanwhile, tells nothing about circumcision except in stories, not in instruction or legal contexts. In J, circumcision is not a law and not a requirement of the covenant. It comes up in two episodes. The first is the strange J story of Moses' Midianite wife Zipporah, who does something to somebody for some reason at a lodging place when they are on the way to Egypt. It is a brief story, only three verses, so here it is:

> And Moses took his wife and his son and rode them on an ass, and he went back to the land of Egypt. And he was on the way, at a lodging place, and Yahweh met him, and he asked to kill him. And Zipporah took a flint and cut her son's foreskin and touched his feet, and she said, "Because you're a bridegroom of blood to me." And he held back from him. Then she said, "A bridegroom of blood for circumcisions."
>
> (Exodus 4:24–26)

If you found that confusing, don't worry. Nobody understands it. Propp and I have suggested utterly different readings of it, and there are plenty more.[58] My goal here is not to solve it but, if anything, to emphasize how enigmatic it is. The story gives no hint of circumcision being a cultural norm, and it derives from a Midianite woman, not from Israel or from the deity.

In the other story, circumcision is *claimed* to be an ethnic norm but turns out to be used as a strategy to disable and destroy someone who has committed an offense against Israel's ancestors. It is the story of Dinah and Shechem (Genesis 34). Dinah is Jacob's and Leah's daughter. Shechem is the prince of the city that is also called Shechem. He has sex with Dinah. The episode is sometimes referred to as "the rape of Dinah," but the Hebrew text is unclear about whether it is a rape, a seduction, or even consensual sex.[59] Still, that does not matter to Dinah's brothers, who are "pained and furious, for he had done a foolhardy thing among Israel, to lie with Jacob's daughter, and such a thing is not done." Shechem and his father, the king of Shechem, come to propose peace and intermarriage between their city and Jacob's clan. Dinah's brothers' strategy: they tell Shechem and his father that they would not give their sister to a man who has a foreskin "because that's a disgrace to us," so all the men of Shechem must be circumcised. The Shechemites agree. Three days later, when the men of Shechem are hurting, apparently handicapped from the surgery, two of Dinah's brothers massacre the city and take back their sister.

This story, like the story of Moses and Zipporah, makes no mention of law or covenant. The brothers just state that they are circumcised and demand the same of the Shechemites "with deception." And one more thing: even in this source, it is just two out of Dinah's twelve brothers who use the circumcision strategy, and one of the two is Levi. And the other J circumcision story that we saw concerns Moses, the most famous Levite of them all, and his son Gershom. And Gershom turns out to be the ancestor of an important Levite clan.[60] Neither of these J stories includes a commandment that all Israelite males must practice circumcision. They simply treat it as a known practice. Circumcision as a commandment for Israel comes only from the Levites.[61]

In fairness we must acknowledge that other ancient Near Eastern cultures had circumcision as well,[62] but still this is worth reckoning as part of the series of connections of culture between the biblical text and Egypt, and the fact remains that it is still only in the Levite sources that circumcision remains as a command and a continuing concern.

So for those who argue that there are no Egyptian elements in early Israel's material culture, that argument, too, has substance only if we are still stuck at the two million number and all of Israel participating in the exodus. Egyptian cultural influences *are* present, but only among the *Levites*.

7. Parallels with Egyptian Traditions

And the list of these connections goes on. The Bible scholar Professor Gary Rendsburg at Rutgers collected a series of known items of Egyptian lore that appear in the story of the exodus. He noted that the story in Exodus 1–15 "repeatedly shows familiarity with Egyptian traditions: the biblical motifs of the hidden divine name, turning an inanimate object into a reptile, the conversion of water to blood, a spell of three days of darkness, the death of the firstborn, the parting of waters, and death by drowning are all paralleled in Egyptian texts, and, for the most part, nowhere else."

He concluded:

In sum, the narrative that encompasses Exodus 1–15 evokes the Egyptian setting at every turn.[63]

Rendsburg is right, and I would add one more thing. What makes these points even more revealing is that every one of them is from the Levite sources E and P. None is from the non-Levite source J.[64] So even if we regard these as just stories and not necessarily as historical, they indicate Egyptian literary connections as well as the Egyptian cultural connections. The exodus story did not come out of nowhere. Its authors knew Egyptian culture, traditions, and literature—but not *all* of its authors, only its Levite authors.

Similarly, many Bible scholars, archaeologists, and Egyptologists have examined the element of the Exodus story that identifies (apparently correctly) two cities by name, cities that the Israelite slaves are said to have built: Pithom and Rameses.[65] Other elements of the story, too, match with known situations in Egypt in the right centuries. The Israelites are said to have been forced to make bricks.[66] They complain about not being given straw to use in making the bricks.[67] Quotas of brick production are imposed on them.[68] Baruch Halpern wrote:

> The brickmaking, too, described as part of the Oppression, reflects close knowledge of conditions in Egypt. A 15th-century tomb painting depicts Canaanite and Nubian captives making mudbricks at Thebes. One text even complains about a dearth of straw for brickmaking—a situation encountered by Israel in Egypt. In Canaan, by contrast, straw was not uniformly an ingredient of mudbrick. Almost every detail in the tradition mirrors conditions under [Egypt's] 19th Dynasty.[69]

I want to emphasize that Halpern was not raising these elements of the story as proof that the exodus was historical. Nor do I take them as evidence of historicity. We should say more cautiously that they show that the biblical authors who told the story had familiarity with conditions in Egypt in the period with which the exodus is associated, the Bronze Age. But again I add the same observation as with Professor Rendsburg's collection of parallels in the biblical and Egyptian sources. In my (and some other scholars') identification of the Bible's sources, every one of these elements is from the Levite sources E and P.[70] None is mentioned in a non-Levite source.

So these other parallels serve only to indicate plausibility; that is, that the biblical writers got many things right about the story's setting. They still do not necessarily constitute proof of what happened. James Hoffmeier made a similarly positive but cautious point, saying that

> while there is no direct evidence to prove the exodus,
> the Egyptian linguistic and cultural background de-
> tails in the Exodus narratives suggest a historical ori-
> gin for Israel in Egypt that is most plausible.[71]

I would restate this that these literary points about the narratives are helpful in showing that the exodus is plausible, yes; but we have also seen tangible evidence that suggests a historical origin not for *all* of Israel in Egypt, but just of the Levites.

8. The Story of the Plagues and Exodus

The literary connection of the story to the Levite authors goes still deeper. It is the sources that come from the Levites—E, P, and also D—that tell the whole story of the plagues on

Egypt, leading to the people's exodus. J, the version that was not written by a Levite, does not tell it at all.[72] If you read the Levite sources E, P, and D, you learn of ten plagues on Egypt: rivers turning to blood, frog infestation, lice, an insect swarm, a livestock epidemic, boils, hail, locusts, a three-day darkness, and finally death of firstborn humans and animals. In these sources you read of the competition with the Egyptian sorcerers who attempt, and ultimately fail, to reproduce the plagues. In these sources you read of the hardening of Pharaoh's heart, which keeps the plagues coming. And then you read of Egypt's capitulation and the people's departure: the exodus. You get all this and more in the Levite sources E, P, and D. It goes on for nine chapters. But if you read J, you find none of this. It jumps from Moses' saying "Let my people go" (Exodus 5:1f.) to the people's already having departed Egypt (13:21). The Pharaoh answers the first demand with "I won't let Israel leave" (5:2), and he is not mentioned again until "He heard that the people had *fled*" (14:5). Who knows what story, if any, came between. The plagues and exodus story comes entirely from the Levite sources.[73] Interestingly, J has a story of plagues in Egypt, but it is set in the time of Abraham (Genesis 12), not in the time of the exodus. So on top of everything else that ties the Levites to the exodus, we now find that *the story itself* comes from them.[74]

9. Be Kind to Slaves

I am among the many readers who love detective fiction. I especially relish when all the different parts of the mystery come together and finally make sense. Similarly here: we have looked at poetry, prose, material culture, traditional lore, and names. And now still another category of evidence comes together with them: law. Only Levite sources (E, P, and D) have laws of how to treat slaves. The Bible does not abolish slavery. It limits it. It gives slaves rights, sometimes (not always[75]) the same rights as free people. It limits the situations in which one can acquire slaves, and it puts certain limits on how long one may keep them. It forbids one from mistreating a slave. If you knock out your slave's eye, or even a single tooth, the slave goes free.[76] If you hit your slave, there is no penalty, but if you strike him or her so hard with an implement that he or she dies, then the slave is to be avenged.[77] If you capture a female in war, you must marry her or set her free, but you may not enslave her.[78] If one acquires a fellow Israelite as a slave, one must let the slave go free after six years, and one must also give the freed slave provisions:

> You shall *provide* him from your flock and from your
> threshing floor and from your wine press; as Yahweh,
> your God, has blessed you, you shall give to him.
>   (Deuteronomy 15:12–14)

And why must one do this?

> And you shall remember that you were a slave in the
> land of Egypt, and Yahweh, your God, redeemed you.
> On account of this, I command you this thing.
>   (Deuteronomy 15:15)

While these laws about treating slaves, which are explicitly traced to having been slaves themselves in Egypt, come up so much in the three Levite sources, there are no laws about slaves at all in the non-Levite source J. Now one might say that this is simply because the J source does not include law codes at all except for the Ten Commandments. That is true, but even there in the J version of the Ten Commandments, its law of Sabbath rest does not include slaves. The other two occurrences of the Ten Commandments refer to slaves both in their very first verse ("I brought you out of the land of Egypt from a house of slaves")[79] and in their Sabbath commandment, which requires that one's slaves are not to be made to work on the Sabbath.[80] But the J Decalogue does not give slaves the day off or show any interest in slaves at all.[81]

In fact the non-Levite J source does not even have the word "slave" any time after Genesis. It is unclear in what way the Egyptians oppressed the Israelites in J. It must be some kind of forced labor because the text refers to "taskmasters," but that is the closest it comes. It has Pharaoh trying to diminish their numbers by killing male babies, and it has Pharaoh refusing to let them leave. But it has no specific reference to slavery. That which is a primary focus of the Levite sources is not mentioned by name in the non-Levite source.

10. Be Kind to Aliens

Over and over—fifty-two times!—all three Levite sources command that one must never mistreat an alien. The first occurrence of the word "torah" in the Torah is the command:

> There shall be one torah for the citizen and for the alien who lives among you.
>
> (Exodus 12:49)

Why should an Israelite not mistreat an alien? What is the reason for this Israelite obsession with not oppressing a foreigner who is in their country? All three Levite sources answer word-for-word the same:

Because you were aliens in Egypt.[82]

Indeed, biblical law forbids an Israelite to disdain an Egyptian. Why?

> You shall not abhor an Egyptian,
> because you were an alien in his land.

This law, too, comes in a Levite source (Deuteronomy 23:8).

Only the non-Levite source, J—by now it should come as no surprise—never mentions this. Indeed, William Propp makes a strong case on the etymology of the very word *levi*, that its most probable meaning is an "attached" or "joined" person, in the sense of a resident alien.[83] This might apply to the Levites as resident aliens during their stay in Egypt, or it may apply to them as attached resident aliens among the Israelite population, where they were not one of the original union of tribes. Either way it fits with the concentration on aliens in every Levite source of the Torah—and never in a non-Levite source. This Levite concern for aliens is unique: unique in the Bible, and actually unparalleled in the laws of all the lands of the ancient Near East. As the Canadian scholar Glen A. Taylor put it:

> In ancient Near Eastern laws, while there is usually protection and provision given to the marginalized (i.e., widows and orphans), there is typically no mention of provision for the sojourner, or foreigner, as Deuteronomy provides. This is an emphasis unique to the Hebrew law codes.[84]

An emphasis unique to the Hebrew law codes. And unique to the *Levite sections* of those Hebrew law codes! Only the Levites preserve the memory of having been outsiders in Egypt, and only the Levites are moved to show fairness to outsiders ever after. This last of the ten bodies of evidence that we have seen may well be the most significant of all. We shall return to it in the final chapter of this book.

In Sum:

So let's do the math:

Eight out of eight Israelites with Egyptian names are Levites.

Two out of two accounts of the revelation of God's name make it to the Levite Moses and are told in Levite sources.

The massive treatment of the Tabernacle, which parallels the Egyptian tent of Rameses II, appears in the Levite Priests' sources.

The ark, which is entrusted to the Levites, parallels the Egyptian barks.

Seven out of seven items of Egyptian lore that come up in the biblical story occur in Levite sources.

Eleven out of eleven references to circumcision in legal context, literal or metaphorical, occur in Levitical sources in the Torah and the prophets. And the two references to it in stories involve the Levite Moses or Levi himself.

Three out of three sources that tell the story of the plagues and exodus are Levite sources.

All texts treating slavery during and after the Egyptian stay are Levite sources.

Fifty-two out of fifty-two references to aliens occur in Levite sources.

Fifty-two references to the sanctuary (*miqdash*) in the Bible, which is where the people in the Song of the Sea go, identify it as the Temple or Tabernacle, the shrines to which only the Levites are allowed access.

The non-Levite source(s) lack all of this.

It took a variety of scholars, each contributing a piece of the puzzle, to arrive at this picture. Homan saw the connection between the Tabernacle and Rameses' tent. Noegel saw the connection between the ark and the Egyptian barks. Rendsburg saw the connection between the Exodus stories and the stories that we know from Egyptian culture. Freedman saw the connection between the Song of the Sea and the Song of Deborah. Propp saw the connection of the word *levi* and the role of aliens. And a host of scholars saw the significance of the presence of Semites, Asiatics, Shasu, 'Apiru (Habiru), Hyksos—Levantine people in Egypt in those centuries. And we can now unite all of this in the context of what we know about the Bible's sources: the texts and the people who wrote them.

OTHER ARGUMENTS ABOUT THE EXODUS

I said above that the study of the Bible's sources and their authors has been a central part of Bible studies for about two centuries. It is remarkable that we have not applied it sufficiently before to the question of the exodus. Perhaps we needed to acquire a certain quantity of archaeological information to go along with it first. For a while we relied on this growing archaeological information in a bubble. We did not see the intersection between it and what we knew of the texts, and that led us astray. But now this combination of textual and archaeological information has proved to be revealing. These ten (a biblical number) points of evidence all support the hypothesis that, while most of Israel was back in the land all along, just the Levites made the exodus from Egypt. How do we relate this to the other evidence and arguments about the exodus?

In the first place there is the dating game. If it was just the Levites, then classic arguments over dates are transformed. One of the turning points in many arguments about the exodus has been the Merneptah stele. Pharaoh Merneptah was the son of Rameses II. He reigned late in the thirteenth century BCE. He erected an inscribed stone, which the archaeologist Sir Flinders Petrie discovered in 1896 at Thebes. It is now in the Egyptian Museum in Cairo. It contains the earliest known occurrence of the name Israel, so it has sometimes even been called "The Israel Stele."[85] Scholars date it to circa 1205 BCE or a little earlier.[86] So, people commonly said, if Israel was a settled people by 1205, then the exodus had to be before that. Also, some pointed out that the Egyptian military controlled the Sinai Peninsula at that time, so a huge mass of escaped slaves slipping by there would have been impossible then. But the flaw in this picture is that it still presumes that all of Israel made the exodus and then arrived in Canaan. If it was just the Levites who made the exodus, while the rest of Israel was back in their land, then this whole argument disappears. If it was just the Levites, then their exodus could have been before or after Pharaoh Merneptah. I am therefore completely in agreement with the historian Abraham Malamat, who said, "This stele has little or nothing to do with the Exodus."[87]

Second, people who challenge the historicity of the exodus frequently point to the absence of any references to it in ancient Egyptian sources. This argument too is dependent on the assumption of a big exodus of a mass of Israelites. There is no reason to be surprised that there is no mention of Israelites in Egypt when, after all, there is no mention of Israelites in the Song of the Sea either! A group of Levites, of unknown size, leaving at an unknown time, under unknown circumstances, did not require a headline in the *Egyptian Daily News*. So when Israel Finkelstein and Neil Silberman say, "We have not even a single word about early Israelites in Egypt" in inscriptions or papyri, it means they are looking for a reference to a specific nation, *Israel*.[88] But no entity named Israel was there. And the group that was there would not necessarily be called "levites" in Egyptian sources either because that might not have been the name by which they were known there. Indeed, if *levi* was in fact a Hebrew word for an attached person, the levite group in Egypt probably was not known to Egyptians by that term. We do not have any idea what they would be called there.

A third old argument figures both ways in this. Some argue that a people would not make up a story that their ancestors were slaves. If they were going to make up a history for themselves, they would say they were descended from kings or gods, not slaves. Why invent a lowly past?[89] I used to use this argument as well. But later I thought that it is really not a very strong argument, and people are right to challenge it. A rags-to-riches story can in fact have appeal. Still, Professor Nahum Sarna of Brandeis University pointed out that rags-to-riches stories are one thing, but "no people, so far as we are aware, has ever suggested that its origins were as *slaves*" (emphasis mine). I would add that the obvious exception is Liberia, a country that does see its origins as slaves, but among Liberia's founders *were* slaves, liberated from

North America. They did not invent it. So that is just the exception that makes the point.

In any case, an essential question for all historians is whether someone would make this up. It still applies here, and it argues in favor of the exodus, because there are other parts of the story that seem even less likely to be made up than slave ancestors. Why make up that Moses was married to a Midianite? Why make up that his father-in-law was a Midianite priest? Why make up that Israel's priesthood was not indigenous? There are some other parts of the story that I, too, would acknowledge were made up. But these basics—some Egyptian experience, the Midianite connection—appear to me to be shoes, not magic pumpkins.

Fourth, some have raised another argument to suggest that the story is made up. Specifically: unnamed pharaohs. I wrote in my commentary on the Torah that there are five pharaohs in the Torah: a pharaoh who thought that Sarah was Abraham's sister, the pharaoh who knew Joseph, the pharaoh who did not know Joseph and oppressed the Israelites, the pharaoh who sought to kill Moses (who may or may not be the same pharaoh who did not know Joseph), and the pharaoh of the exodus. Why are not any of their names given? Names of pharaohs do appear in later books (Shishak, Necho).[90] Their absence in the Torah gives the narrative a nonhistorical quality, which is contrary to the manifest aim of the authors to present history. So some argue that this is evidence that the stories are not true, that they were invented by writers who could not name these kings because they had no idea of the names of ancient pharaohs.[91] In the case of the two pharaohs in Genesis we have hardly any evidence to argue for or against this. But in the case of the exodus pharaohs, we have seen sufficient likelihood that the oppression and exodus are historical so that we must at least consider whether there could be other reasons why the pharaohs are not named. My friend Jonathan Saville suggests that perhaps the reason, consciously or not, was to downgrade the pharaoh, as when people sometimes avoid saying the name of someone to whom they feel hostile. I also keep in mind a lesson I learned from my teacher Professor Cross, who used to say: the most banal explanation is usually the right one. Perhaps the names of the pharaohs simply were no longer preserved in memory or written tradition by the time the stories came to be written. The authors no longer had any sources that recorded (or cared about) the pharaohs' names. They cared about preserving names that mattered much more to them: Levi, Moses, Aaron, Miriam, Zipporah, even the midwives Shiphrah and Puah. These are the names of the story's heroes. But did the authors care whether it was Pharaoh Rameses II or Rameses III? Or Merneptah? Apparently not. An absence of pharaohs' names does not mean an absence of an exodus.[92] Indeed, there may not have been any single pharaoh's name to remember. What we have seen is the likelihood that there were Levites, "attached" outsiders, living in Egypt through centuries, who then left. We do not know if any one pharaoh stood out as their prime oppressor.

Fifth, some have argued that the biblical accounts were written a long time—many centuries—after the time of the exodus, so we cannot rely on them for facts. And that brings us back to the question of sources. If some or all of the biblical authors did not see the exodus themselves, how did they know what happened? Some scholars have argued that the Bible's story of the exodus comes from very late writers. Probably most prominent among these scholars are the archaeologist Israel Finkelstein and the Egyptologist Donald Redford. Redford says that geographic details in the story reflect locations in the seventh and sixth centuries BCE, which is at least five or six hundred years after the suggested time of the exodus.[93] Finkelstein cites all of Redford's evidence and concludes, "All these indications suggest that the Exodus narrative reached its final form during the time of the Twenty-sixth Dynasty, in the second half of the seventh and the first half of the sixth century BCE."[94]

In the first place, "reached its final form" covers a lot of sins. At most it means that some names of persons and places that fit that period were changed or added to the text at that period. I respect Finkelstein as an archaeologist, and I respect Redford as an Egyptologist. But they are not expert in biblical source criticism. When they date the composition of the texts about the exodus to the seventh or even sixth century BCE because they say that some geographic details in the story reflect that century,[95] and when others date it even later, they have to feel compelled at least to *try* to explain how those places and details found their way into texts that show so many signs of having been composed during the time when both Israel and Judah existed as two countries side by side. That was *centuries* earlier: between the tenth and eighth centuries BCE.[96] These scholars have made no attempt to account for this. Our main sources—the Song of the Sea, the Song of Deborah, J, E, P, and most of D (the law code called Dtn in Deuteronomy 12–26; and the songs in Deuteronomy 32 and 33)—all come from before the end of the eighth century BCE, and some come from as early as the twelfth century BCE. Finkelstein and Redford just do not address source criticism of the Bible. They likewise do not come to terms with the linguistic evidence that confirms that these sources were written in a Hebrew that comes long before the time that they imagine.[97] Redford wrote back in 1992, "Any scholar who exempts any part of his sources from critical evaluation runs the risk of invalidating some or all of his conclusions," but that is exactly what he has done. Our various biblical sources referring to the exodus range all the way from the twelfth century to the fifth. So ancient authors were writing about the exodus all through the biblical period.

And there is an even larger point of method here. At the San Diego conference, Professor Rendsburg questioned the archaeologists. He noted that the Bible says, "Didn't I bring up Israel from the land of Egypt, and the Philistines from Caphtor?"[98] The archaeologists agreed that the Bible was right about this: the Philistines did in fact come to the region of Canaan/Israel from across the Mediterranean Sea (Caphtor, which is possibly Cyprus or the Greek Islands). So, Rendsburg asked, if the Israelites could remember the history of the Philistines four hundred years back, why should we think that they could not remember their own history that far back?! Rendsburg addressed the question to two of the leading archaeologists of the United States and Israel, and neither one of them gave him an adequate answer. Late sources do not necessarily mean *wrong* sources. (Rendsburg, being an honorable scholar, later wrote to me that he had learned that the biblical scholar and archaeologist James Hoffmeier had also made this point in print. Hoffmeier wrote, "It would be inexplicable for the prophet (and his audience) to know the origins of the Philistines and Arameans but be wrong about Israel's origin!" It is reassuring when two scholars independently make the same observation.)[99]

The likelihood that the Levites were the ones who experienced the exodus forces us to reexamine many of the classic arguments. Either these arguments involve a mass exodus, which need not be the case, or they do not come to terms with connecting the archaeology with the texts and their authors.

DON'T MESS WITH THE LEVITES

So, in this scenario, what happens when these Levites leave Egypt and arrive in Israel? The ten tribes of Israel (and two more—Judah and Simeon—to the south) have their territories, and none is about to give its territory to these newcomers. The tribe of Ephraim tells Issachar, "Give them some of yours." Issachar says, "You give them some of yours." The tribe of Dan says, "Manasseh has more than we do. Let them give some." Manasseh says, "In your dreams!" Nobody wants to part with land to give to these immigrants from Egypt.

Ah, but the Levites are not people to whom one says "No." The stories about them in five different sources connect them with violence:

Levi is one of the two brothers who massacre the men of Shechem in that circumcision story about Dinah that we considered earlier (Genesis 34).

Levi (along with Simeon) is cursed for his violence in Jacob's deathbed testament:

> Implements of violence are their tools of trade.
> Let my soul not come in their council;
> let my glory not be united in their society.
> For in their anger they killed a man,
> and by their will they crippled an ox.
> Cursed is their anger, for it's strong,
> and their wrath, for it's hard.
>
> (Genesis 49)

The Levites massacre around three thousand *Israelite* people in the golden calf episode:

And Moses stood in the gate of the camp and said,
"Whoever is for Yahweh: to me!" And all the children of Levi were gathered to him. And he said to
them, "Yahweh, God of Israel, said this: 'Set, each
man, his sword on his thigh; cross over and come back
from gate to gate in the camp; and kill, each man, his
brother and, each man, his neighbor and, each man,
his relative.' " And the children of Levi did according
to Moses' word, and about three thousand men fell
from the people in that day.

> (Exodus 32:26–28)

The Levite Phinehas sees two non-Levites, an Israelite man
and a Midianite woman, enter the Tabernacle when the Israelites are encamped in the wilderness. No one but a Levitical
priest is allowed in the Tabernacle. The two intruders are apparently engaged in an activity in which they are positioned in such
a way that Phinehas can kill both of them with a single spear:
it goes through the man and into the woman. According to the
text, Phinehas is rewarded for his zeal in this action. He later
becomes Israel's high priest (Numbers 25:6–15).

And there is the old poem at the end of the Torah, the Blessing of Moses (Deuteronomy 33), that we discussed earlier. It asks
God to

pierce Levi's adversaries' hips, and those who hate
    him,
so they won't get up.

> (Deuteronomy 33:11)

Is any of this historical? Did Levi and/or his descendants really
do any of these things? Watch carefully. You are about to read

a scholar saying the words "I don't know." But I do know this much: even if they are fiction, they represent a common understanding about the Levites in ancient Israel. Two poets and three prose writers all shared that understanding. You do not mess with the Levites.[100] If you do, you find a horse head in your bed. So they reach an accord: the resident tribes keep their legacies, their territorial portions of the land. But the Levites have no tribal territory; so they get a few cities and 10 percent (a tithe) of the Israelite tribes' produce. And then this is set in a context of religion. The Levites collect their 10 percent in their role as the priests of Israel.[101] In some early texts, the word "Levite" itself implies a priest. So, for example, we have a story in the book of Judges that takes place early in Israel's history in the land. A man has a religious shrine at his home, and a Levite passes through. The man says, "Be my priest," and blesses God for giving him a Levite so he will have a priest.[102] It is naturally understood that Levites are clergy. It would be as if in some small American town that had no church a minister would pass through town. They would have him performing weddings in no time.

PRIESTS AND TEACHERS

One more thing: the Levites were not just priests. The Bible emphasizes their role as *teachers*. Another of the oldest texts in the Bible that we discussed besides the Song of the Sea and the Song of Deborah was the Blessing of Moses (Deuteronomy 33). Already at this very early point in the national history, this song says of the Levites, "They'll teach your judgments to Jacob and your torah to Israel."[103] Leviticus likewise commands that they are to teach what God spoke through Moses.[104] And the Levites, as the teachers of the religion, taught everyone about the wonderful miraculous departure from Egypt. And within relatively few generations, the teachers had everyone growing up with the story—and sharing in it. The Levite author of E taught:

> And it will be, when your child will ask you tomorrow, saying, "What is this?" that you'll say to him, "With strength of hand Yahweh brought **US** out from Egypt, from a house of slaves."
>
> (Exodus 13:14)

The Levite author of Deuteronomy taught:

> When your child will ask you tomorrow, saying, "What are the testimonies and the laws and the judgments that Yahweh, our God, commanded you?" then you shall say to your child, "**WE** were slaves to Pharaoh in Egypt, and Yahweh brought **US** out from Egypt with a strong hand. . . . And He brought **US** out from there in order to bring **US** to give **US** the land that He swore to **OUR** fathers."
>
> (Deuteronomy 6:20–23)

They taught the people that they had to take from their first fruit and set it before their God and share it with the Levites. And when they would do this ceremony they each had to say the credo:

> My father was a perishing Aramean, so he went down to Egypt and resided there with few persons and

became a big, powerful, and numerous nation there.
And the Egyptians were bad to US and degraded US
and imposed hard work on US. And WE cried out
to Yahweh, OUR fathers' God, and Yahweh listened
to OUR voice and saw OUR degradation and OUR
trouble and OUR oppression. And Yahweh brought
US out from Egypt. . . . And He brought US to this
place and gave US this land.

(Deuteronomy 26:5–10)[105]

They taught the people ten commandments, and the premise
that preceded all of them was this:

I am Yahweh, your God, who brought YOU out from
the land of Egypt, from a house of slaves.

(Deuteronomy 5:6)

Now consider: How long did the Levites have to teach these
things—one generation? two? three?—before all the children
in Israel grew up with them, accepting them as their own history and legacy? When your child asks what it is all about,
you say, "Yahweh brought *us* out from Egypt." Compare the
observance of Thanksgiving in the United States. Not many
of us are descended from Pilgrims or the Wampanoag native
Americans, but most of us have come to participate in some
way in the event. The specific event—the first Thanksgiving
dinner—in the story may not even be factual, but there are
some real historical events behind it. So with the exodus:
Something happened. It may not have included the sun going
dark for three days or sticks turning to snakes. It may not have
had two million people. But it did include some core of the
future people of Israel departing Egypt.[106]

A number of my colleagues in the field of biblical scholarship have added pieces of the puzzle that may further help to explain how all of Israel came to accept the idea that the whole nation had been slaves in Egypt. They each put it in different ways, but they all focused on the fact that Egypt had ruled the region of Canaan, which became Israel, for around four hundred years. (That does in fact happen to be the amount of time that the Bible says the slavery in Egypt went on.[107]) At times this period of Egyptian hegemony over the land even included enslavement of some of the population. Ronald Hendel of the University of California, Berkeley, proposed that this memory of oppression by the Egyptians could have attracted the Israelites to embrace the story of the enslavement and exodus from Egypt. He wrote:

> But—and this is the important point—for the exodus story to take root in early Israel it was necessary for it to pertain to the remembered past of settlers who did *not* immigrate from Egypt.[108]

Of the other scholars who made this connection between the Egyptian empire in Canaan and the Israelites' view of the exodus, the one who took it the furthest was David Sperling. Hendel and the Israeli scholar Nadav Na'aman and others had offered this connection as a possible explanation of why Israel accepted the exodus as their history.[109] Sperling went the full distance and claimed that there was never any enslavement in Egypt or exodus at all. Sperling said that the whole exodus story was fiction, invented as an allegory for those four hundred years of Egyptian domination. Instead of slaves *to* Egypt, they were now pictured as slaves *in* Egypt.[110] In my debate with Professor Sperling in New York, I questioned the idea that the Bible's authors were making an allegory to Egypt's enslavement of the people in the region of Israel. I looked first at how the prophets in the Bible treat the subject. Seven books of the prophets refer to the *exodus* in thirty-three verses, but they mention the *slavery* in only two verses.[111] Now, if they were inventing an allegory to Egyptian slavery, why is almost their entire emphasis on the exodus and not on the slavery? Likewise in the book of Psalms, five of the psalms refer to the exodus, but they never refer to the slavery.[112] We could even say the same of the Bible's story in the Torah itself. After the point of the departure from Egypt, the books of Exodus, Leviticus, and Numbers refer to the exodus in sixty-five verses, but they mention the "house of slaves" in only three.[113] How could they put all this emphasis on the departure and hardly ever mention the slavery if the whole thing was fashioned as reinventing the enslavement in the land to the Egyptians?! And further, we still have the matter of those fifty-two references to aliens. Why emphasize *aliens* if it is an allegory for slavery *in their own land*?! The emphasis on exodus and on aliens leads to the conclusion: They cared about the slavery, of course, but their chief concern in formulating their story was not only with being enslaved to Egypt. It was with being aliens there! Hendel's view is attractive as a middle ground between Sperling's view and mine. It takes account of the years of Egyptian domination, but not as a basis for making up the whole exodus but rather as a reasonable historical explanation for why all of Israel would have been attracted to accept the basic story. Only the Levites may have experienced the exodus, but all of Israel adopted it and told it and retold it, from some point around three thousand years ago to the Passover celebrations of Jews to the present day.[114]

TWO COROLLARIES

We are close, but not quite done. Israel's acceptance of the doctrine over time that they *all* had come from Egypt required two more corollaries. First, it meant that, if all of Israel had participated, then the group that had experienced the exodus had to have been much bigger. So at least two centuries after such an arrival of Levites would have occurred, the Levite E source had the Pharaoh in its story say, "They are more numerous and powerful than we" (1:9); and it added, "The more they degraded it, the more it increased, and the more it expanded" (1:12); and it added, "And the people increased, and they became very powerful" (1:20); and by the end of the plagues it concluded, "The men, apart from the infants, were about six hundred thousand" (12:37). That opened the door for another Levite/Priestly source, P, after another century or two had passed, to include a census and get the number up to 603,550 adult males, from which we derived a total of some two million. Our earliest poetic source (the Song of Miriam) and our earliest prose source (J) had not mentioned any numbers at all. It is the latest source, P, the farthest source from the event, that added a census and a giant, specific number. That is the answer to the detective question that we asked at the beginning of this chapter: how do two million people disappear? The biblical authors did not make up the exodus. But they *had to* make up the numbers. And that is what got us up to two million people, whom our archaeological colleagues have been combing in vain to find.

And the second corollary of the acceptance of the doctrine that all of Israel had come from Egypt was that this opened a question of how all these people had arrived and come to be living all over the land. So the authors of the book of Joshua imagined that there had to have been a great conquest. They imagined that Joshua fit the battle of Jericho, walls came tumbling down, the sun stood still in the sky, and Canaanite cities were destroyed. They even introduced the idea that Joshua circumcised all of Israel in preparation for that conquest, because they now envisioned all of Israel, not just the Levites, practicing circumcision.[115] They needed the mass numbers, they needed the conquest, and they needed circumcision. In this case our archaeological evidence indicates that no such arrival of conquering masses ever took place—the destruction layers are just not there on the sites—and our earliest source, the Song of Miriam, does not mention it. Where we do find a destruction layer is at the site of the city of Hazor, but that fits better with the account of Deborah's defeat of the king of Hazor, to which we referred earlier, or it could have happened at some other time.[116] Without all the other cities, it does not add up to Joshua or a widespread conquest of the land. The archaeologists are right: there was no conquest.[117] (And thank heavens for that. It is a story of violent destruction, and the Jews have been denigrated for it; but it never happened.) We might ask: would these ancient writers have really made this up? Would they invent a genocide that they never committed? But consider the earliest references to Israel in archaeological sources. We already know the first: the Merneptah stele. Pharaoh Merneptah says, "Israel is wasted. Its seed is no more." The second is the stele of the Moabite King Mesha. It is standing in Paris in the Louvre. Mesha, who is known from the Bible, acknowledges that, as the Bible reports too, Israel conquered and dominated his land. But, he says, he broke Israel's yoke, and now "Israel is destroyed." These two of the earliest mentions of Israel outside of the Bible both claimed that Israel is gone, erased. Neither was true. That was just what you said in that world. "We killed 'em." "We slaughtered 'em." Egypt said it. Moab said it. And so did Israel. They said it, but they did not do it. The conquest never happened. People have used this as proof that there was no exodus either. But it is the opposite. It argues against the historicity of a *mass* exodus, but it is consistent with our picture of an exodus of a smaller group that then transformed and taught it as the experience and heritage of all of Israel. The archaeologist William Dever saw the same thing. He wrote, "Some of Israel's ancestors probably did come out of Egyptian slavery, but there was no military conquest of Canaan."[118] And the biblical historian Baruch Halpern, too, saw the need to follow the exodus account with a tale of conquest of the land by the arriving masses from Egypt. He wrote, "The Exodus, without the conquest, would never have survived as a story."[119]

THERE WAS AN EXODUS

Do you really think that the Israelites made up a story that they were descended from slaves?

Do you think that they completely made up a story that they were not indigenous in their land—that they had become a people someplace else?

Do you think that they made up a story in which their priests had Egyptian names—and then forgot that they were Egyptian names?

Do you think that they made up Moses?

Do you think that they made up a story that Moses had a Midianite priest as his father-in-law?

Do you think that the architectural match of their Tabernacle—their central shrine—with the battle tent of Rameses II was just coincidental?

That the similarity of their ark to the Egyptian bark was also coincidental?

Was the Egyptian practice of circumcision being commanded only in the Levite sources coincidental?

Were fifty-two references to being good to aliens and four times saying that this was "because we were aliens in Egypt" unrelated to ever having actually been in Egypt?

Are four hundred years of presence of Western Semites as aliens in Egypt, and then those fifty-two references about how to treat aliens, a coincidence?

Do you think that two different stories, from two different authors—both of them Levite authors—that both have the name of God unknown until the time of Moses and the exodus have nothing to do with this?

Do you think that *not* finding thirty-three-hundred-year-old evidence in the Sinai wilderness in surveys in the twenty-first century CE outweighs all of this?

———— ⌾ ————

So the picture that is proposed here is that there was an exodus. There was not a conquest. There was an introduction and merger of Yahweh, the God of the exodus experience, with El, the God of the Israelite experience. That merger was—it had to have been—a crucial step in the formation of monotheism. Whether you think that the formation and ultimate victory of monotheism was in the twelfth century BCE or the eighth or the seventh, sixth, or fifth, it is hard to see how it would have happened if Yahweh and El had long been two distinct gods of Israel. If there was an exodus, it was necessarily small in numbers. Does it really ruin your day if the exodus was historical but not *all* of the Israelites were in it? It was more than an escape or even a liberation. It was, unknown to the people who experienced it, a necessary part—a *foundational* part—of religion, literature, and history ever after.

CHAPTER THREE

THE MYSTERY OF ISRAEL

What Did They Find When They Came There?

THERE WAS A THERE THERE

If the exodus was historical, that is not the end of the story. It is the start. When the people who experienced the exodus from Egypt arrived in the breathtaking land that lay on the east shore of the Mediterranean Sea—the point where Europe, Asia, and Africa all converge—what did they find, and whom did they meet? They found two regions: one in the north, called Israel, and one in the south, called Judah. The people of Israel were the Israelites. The people of Judah were the Jews, or Judeans.[1] Sometimes they were two separate countries. Sometimes they were one united kingdom. That Israel and Judah were there is no mystery.

Not so fast. On September 24, 2012, the president of Iran informed reporters that Israel has "no roots there in history" in the Middle East. Now a lot of jokes came to mind at the expense of that clueless man, but, seriously, he at least conveyed an important truth: he recognized that Israel's historical presence in that world since antiquity matters—matters enough to deny it. The current issues of the Middle East have injected even sharper interest in the historicity of the Bible's record than we had already. But this chapter is not about contemporary Middle East politics. Our business is much earlier, back near the beginning. Our concern is what the Levites would have encountered when they arrived there over three thousand years prior to our time and issues.

The Bible pictures the Israelite and Judean populations and their governments there starting at least in the twelfth or thirteenth century BCE and continuing until the end of the Hebrew Bible's history about eight hundred years later. But, just as we asked in Chapter 1, how do we know if this is true? As scholars, we cannot just say, "The Bible tells us so." We need to see evidence that could be presented to any honest person, whether that person is religious or not, Jewish or Christian or from some other religion or no religion, or from Mars. If we want to know what the Levite immigrants found there, we have to see how we know that there was a there there.

INSCRIPTIONS IN HEBREW

First, the land is filled with inscriptions in Hebrew. I do not mean just an occasional message on a piece of pottery or carved in a wall. Nor should we even start with one or two of the most famous archaeological finds. Rather, we have thousands of inscriptions. They come from hundreds of excavated towns and cities. They are in the Hebrew language. From whatever the point that Yahweh was introduced in the land, the inscriptions include people's names that bear forms of the name of their God, Yahweh (thought to be pronounced *Yahwéh,* with the accent on the *second* syllable). This means names like:

Hoshaiah	which means	"Yahweh Saved"
Ahijah	which means	"Yahweh Is My Brother"

Shemariah	which means	"Yahweh Watched"
Gemariah	which means	"Yahweh Accomplished"
Ge'alyahu	which means	"Yahweh Redeemed"
Azaryahu	which means	"Yahweh Helped"
Hilqiyahu	which means	"Yahweh Is My Portion"
Berekhyahu	which means	"Blessed by Yahweh"
Shelemyahu	which means	"Made Whole by Yahweh"

The inscriptions also refer to their rulers. Both Israel and Judah had kings. The inscriptions include stamps and seals from official documents. The seals were people's engraved names, which were imprinted on small chunks of clay, producing a stamp, also called a bulla. The inscriptions also come from tombs where that land's people were buried. They name people who appear in the Hebrew Bible. Just while I was writing this chapter, a beautiful clay stamp was made known that had been discovered in Jerusalem bearing the name of King Hezekiah son of King Ahaz. Hezekiah and Ahaz are two of the most prominent kings in the Bible, appearing in the books of Kings, Chronicles, and Isaiah.[2] A seal at Ezion Geber (the contemporary city of Eilat) says "*lĕyōtām*," meaning "belonging to Jotham," which was the name of the king-regent, son of Uzziah, who is reported in the Bible to have built Ezion Geber.[3] A seal at Megiddo says, "Servant of Jeroboam." Jeroboam is the name of a king of Israel in the Bible.[4] We have found pottery jars and handles stamped with the word *lmlk,* which means "By the King" or "According to the King." They are like stamps of government-approved measurements on bottles and packages today. Altogether there are thousands of *lmlk* seal impressions on jar handles.[5]

Some of the bullae identify the person as "Who Is over the Building" (*'ašer 'al habbayit*) or "Who Is over the Work Force" (*'ašer 'al hammas*), which are titles for officials in the government. Some identify the person as "The Scribe" (*hassōphēr*); or as "Servant of the King" (*'ebed hammelek*), which is another term for a royal official; or as "Son of the King" (*ben hammelek*), meaning a prince; or as "Mayor of the City" (*śar hā'îr*); or as "Officer of the Army" (*śar haṣṣābā'*).[6] These references to titles of civil and military officials are not just a matter of getting some people's names from those times. They are specific signs of the existence of a government, of official organization and administration.

In the City of David excavations of Jerusalem, where I spent four seasons with my students from the University of California, San Diego, fifty-one bullae were found, many with names ending in *-yahu*. And one of them had the name Gemaryahu ben Shaphan. He was a man mentioned by name in the book of Jeremiah.[7]

Inscriptions include wording that also appears in the Hebrew Bible. They reflect a widespread community whose dominant language was Hebrew and who worshipped a God named Yahweh.

I happened to be present at the time of the discovery of another important inscription in Jerusalem, though I didn't know it until years later. In the summer of 1979 I was staying in Jerusalem at the Scottish hospice, a guest house connected with the Church of Scotland. One morning I looked out my window and saw people engaged in archaeological work below. Since I am in the business, so to speak, I went out and chatted with them. I learned that they were doing an excavation under the direction of the archaeologist Gabriel Barkay of the University of Tel Aviv, and they had uncovered some tombs from the seventh century BCE. In one of these burial caves they found a cylindrical object made of silver. The silver had been beaten into a flat sheet like foil. Words were inscribed in it, and then it was rolled up so a string could be placed through it and it could be worn like a necklace. The problem was that it was twenty-seven-hundred-year-old silver, and whenever anyone tried to unroll it to see what it said, it cracked. (It was sort of the archaeological equivalent of the Heisenberg uncertainty principle. If you looked, then it could not be seen.) So it appeared that we might never know what was inscribed in it. But Ada Yardeni, a curator and conservationist at the Israel Museum, would not give up. She put a concoction of thick glue around the cylinder and then opened it a tiny fraction of an inch. She then applied more of the concoction and then opened it another minuscule amount. This process was painstaking and slow, but she finally unrolled the silver. And this is what she read:

> May Yahweh bless you and keep you.
> May Yahweh make his face shine to you and give
>   you peace.

It is the words of the Priestly Blessing in the Hebrew Bible. You will find it in Numbers 6:24–26. It is thus the oldest text known from the Bible ever found.[8]

That was just one inscription. In a Harvard expedition at the city of Samaria in 1910, over sixty were found. Later excavations brought the number to 102.[9] In the excavation of the city of Lachish, a British archaeologist, J. L. Starkey, found twenty-one drafts of letters in Hebrew on pottery shards (ostraca) in 1935. Lachish was the second biggest city in Judah after Jerusalem.[10]

At the city of Arad, the archaeologist Yohanan Aharoni, of Tel Aviv University, discovered over one hundred inscribed Hebrew ostraca. Those ostraca range across centuries. They include three personal seals of one of the Judean commanders of the fort there, a man named Elyashib son of Ashyahu—another name with a theophoric element of the name Yahweh.[11] On ostracon number 18 at Arad are the words "House of Yahweh," meaning a Temple.[12] An inscription on a bowl there refers to the sons of Korah. The Bible identifies the sons of Korah as composers of psalms.[13] It lists them as a Levite clan, the descendants of Korah, a first cousin of Moses and Aaron who challenges their leadership in a story in the book of Numbers.[14] Twenty-eight inscribed ostraca in Hebrew were found at Horvat 'Uza.[15] Ostraca with Hebrew inscriptions on them were also found at Yabneh-yam, at Tel 'Ira, and at Beer Sheba.[16]

The distinguished scholar Jeffrey Tigay of the University of Pennsylvania summed up: "The names of more than 1,200 pre-exilic Israelites are known from Hebrew inscriptions and foreign inscriptions referring to Israel." Of these, 557 have names with Yahweh as their divine element, and seventy-seven have names with El.[17]

The existence of this many inscriptions means that there had to be a fair number of people who could write them and read them. One of the indicators that people were learning and practicing writing is the discovery of texts with the alphabet written on them. These are called "abecedaries." People would just write out the alphabet in order. These may have been school texts, they may have been for practice, or just graffiti. Some scholars think they may have also had a magical purpose. They range through nearly the entire biblical period, from the twelfth century (or tenth at latest) BCE forward.[18] The 'Izbet Sartah inscription, dating from the twelfth century, was found in 1976.[19] The

Tel Zayit inscription, dating from the tenth century, was found in 2005 in excavations by the Pittsburgh Theological Seminary directed by the archaeologist Ron Tappy.[20] My former student Michael Homan, now Professor of Theology at Xavier University of Louisiana, who made the connection between the Tabernacle and Rameses' Tent (Chapter 2), was the supervisor of the area where it was discovered. He wrote about what transpired on the day of the discovery:

> The square that I supervised was O-19, right on the shoulder of the tel. Ron was in a metal basket suspended over the site by a tractor arm for taking pictures. While we were waiting up on top for Ron to finish photographs of the Trench, a volunteer named Dan Rypma from Colorado State approached me. Dan said he had seen some scratches on a rock while he had been sweeping the stones in a wall the day before. He said he wasn't sure what these scratches were, but he had thought quite a bit about them the night before and he wanted to make sure that we didn't leave the site without at least pointing them out to me. We carefully went into the square into this Iron Age room that had cobble stones and well preserved walls. Just over a meter up, sitting in the wall, was the stone Dan wanted to show me. I could see, sure enough, the scratches Dan mentioned. But, looking carefully at the stone for quite some time, I could recognize what appeared to be the letters *mem* and a *nun* in an ancient West Semitic script. Let me be clear in stating that these letters and the others that we saw shortly thereafter were HARD to see, as other scholars who saw the stone in more favorable conditions have attested.

The light had to be coming from the side just right. It reminded me of Indiana Jones and the staff of Ra. So here I was, the first person in nearly 3000 years to read letters carved on the stone. I was extremely overcome with excitement. I'm not the type of person who jumps up and down though. I just kept telling Dan and the assistant supervisor Dale Swindel how amazing all of this was. I told Gabi Barkai that I thought we had an inscription in a stone in the wall. He was of course very excited, as the wall provided a great archaeological context, and the thought of a 10th century BCE inscription in Judah is rare. Impossible some would have argued. When Ron was lowered back to the ground, I told him about Dan's amazing find, and we led him and Gabi over the rock. Then we celebrated, and then the entire team celebrated, and then we took a bajillion pictures of the rock *in situ*. We excavated the top of the wall down to the stone, and when we were set to remove it, my hand felt that the bottom was carved out. That was even more exciting, as the inscription was on some sort of a stone bowl, or mortar, or something. Dale and I had the privilege of carrying the soon-to-be-famous stone down the tel. I remember asking Dale "Are you ready for one of the most important walks of your life?" It was a few days later, after the stone was photographed and drawn by an expert, that Ron was able to discover that it was in fact an abecedary (the entire alphabet from *aleph* to *taw*).[21]

We often hear claims that there was very little literacy in early Israel. That is patently false. A recent study of pre-exile inscriptions further confirmed this.[22] It made the international media, so perhaps we can hope that these claims will finally be put to rest. This was a land where people were writing the alphabet. This was a land where there were people who were literate. They read. They wrote. And they left their writings, large and small, for us to find.

INSCRIPTIONS FROM OTHER COUNTRIES

Imagine the excitement of finding such things. Mike's and Dan's experience has happened to thousands of participants in excavations from dozens of countries. And that is just the Hebrew inscriptions from the lands of Israel and Judah. Plus we have those foreign inscriptions that Tigay mentioned. Texts from the neighboring lands refer to the people, to their kings, to their government, to their armies, and to their cities. The basic fact is: everybody knew that Israel was there: the Egyptians, the Assyrians, the Babylonians, the Arameans, the Moabites, the Persians.[23] In the last chapter we spoke of Pharaoh Merneptah (1213–1203 BCE), who refers to the people of Israel in a stone stele.[24] Pharaoh Shoshenk I, in the tenth century BCE, describes his campaign in which he refers to cities in Israel (including Ayalon, Beth-Shan, Megiddo, Rehob, and Taanach).[25] Assyrian King Shalmaneser III, in the ninth century BCE, names King Ahab "the Israelite" among his opponents in his Kurkh monument and names and pictures King Jehu of Israel on his Black Obelisk, which is now in the British Museum.[26] The Assyrian emperor Sennacherib, in the eighth century BCE, describes in detail his siege of Jerusalem and its king "Hezekiah the Judean,"

also in the British Museum.[27] Six other Assyrian emperors refer to
Israel and Judah as well and name kings whose reigns are also recorded in the Bible. The Babylonian sources, too, refer to the Jews
and their monarchy in the years after the Babylonians replaced
the Assyrian empire. And the record continues when the Persians
replace the Babylonians, as documented in the Cylinder of Cyrus,
the Persian emperor. Cyrus' decree in 538 BCE let the exiled Jews
return to their land. It was followed by an influx of Jewish population. There was population growth from the reign of Darius I
to Artaxerxes I. The country that the Babylonians had conquered
was reestablished as a state of Judah (*yehud medintha*) within the
Persian umbrella. You want irony? Persia, today called Iran, the
country that reestablished the Jews' country in biblical times, had
a president who said that Israel has no roots there.

Also from that period come the Elephantine papyri, a collection of documents that include letters from the Jewish community in Egypt in the fifth century BCE to the Jewish community
back in Jerusalem.[28]

Closer to home, right across the Jordan River from Israel, was
Moab, in what is now Jordan. In the ninth century BCE, its king
Mesha erected a stele referring to Israel and its king Omri, which
I cited in Chapter 2. He also refers to the royal House of David.[29]
An inscription erected by an Aramean (what is today Syria) also
refers to a king of the House of David.[30] In all, these ancient texts
refer to fifteen kings of Israel and Judah who are known from the
Bible, and all of them are referred to in the right periods.

MATERIAL CULTURE

Material culture (in other words: stuff) fills out this picture.
Thousands of people have now walked through the Siloam

Tunnel in waist-deep water under Jerusalem. It is a major feat of engineering. It is a passage nearly six football fields long underground. A tremendous project like this and others that we shall see reflect a major organized society with a government that could bring such an undertaking off. If it were done today, the governor would be there for photo opportunities, and the architect and builder would be honored. When it was done twenty-seven hundred years ago, it took a substantial number of workers and tremendous cost. Also, in 1880, an inscription was found in its ceiling. The Siloam inscription is now in the Istanbul Archaeology Museum. It actually describes how the tunnel was built. The tunnelers were in a hurry, so they started digging from both ends at the same time, planning (or hoping) to meet in the middle. There are old jokes about that: that the way to build a tunnel is to have two teams of men start from opposite ends and meet in the middle. And what if the two teams don't meet? Then you have two tunnels! Just a joke, but apparently that is almost what happened in Jerusalem. According to the inscription, the two teams were not quite on track to come together, but they heard the sounds of each other's tools. They followed the noise, and they met! We can date the Hebrew script of that inscription to the eighth century, which fits with King Hezekiah, the king of Judah who, according to the Bible, in fact built a water channel at Jerusalem (c. 715–687 BCE),[31] the same Hezekiah whose stamp was made known this year.

Likewise, when my students joined in the City of David Project archaeological excavations of Jerusalem under the archaeologist Yigal Shiloh in the 1980s, they uncovered the now-visible "stepped stone structure." Whatever purpose it served—defense, soil or water retention, a platform for some other major structure—it was a huge project. It was not something that a couple of friends assembled. It required community organization, planning, design, a large number of construction workers, and funding. Then, in 2005, farther up the hill, the archaeologist Eilat Mazar uncovered the remains of a monumental building that was constructed along with the stepped stone structure. She identified it as King David's palace. This caused much controversy at the time, as many people thought that she had overstepped the limits of the evidence.[32] Maybe it was a royal palace. Maybe it was something else. What we do know, though, is that it is a construction of monumental architecture from an extremely early period in Israel's history. And again, this was not built by some children as a playhouse. It reflects an enormous undertaking by an established organized society.

This is the kind of thing we find in other cities as well. At Dan, the northernmost city of ancient Israel, we find a planned city, with a massive gate (over twenty-two feet high), fronting on a plaza and leading to a temple with adjoining halls for priests, plus cobblestone streets and other public buildings.[33] At Hazor we find public buildings, a granary, and an underground water system.[34] We also find underground water systems at Megiddo, Taanach, Ibleam, Beer Sheba, and Bet Shemesh. We find massive fortifications at Lachish and other cities.[35]

Three of these cities proved not only revealing in themselves but truly astonishing as a group, a *connected* group. When the archaeologist Yigael Yadin excavated Hazor, he uncovered a tremendous gate made of six chambers. Then, when he excavated Megiddo, he found the same thing: a tremendous six-chambered gate. Now, a biblical verse refers to these two cities in a report about King Solomon. It says that, in addition to his building the Temple and his palace and other structures in Jerusalem, Solomon also had constructions at three cities: Hazor, Megiddo, and Gezer.[36] Yadin therefore proposed an examination of the site of the third city, Gezer, to see if it had the six-chambered gate as well. And it did. So the archaeological picture and the biblical picture matched. It was one of the great early cases of finding archaeology and text corresponding to each other. Now, since then, some archaeologists have challenged this (which should come as no surprise). Our friend the archaeologist Israel Finkelstein, co-director of subsequent excavations at Megiddo, questioned Yadin's view that King Solomon built up these three cities. He argued that these structures were from a later period and that we should attribute them to a later king, perhaps King Ahab (ninth century BCE) or King Jeroboam II (eighth century BCE).[37] Finkelstein's co-director at Megiddo, Professor Baruch Halpern, disagreed and still supports Yadin's original conclusion: King Solomon built these cities. I sat with Halpern on the top of that gate at Megiddo and went over the facts in light of its structure, and Halpern published his findings in a lengthy article.[38] I am persuaded that Yadin and Halpern are more probably right. But for our purpose here, we do not need to argue those fine points of archaeology. The revealing point is: all three major cities were constructed according to a common plan. When we see several schools in a town today, all built according to nearly identical architectural plans—or several post offices or government buildings looking the same around the country—we know what that means. A central government planned and carried it out that way. In the case of Israel, our concern here is not the debate over whether that central government was in the tenth, ninth, or eighth century. It is the fact such a central government existed. Early in the world of biblical Israel, there was a large population living in major cities with a common government.

The archaeologist John S. Holladay Jr. thus speaks of the "archaeologically discernible characteristics of a state" from the

tenth century BCE on. These include a pattern of urban settlements in a hierarchy of size: cities, then towns, then villages,
then hamlets. They have primary seats of government (i.e., capital cities): Jerusalem as capital of Judah, and Samaria as capital
of Israel. Then they have major cities as regional centers: Hazor,
Megiddo, Gezer, and Lachish. They have centralized bureau-
cracy. They have frontier defenses. They have standing armies.
They have economics based on tribute, taxes, and tolls. They
have a writing system. Holladay lists all of these and more in
showing how we know that there was a populous society with a
central government from this early stage of the biblical period.
Holladay published this in 1995.[39] We can now add more: central
planning of the architecture and layout of towns, a distinctive
alphabet, standard weights and measures.

And we can add that the Israelite sites lack pork bones.[40]
The archaeologist Elizabeth Bloch-Smith seconds the point, that
the material culture is clearly Israelite starting from the Iron II
period (950–600 BCE) at the latest.[41] These were established
countries, made of hundreds of towns, with a population whose
language was Hebrew, whose God was Yahweh, and who did
not eat pork.

EPIGRAPHY

We can also see the changes in the Hebrew scripts on the inscriptions developing through time, and we can actually date
texts based on this. (The first letter of the Hebrew alphabet is
aleph. An eighth century letter *aleph* does not look the same
as a seventh or sixth century *aleph.*) The study of these scripts
and the inscriptions is called epigraphy. Many biblical scholars

go through training in this field. I still recall taking my final exam in this field in my doctoral studies at Harvard. We were given a drawing of an inscription and had to date it by the way the letters were formed. (I passed.) The point is that this does not happen overnight. It takes centuries for these scripts to go through all these changes. So (1) we can date texts, and (2) we know that the Hebrew of these inscriptions was the language of the people of Israel and Judah, not just for a year or a decade or a century, but for many centuries.[42]

LANGUAGE

In parallel, we can trace the development of the Hebrew language as found in the Bible and the other ancient texts. We did not move from Shakespearean English to Valley Girl English overnight. That takes centuries. Likewise, the Hebrew of the Song of Miriam and the Song of Deborah, which are the two oldest texts in the Bible, is different from the Hebrew of the Court History of David in the book of 2 Samuel. And the Hebrew of the Court History is different from the Hebrew of the late book of Nehemiah.

We can verify this with outside controls. The texts in the Hebrew Bible that we trace to the early centuries of Israel's history—the time before the Babylonian exile of the Jews in 587 BCE—have parallels with the Hebrew of the inscriptions that we have dug up from those early centuries. The biblical texts that come from later centuries of Israel's history have parallels with the Hebrew of later works (the Dead Sea Scrolls and the Mishna).

Now you might say that maybe it was someone from a late period deliberately writing to make his or her work look early.

That is a fair question to raise. After all, could we not write something today imitating Shakespearean English? There are probably hundreds of high school teachers who have assigned their students to try doing just that as an exercise or just for fun. It is called archaizing. So how do we know when a biblical text is genuinely archaic and when it is a late writer archaizing?

The fact is that there is occasionally some archaizing in biblical texts, where a writer uses some older term for effect or elegance, just as we might throw in a word like "thou" or put up a sign saying "Ye Olde . . ." for fun or elegance. But no writer of Hebrew in a late period, for example the Persian or Greek period, could have written an entire long work in pre-exilic Hebrew. That would not have been possible because they could not have *known* pre-exilic Hebrew without having dug up a lot of inscriptions archaeologically and then derived the entire language from them.

The evidence is now substantial: Hebrew existed as a language that went through all the natural stages of development that we find in any language that people continuously speak and write over very long periods of time.[43]

LITERATURE

And then there is the literature itself. What we now know of who wrote the Bible reflects, conservatively, that there were seventy-five to one hundred authors and editors of the Hebrew Bible, and quite possibly a lot more. The literary study of the Bible that has blossomed in the last forty years (a biblical number) has revealed the artistry in so many of these works. Such a huge quantity of prose, poetry, and law did not materialize overnight. Or in a year. Or in a century. It had to take centuries and a thriving culture to compose. (From the oldest literary works in the Hebrew Bible, the Song of the Sea and the Song of Deborah, to the latest work, the book of Daniel, is about a thousand years.) Great literature, like a bacillus, can develop only in a culture. It is not chance that Russia produced so many superior novels, or that the British isles produced so much superior poetry. For ancient Israel to have produced so many fine authors required a culture that welcomed and fostered such literature over centuries. And the linguistic evidence confirms this, and so does the epigraphic evidence, and so does the archaeological evidence. This is a real showpiece of the evidence from the text and the evidence from archaeology coming together.

The point of this is how vast the array of the evidence is. This is not a vague hypothesis. It is not formulated by overestimating or overinterpreting a single little find. It is not like an Indiana Jones movie (though I like them a lot), in which the archaeologist goes tracking down a single object. This is a civilization: between four hundred and five hundred cities and towns excavated, hundreds of years, thousands of items in writing, millions of people. This evidence was not discovered by an individual or even by a small group. It was assembled by hundreds of archaeologists, with tens of thousands of workers, coming from many religions and many countries. Some archaeologists hoped to confirm the Bible. Some seemed to take pleasure in throwing the Bible into doubt. There have been frauds, and there have been mistakes, aplenty, as in any other field. But the mass of the evidence remains available to all. We can see and continually refine a picture of ancient Israel.

We can (and do) have a million arguments about almost every aspect of the Bible. But what we cannot deny is the existence of the world that produced it. That fact is not true just because the Bible says so. It is true because practically everything says so.

AND THEN THE LEVITES ARRIVED

Israel and Judah were there for hundreds of years. Still, the mystery is from where they came—and we just do not know. That is one of the raging battles and biggest unknowns in Bible and archaeology.[44] But what we do know is that they did not all come from Egypt. The group who came from Egypt, whom the evidence suggests were the Levites, found Israel and Judah already there. Pharaoh Merneptah's stele seems to have Israel there by 1205 BCE at the latest.

The Merneptah stele confused things as long as people were picturing the entire nation of Israel making the exodus. They had to picture the exodus taking place long before Merneptah's time: with millions leaving Egypt, journeying through the Sinai wilderness for a whole generation, arriving and conquering and settling in the land, all without leaving a sign in Egypt, Sinai, or Israel of any of those things happening. But as we saw in Chapter 2, if it was just the Levites, then their exodus could have been before or after Merneptah. The stele is still important. It just does not happen to be evidence for the date of the exodus. It is not evidence that Israel was in Egypt. It is evidence that Israel was in Israel! What matters—matters enormously—is that Israel the people was already there when the Levites arrived. Archaeologists and critical biblical scholars have been persuaded for a long time—correctly—by evidence that Israel was there all along in the land and not in Egypt. This seemed to bolster the conclusion that there was no exodus from Egypt. But Israel's presence in the land had nothing to do with the exodus, not if the Levites were in Egypt and Israel was in Israel.

The Levites would have had to arrive during the first couple of centuries of Israel's existence in the land. The early song of Deborah does not include them. We saw that in the last chapter. We were not certain if that omission was because the Levites were still in Egypt or because they were priests, not a tribe. But the Levites *are* mentioned in the next earliest poetry and in all of the earliest prose. The poetry includes the Blessing of Jacob in Genesis 49 and the Blessing of Moses in Deuteronomy 33.[45] The prose includes all of the sources of the Torah: the texts that we call E, J, P, and D. All of these prose and poetic sources treat the Levites as one of the tribes of Israel, a tribe that is assigned the priesthood. And the Levites continue to figure through all the books of biblical narrative: through Joshua, Judges, Samuel, Kings, and Chronicles, all the way down to the Bible's fifth-century BCE works: the books of Ezra and Nehemiah. In the early works, all Levites are recognized as priests. In later works, only one Levite clan are priests (the Aaronids, or Zadokites), and the rest of the Levites are identified as ancillary clergy.[46] That is the situation to the present day. The Levites may have been just a group of Asiatics who became "attached persons" from Egypt. But the early biblical writers transformed them, claiming that they were a tribe like any of the tribes of Israel and Judah, changing them from "attached persons" to a related clan, a tribe, genetic descendants of a man named Levi.

GENETICS: AN UNEXPECTED
CONFIRMATION

As I began writing and lecturing about the exodus, people occasionally asked me if I had considered genetic evidence. I had not. Having no expertise in genetics, I was reticent to go there. But, following a public lecture I gave about the exodus and the Levites, I spoke with Dr. Paul Wolpe, who is the Asa Griggs Candler Professor of Bioethics and the Raymond F. Schinazi Distinguished Research Chair in Jewish Bioethics at nearby Emory University. Dr. Wolpe had looked into genetic studies relating to the Levites, and he told me cautiously that they *might* provide evidence that supported my conclusions. I could not ignore a body of evidence if it existed and shed any light on this. So I contacted a friend, Dr. Geoffrey Wahl, doing genetic research at the Salk Institute in California. He generously made contact for me with a researcher at the Weizmann Institute in Israel, Dr. Moshe Oren, who replied that the person who is probably the best in the world to contact on that matter is Professor Karl Skorecki at the Technion in Haifa. He, likewise generously, made the contact with Dr. Skorecki. And, the next thing I knew, I was talking with Karl Skorecki by Skype. As different as our fields are, it appeared that we each had come upon possible confirmations or explanations of the other's findings.

A Brief Recap

To recap the archaeological and biblical side of this, here is what we have observed with regard to the Levites and the exodus:

A root meaning of the word *levi* in Hebrew is "attached" or "joined." This term applied quite suitably to the people who made the exodus from Egypt. They were an outside group attached to society in Egypt. And later they were an outside group attached to society in Israel and Judah. They need not have been a family, not a clan, not all kin to each other. What they had in common was rather a particular social status, this outsider alien status in Egypt. Later, after these levites settled among the people of Israel and Judah and became their clergy, they came to be thought of as a full-fledged tribe of Israel like any of the existing tribes there. This must have happened very early. We saw, in the previous chapter, the early poem known as the Blessing of Jacob (Genesis 49). It identifies Levi as one of twelve sons of the patriarch Jacob. Each of those twelve sons is pictured as the ancestor of a tribe. Dan is the ancestor of the Danites. Reuben is the ancestor of the Reubenites. So the Levites are also understood to be descendants of a particular man named Levi. This "adoption" of the Levites and calling them a tribe, descended from a single ancestor, had the effect of treating them as *related* to each other. And this has been the accepted picture of the Levites in Judaism down to the present day.

Then one more crucial historical development occurred: at a certain point in the history of ancient Israel, one family of these Levitical priests was singled out from the others. This family traced themselves to a single ancestor: Aaron. They identified Aaron as the elder brother of Moses.[47] Among both traditional and critical scholars there are differences about when the singling out of this family took place, but sometime during the time when the first Jerusalem Temple was standing (the Temple of Solomon, between the tenth and sixth centuries BCE), these "Aaronid" Levites became the official Temple priests. After this,

just the Aaronids were called the "priests." In Hebrew the word
for priests is *kohanim,* sometimes spelled *cohanim.* The Aaronids
were the priests, the *cohanim.* The rest of the Levites were just
plain Levites. They were lesser clergy, with religious duties but
without priestly status. And this too has been the accepted picture of the Levites in Judaism down to the present day. All Jews
who can trace their lineage, through whatever number of generations, are identified as in one of three groups: cohanim, Levites,
or Israelites. The general term "Israelites" is used for everyone
who is not identified as a cohen or a Levite.

The Cohen Gene

I was aware that there had been genetic research on the cohanim, but I was not aware of any work specifically on the
Levites. Karl Skorecki was among the group who had done the
research on the cohanim. And, I learned, they had in fact done
research on the Levites as well. This was a distinguished group
of scientists from the University of London, the Technion in
Haifa, and Oxford. They published their studies in the journal
Nature in 1998.[48]

First, regarding the cohanim: we find them among Jewish
communities around the world. The two most prominent communities in the Jewish diaspora are the Ashkenazi and the Se-
phardi. Ashkenazic Jews derive mainly from central and eastern
Europe. Sephardic Jews derive mainly from Spain, Portugal, and
the Middle East. Both have now spread to other places around
the world as well. What the researchers found was that people
who identify themselves as cohanim have features in common
genetically, distinguishing them from Israelites. Their common
genetic characteristics occur whether they are Ashkenazic or

Sephardic. Find cohanim anywhere in the world, and they will disproportionately show signs of kinship. In the scientists' more technical terminology:

> Despite extensive diversity among Israelites, a single haplotype (the Cohen Modal haplotype) is strikingly frequent in both Ashkenazic and Sephardic Cohanim.[49]

Early reports of this study understood it to have traced cohanim to a single male ancestor who lived around three millennia ago. Subsequent studies more carefully spoke of a small group of ancestors, not just a single individual. Dr. Skorecki told me more succinctly: "Not a *single* paternal lineage, but a very small number." The researchers were able to track this *paternal* lineage, from *male* ancestors, because Israelite priesthood passes only from father to son. So the research could focus on the Y, male chromosomes.

The Levite Genes

That is very interesting, and noteworthy. But what about the Levites? When the researchers looked at the Levite genetic picture, Dr. Skorecki said, "We found the Levites to be all over the place, not uniform across diaspora communities." That is, unlike the cohanim, Levites do not go back to a small group of ancestors, and they certainly do not go back to a single common ancestor. They do not descend from a single man, a theoretical Levi. The researchers recognized the distinction:

> Levite Y chromosomes are diverse, Cohen chromosomes are homogeneous.[50]

Another member of the group, Dr. David Goldstein, wrote:

> Those studies also gave us an inkling that the Y chromosomes of the Ashkenazi Levites are different from those of the Cohanim, the Israelites, and even the Sephardi Levites. What they did not do was reveal a clear Levite-specific genetic signature comparable to the Cohen Modal Haplotype.[51]

Simple and straight: Levites are not all related genetically—not to cohanim, not to Israelites, not even to each other. They do have roots in the ancient Near East,[52] but they do not come from a common tribe, let alone a common individual. The group's conclusion:

> Levite Y chromosomes have heterogeneous origins. Contemporary Levites, therefore, are not direct patrilineal descendants of a paternally related *tribal* group.[53]

Dr. Harry Ostrer, a medical geneticist at the Albert Einstein College of Medicine, concluded likewise:

> Y-chromosomal analysis of Levites has demonstrated multiple origins that depend on the Diaspora community from which they came—they are not all the descendants of tribal founder Levi.[54]

This conclusion was perplexing. Cohanim showed common ancestors, just as we would expect from the Bible. They could all be descended from that small priestly group that was singled out from among the other Levites. But the Levites overall did not show common ancestors. They were not related. No way. Skorecki had written to me, "There has been a significant amount of work and several publications pertaining to the Y-chromosome lineages of contemporary Levites, and the many hand-waving explanations that have been proposed regarding these perplexing findings (in contrast to the lineages of Kohanim and Israelites)." The proposed explanations were indeed far stretches. Goldstein cited two works, writing:

> Thus, the genetic evidence appears to favor the suppositions of John Bright (*A History of Israel*) and Risto Nurmela (*The Levites*) that it was much easier to become a Levite than it was a Cohen. To become a Cohen usually required a father who was a Cohen. To become a Levite probably required no more than faith and conviction (and perhaps the occasional well-placed bribe).[55]

With due respect to the late, respected historian John Bright, the genetic evidence favors no such thing. These were indeed "suppositions." Nothing more. We have no reason at all to think that it was easier to become a Levite in biblical times than it was to become a priest. On the contrary, we have evidence from the text that the opposite was the case. In the book of 1 Kings, after King Solomon dies, the country splits back into two kingdoms: Israel and Judah. The Temple and the Aaronid priesthood are in Judah, ruled by Solomon's son, King Rehoboam. Israel meanwhile gets its own king, Jeroboam I. King Jeroboam establishes alternative places of worship rather than the Temple. But, at least as important, he establishes an alternative priesthood. The biblical account does not tell us who these new priests were, but it definitely tells us who they were *not*.

> And he made priests from the lowest of the people,
> who were not of the children of Levi.
>
> (1 Kings 12:31)[56]

This is the best example we have from the biblical histories, and it is the exact opposite of what Bright had speculated. King Jeroboam chose people who were not Levites as Israel's priests. He is criticized in the text for doing this—but he gets away with it. This story may be history or it may be fiction. (In any case, Jeroboam's priests are never connected in any way with the Aaronid priesthood in Judah, and they are lost to history, so any descendants of theirs would never have been counted as priests among the Jews, and they would not figure in our genetic researches at all.) But either way the story reflects the fact that one could imagine an ordinary person becoming a priest. Someone who was not born a priest might get to be a priest, a *cohen,* maybe by just faith or by that well-placed bribe. But there was no case, no way that one who was not born a Levite could become a Levite. That identification was passed down from those original Levites, from father to son. After that original generation of Levite immigrants from Egypt, it was easier to become a king or a prophet or, for that matter, a shepherd than it was to become a Levite.[57]

If this is right, then what should we expect genetically? *Cohanim,* starting from a small group, perhaps a family or clan, should be related genetically. Levites, starting from a large, diverse group of immigrants from Egypt, should be diverse genetically. Cohanim are related by DNA. Levites are not related by DNA; they are related by common history.[58]

And that is just what the genetic research showed.

THE MERGER AND THE EXODUS

They came. They met. They joined. The Levites became part of Israel, part of the Jews, forever after. But after that merger the exodus was never forgotten. On the contrary, the nation observed it as a holiday: Passover. They sang its story in songs and wrote it down in prose histories. People were directed to teach it to their children. It inspired ceremonies, sacrifices, prayers. It reached a point at which a scholar in our own era could write, as I quoted at the beginning of this book: "The story of Israel's flight from Egypt is the most important in the Hebrew Bible."

WRITING HISTORY

Now while we are arguing (or let us say: investigating) whether all these biblical texts are right or wrong, true or false, history or fiction, we should also ask: why do we even have these texts? Why did ancient Israelites and Judeans write them? For some reason, the people of these lands, these cultures, felt that they had to tell the story. Perhaps it was another corollary of their particular experience. A small group joins a much larger group just around the time that they become a nation. They make a revolutionary consensus about having one major God, not two. They make a revolutionary union in which the small group become the priests of the larger group. And these priests teach that this one God had intervened in human affairs on earth. In the pagan religions of the ancient Near East, the gods and goddesses were the forces of nature: sky, earth, sun, moon, storm wind, fertility, sea, grain, death. But this nation's God is different. He is not the sun or the wind or the sea or any other one thing in nature. He is outside of nature, above nature, able to move those forces as He sees fit. Already in the early Song of the Sea, He is toying with the wind and the sea. Yahweh is not a God known through nature. He is a God known through His acts in history.[59] The movement of time in pagan religion is cyclical. This is, presumably, because its gods are known in nature, and nature is cyclical: the moon goes through its phases, the seasons recur in order, the sun also rises and sets. But history is linear. Teachers of history to children often draw a line. Books about history often have charts showing things along a line. Events follow on that line. We speak of "the arrow of time" following a linear course. And so the members of this new religion, with its new idea of a God who has acted in history on Israel's behalf, were moved to tell history. They traced a record of events along a line, with cause and effect. They found a new way to do this, a way to tell a story that, as far as we know, had never been done before on earth: writing history in prose. I say "as far as we know" because we cannot know if there were a thousand other prose works that were written before the ones in the Bible but that just did not survive. As far as we know, though, these ancient writers invented something new. They did not tell their story in poetry. They told it in prose. They occasionally inserted a poem or song and a law code, but their work was mainly prose. Herodotus is called the father of history, but the oldest prose accounts of history in the Bible were written when Herodotus' great-grandmother was not yet in preschool.[60]

So they wrote their story. They may have told it orally for a generation or two first. We cannot really know this because oral history is, after all, oral. Without a time machine we cannot go back and see them telling early versions of their story around their campfires. (I don't know why, but somehow someone always mentions campfires when we talk about this. Israel and Judah were urban. I don't think anybody told campfire stories unless they were in the scouts.) The prose texts, moreover, show signs of written rather than oral composition. For example, they contain puns that make sense only on a written page. Take the story of Joseph. His name is pronounced *yoseph* in Hebrew. The text says that after Yoseph tells his brothers a dream that offends them, they "added to their hatred" of him. "Added" in Hebrew is *yôsiphû*. Any ancient Israelite hearing the story orally in Hebrew could get the pun of *yôsēph* and *yôsiphû*. Then the story says that he "told" them a second dream. "Told" in Hebrew is *yĕsappēr*. Maybe not everyone, but at least some of the audience might have heard the root of the name *yôsēph* (*ysp*) lurking there as well. But the text also says that Yoseph's father Jacob gives Yoseph the famous "coat of many colors." Scholars have argued over that coat, about whether the word means striped, polka-dotted, long-sleeved, or whatever. But a more important point than the garment's style, I think, is that the Hebrew word that we are struggling to translate there, whatever it means to a haberdasher, is *psym* (pronounced *passîm*), which contains the root letters of the name Yoseph (*ysp*) backward. No audience could possibly get that pun orally. You have to see the letters on the parchment. These puns surface five times in just a few verses (Genesis 37:3–10).[61] One might respond that finding a pun in letters that are reversed is going too far. But in the same passage the text says that Joseph's brothers were not able "to speak to him of peace" (verse 4). "Peace" in Hebrew is *shālōm,* and later Joseph's father sends him to check on the *shālōm* of his brothers and the *shālōm* of the flock (verse 14). In between those, the angry brothers ask Joseph if his dream means "Will you *dominate* us?!" (verse 8). "Dominate" in Hebrew is *māshôl,* which is a reshuffling (called a metathesis) of the letters of *shālōm*. It, too, is a visual pun, not an oral one. There are many of these metatheses in the Bible, and this implies written, not oral, composition.[62]

In any case, whether they had some oral forerunners or not, the stories that we know are the ones that ancient Israelite and Judean authors wrote down. The fundamental thing is that by the time that these authors wrote them, the Levites' arrival and fusion into the community had already taken place. The teaching of the exodus as *national* history, the common experience of all the tribes, had already taken hold. I do not know what made them start writing their national story in prose. Once they started writing that way, though, it germinated into works of such virtuosity, such craftsmanship, that we are still reading them, arguing about them, believing in them, doubting them, and writing our own books about them. One of those early literary artists was a man or woman from the royal court in Judah. That genius wrote the text that we now call J. Another artist, no less talented than the first in my opinion, was a Levite in the kingdom of Israel. He wrote the text that we call E. A third writer, of different but equivalent talents, was a Levite priest in Judah sometime later, after the neighboring kingdom of Israel had been conquered by the Assyrians and ceased to exist. He wrote the text that we call P. Yet another writer, a century later in Judah, gave us the (composite[63]) text called D. We have already begun to see the literary results of these compositions and the editing process that preserved them together. These writers produced stories of the enslavement of all of Israel and their liberation from Egypt. They wrote that all of Israel, millions of people, made the journey to the promised land. They wrote that the name of their God, Yahweh, was known to all of the Israelites by the time that they arrived in that land. They wrote that Joshua led the millions into the land and conquered it. That is the story that they told, the first prose writing known to us in human experience. It is part story and part history. What we have been trying to do here is to see both: the story and the history of the world that produced it.[64] What we have found is that, even if much of the story is fiction, it still has clues embedded in it. Those clues, together with archaeology, have begun to enable us to look behind the stories and exhume history.

THE STORIES THEY TOLD

They told stories of their patriarchs and matriarchs: Abraham, Sarah, Isaac, Rebekah, Jacob, Leah, Rachel. These were stories of a family, from a time that was a distant memory even to them. They told stories of Abraham and Sarah's son Isaac, who was nearly sacrificed. They told stories of Isaac and Rebekah's son Jacob, who displaced his twin brother Esau. They told stories of Jacob's two wives, Leah and Rachel, and his two concubines, Bilhah and Zilpah, who altogether gave birth to a daughter and twelve sons. And they identified one of those twelve sons as Levi, the ancestor of the Levites, thus embedding the Levites in Israel's story long before the exodus. They were no longer *levites*, meaning "attached persons" who came to Israel from Egypt. Now they were Levites, meaning a tribe of people descended from a man named Levi. And they told a story of another of Jacob's sons, Joseph, a man who was carried off to Egypt as a youngster and sold as a slave, but who rose to Egypt's highest office after the Pharaoh. That led to the entire family's migration to Egypt. The family had grown into a clan. The clan grew into a nation. And this story was the prequel to the great story with which we started back at the beginning of this book: the enslavement, the exodus, the journey back to the land, the conquest.

But then those authors did something truly remarkable. They wrote a history that went all the way back to the beginning of their world. They took the story all the way back to creation. So in the final version of their story, Yahweh was not a God who became known in Midian, or in Egypt, for the first time. This God was already known to Adam and Eve, to Cain, to Noah. And then this God appeared and spoke to Abraham, to Isaac, and to Jacob. In their story, the exodus remained a turning point in divine and human history, but it now took its place on a line that went all the way back to creation.

Why did the authors do that? If any of us were asked to write a history of our country, would we begin it: "Well, first there was the Big Bang. And then a fraction of a second after that there was the breaking of cosmic symmetry. And then there was the continued expansion of the universe. And then. . ." And eventually we would get to the birth of our nation? Why did biblical authors feel a need to start their story with the creation of the whole earth and heavens? I believe we can know the solution to this mystery too. We shall come to it in Chapter 6. But for now we can just stand in awe at their early masterpiece of literature and history. It was the story of a people, and it was the story of the earth. And one more thing: in a profound and lasting way, it became the cornerstone of the story of the one and only God.

CHAPTER FOUR

THE MYSTERY OF MIDIAN

From Where Did God Come?

THE GOD OF THE EXODUS,
THE GOD OF ISRAEL

In beginning to grasp the exodus, we get more than just an idea of historical events. We get perspectives that help us see the off-spring of those events. The evidence led us to this hypothesis: An exodus occurred. It involved Levites. The Levites had been aliens in Egypt. The Levites came to merge with the people of Israel and Judah and became their priests and teachers. If this is correct, then these events had consequences. The consequences include our coming closer to uncovering the origins of the Western religions and of monotheism in particular. The picture that we formulated in Chapter 2 was that the exodus was fol-lowed by a fusion of Yahweh, the God of the exodus experience, with El, the God of the Israelite experience. And we said that this fusion was a necessary step of the formation of monotheism. It is difficult to see how monotheism would have happened in Israel if Yahweh and El had long been two distinct gods there. Call it duo-theism, bi-theism, or invent some new term. A dual theology by any other name is still not monotheism. And the dif-ference between a religion with one god and a religion with two is more than just arithmetic. It is all the difference in the world. The history of the whole world for at least two thousand years would have been different, for better or worse, in ways we can hardly imagine, if it had been grounded in two-theism. Would we have had temples, churches, synagogues, and mosques dedicated to one particular god while other temples, churches, synagogues, and mosques were dedicated to the other? Or would all be dedicated to both? Would we have developed a whole set of stories (myths) of the two gods' interactions? Would people pray to one or the other? If a person's prayer to one did not work, would/could he or she try the same prayer to the other one? In war (or sports), would each side seek the favor of a different god? What would be the impact on our art? On our literature? On theology! Would people be more accepting of other people's beliefs? Or would they fight more about them? Would it be easier (or harder) to account for suffering in the world? Would it affect our beliefs in what happens after death? How would we picture each god? What would be the main differences between them? And on. And on.

But it did not happen that way. How did we get here? Yahweh and El merged. "The LORD is one." Let us look closely at that. The people who left Egypt behind and came to Israel and became its priests worshipped the God Yahweh. But where did they get the belief in this God? There are several possibilities, all of them tantalizing.

1. MOSES THE MIDIANITE

One possibility that many scholars have weighed over the years: Israel learned it from the Midianites.[1] I mentioned that some of the Western Asiatic people who lived in Egypt were known as "Shasu." We have two inscriptions from Egypt that refer to the "*Shasu* of yhwh" (Egyptian *yhw3*).[2] They are the oldest known references to Yahweh outside of the Bible. William Propp notes that these people are located "in the rough vicinity of Midian"[3]—southeast of Israel, near the land of Edom. The Egyptologist Donald Redford says of one of these references to the *Shasu* of Yahweh:

> The passage constitutes a most precious indication of the whereabouts during the late fifteenth century B.C. of an enclave revering this god.[4]

Redford does not picture all of Israel making the exodus from Egypt and coming to this region any more than we did in Chapter 2. He says:

> The only reasonable conclusion is that one major component in the later amalgam that constituted Israel, and the one with whom the worship of Yahweh originated, must be looked for among the Shasu of Edom.[5]

Just one major component—not all of Israel. A component that worshipped Yahweh. A component from the Shasu. We could not agree more. What we have added here is the evidence that this "one major component" was the Levites. Now, what connects the Levites to the region of Midian or Edom and to Yahweh?

Moses and Midian in a Levite Source

In Chapter 2, I gave a brief introduction to the various texts that editors put together to make up the Bible's first five books. Aside from everything else that we think about the Bible's source texts, I just wanted to underscore there, and now here, that we can trace some of the texts to Levite authors and some to non-Levite authors. Now, in the oldest Levite prose text that we have, which is the text called E, Midian periodically emerges in the story. When we separate out the E story and read it, here is what we get involving Midian:

In the book of Genesis, all of the sources say that Abraham, the patriarch of Western religion, has a wife named Sarah and a concubine named Hagar. Sarah gives birth to a son, Isaac. Hagar, too, gives birth to a son, Ishmael. But the E source adds something that you will not find in the other sources. E says that Abraham takes *another* wife (or concubine), named Keturah, in addition to Sarah and Hagar.[6] Abraham and Keturah have six sons in E, and one of those sons is Midian.[7] So the author of the E text wanted us to know that the Midianites (descended from Keturah), like the Israelites (descended from Sarah) and the Ishmaelites (descended from Hagar), are of the lineage of Abraham. Later, in the story of Abraham's great-grandson Joseph in Genesis, in the E version of the story Midianites are prominent. Joseph's brothers have left him to die in a pit, but the Midianites save him by stealing him away and sell him as a slave in Egypt. Apparently unwittingly, they thus end up saving his life and setting in motion the chain of events that lead to the exodus.[8]

But most striking of all: the first time that Moses appears in this Levite E story, he is in Midian—not in Egypt!

I want to make this as visible as possible, so I have translated this first E episode about Moses in its context among the other sources in the first chapters of Exodus. It appears in Appendix A at the end of this book.[9]

In the Levite author's E story at the start of the book of Exodus, we read: a new king came to the throne, he oppressed the

Israelites, and he tried to reduce Israel's growing numbers by in-
fanticide, but two midwives thwarted his tactic. Then suddenly,
the very first time that we hear about Moses, we read:

> And Moses had been shepherding the flock of Jethro,
> his father-in-law, priest of Midian.
>
> (Exodus 3:1)

If we had nothing but this source, we would understand Moses
to be a Midianite, not an Israelite! Never a slave, never a baby
in a basket, never a prince, *never in Egypt,* his life before this
moment would be unknown. It is possible, of course, that some
biblical editor excluded a piece of the original E text that came
before this. Maybe Moses had started out in Egypt and somehow
made his way to Midian. In favor of this possibility, Moses later
tells his father-in-law, "Let me go back to my brothers who are
in Egypt."[10] "Go back" implies that he has been there before.
And still later in E we read that he had named his son Gershom
(which is taken to mean "Alien There") because he said, "I was
an alien in a foreign land."[11] This too implies that he came to
Midian from some other place where he was not a native. So, as
honest detectives, let us not rule that possibility out. But we read
on. God calls to Moses from inside a bush on a mountain and
says: "I've seen the oppression that Egypt is causing them. And
now go, and I'll send *you* to Pharaoh, and *you* shall bring out my
people, the children of Israel, from Egypt." To which Moses re-
sponds: "Who am *I* that *I* should go to Pharaoh and that *I* should
bring out the children of Israel from Egypt?"

That is a fair question for a man in Midian: What does this
have to do with me?! We have usually read Moses' words here
("Who am I . . .") to express humility (or fear). That makes
sense when we read the full Bible in its present united context

because this E story has the two other stories wound around it. That combination provides a whole life for Moses back in Egypt before this—born a slave, a baby in a basket, raised as a prince, killing an Egyptian, fleeing Egypt—so naturally we understand that Moses could be afraid to go back to a land that he left. But if we read just the Levite E story, we do not need to imagine psychological reasons for Moses' reluctance to go save people in Egypt. On the face of it, his reluctance is as natural as can be: "Egypt? Who am I that I should go there? Why me?! I'm a Midianite!" And the deity's answer makes sense as well: because you are going to bring the people from Egypt to serve me *here,* on this mountain, in this land. As my teacher Frank Moore Cross affirms, "This text presumes that the mountain is in Midianite territory." If the divine plan is to bring the people to a mountain in Midian, send a Midianite![12] And as the deity informs Moses: He is not just the God of Abraham and Midian. He is also the God of Abraham and Isaac and Jacob. The oppressed people in Egypt are Moses' kin, from whom the Midianite clan had separated. That might also explain why Moses would say, "Let me go back to my brothers who are in Egypt." It need not denote "go back to Egypt." It can denote "go back *to my brothers.*"

Also, in this source Moses will then go on to protest that he cannot go to Egypt because he is "heavy of tongue."[13] Readers have often assumed this expression to mean that Moses has some sort of speech defect. But the first step when encountering an expression for the first time in the Bible is to see if it occurs anywhere else in the book. This idiom occurs in one other place. It is in the book of the prophet Ezekiel. God tells Ezekiel that He is not sending him to nations who are "deep of lip and heavy of tongue," whose words Ezekiel cannot understand. God says that those "heavy of tongue" people would listen but that, ironically,

Ezekiel's own people, Israel, will not.[14] "Heavy of tongue" there means people who speak foreign languages. So back in Exodus, Moses' protest would be understood to mean that he cannot go on the mission to which God is directing him because he does not speak the language. What language? Our first thought would naturally be that he does not speak Egyptian. But the text before this rather says that God tells Moses to gather and speak to *the elders of Israel*.[15] And the text after this says that God gives Moses an interpreter, Aaron, and God says, "He will speak for you *to the people*."[16] The problem is not that Moses does not speak the language of the Egyptians. It is that he does not speak the language of the people whom he is being sent to save. Moses, the shepherd in Midian, does not speak Hebrew, the language of the people in Egypt.

And, after all, as we said in Chapter 2, why would anyone make up that Moses was married to a Midianite? And why make up that his father-in-law was a Midianite priest? Why would the author of E place him in Midian if Moses did not in fact have some connection back to Midian? The archaeologist and biblical scholar Carol Meyers of Duke University writes, "These highly unusual and positive features of the Midianite connection, especially in light of the genealogical connection between Israel and Midian (Gen 25:1–4), suggest a note of validity for a formative Midianite role in Israel's past."[17] And we can now add to this the fact that those earliest archaeological references to Yahweh locate Him in or near this region as well.

Moses and Midian in the J Source

Now let us go back and see those other texts that are wrapped in between this E text. From around the same period as the

E story's composition, we have the author of the J story. We are already familiar with part of this story from Chapter 2, the part about the baby in the basket. This story largely involves women: Moses' mother, his sister, the Pharaoh's daughter, her girls, her maid, Moses' wife Zipporah, and Zipporah's six sisters. The prominence of women in the J text was one of the reasons that first led me to propose that its author might have been female herself.[18] In this version, Moses is from Egypt, not Midian. But—and this is very important—this author still recognized the importance of Midian. Midian had to be in the story. This author had a different name for Moses' father-in-law: Reuel (the E author had called the father-in-law Jethro), but this J author still identified that father-in-law as priest of Midian. The J text thus affirms the importance of Midian and its priest, and it affirms that Moses was there, and not in Egypt, when he received the divine call. This author made sure we knew that Moses was an Israelite, born among the slaves in Egypt, but the author also needed to get Moses to Midian. So the J author gave a background that we do not find in E: Moses grew up in the royal house of Egypt, he killed an Egyptian, he went to Midian because he was a fugitive from Egypt, he settled and married in Midian, then God summoned him to go back to Egypt to save the people, *his* people, the people from whom his father and mother came. The point is that the J and E versions of the story are different in many ways, but one element of the story was necessary to both: the link to Midian, and especially to a priest there.

Moses and Midian in the P Source

And then comes the third of the sources, the Priestly source, P. It is the strangest—and in some ways the most revealing—of all.

It has nothing about Moses' birth or early life. Nothing about being a prince of Egypt. And absolutely nothing about his ever having been in Midian. Nothing about a Midianite wife (or any wife). Nothing about a priest father-in-law. Nothing about his having any children. No shepherding. No bush. In the P context as we have it, in the first encounter between God and Moses, Moses is in Egypt! (Exodus 6:2ff.)[19]

Now again we might say that perhaps the Priestly story had something about Moses in Midian and that an editor removed it. But in fact we have reason to believe that the explanation is rather that the Priestly author deliberately painted the Midianite connection very differently. Moses' starting location in Egypt does not mean that Midian has no place in the P story. Midian does occur in P, but it is not until years later in the story, and not until two books later in the Bible, in the book of Numbers.

In Numbers 25 a Midianite woman has an apparent sexual encounter with an Israelite man. The text indicates that they pass right before the eyes of Moses and the whole community and are intimately close in the inner part of the Tabernacle, the most sacred place. This initiates a deadly plague.[20] In one of the most blood-curdling sexual depictions in literature, Phinehas, the future high priest, goes in and drives a spear through the man and into the woman. The plague is stopped but only after twenty-four thousand people have died. I mentioned this episode of Phinehas in Chapter 2, but I did not tell there what comes next in the story. Yahweh then commands Moses to strike the Midianites. And strike them he does. Six chapters later, Moses orders the people to avenge what Midian has done. Here the story becomes more horrific. The Israelite army kills all of the men of Midian. But then Moses arrives and is irate that they did not kill all the women as well. He orders that they kill all women who have had sex with a male, but not virgins. So in this P source, Midianites are bad, and Midianite women are particularly bad. And Moses himself gives the order to kill the Midianite women. And this source does not include the little fact that Moses has a wife who happens to be a Midianite woman.

This P version may be more telling than the other two. P doth protest too much. It would be one thing if P were merely silent about Midian. But P is hostile to Midian. Its author tells a story of a complete massacre of the Midianites. He wants no Midianites around. And he especially wants no Midianite women around. This author buried the Moses–Midian connection.[21] We can know why he did this. Practically all critical scholars ascribe this Priestly work to the established priesthood at Jerusalem. For most of the biblical period, that priesthood traced its ancestry to Aaron, the first high priest. It was a priesthood of Levites, but not the same Levites who gave us the E text. Some, including me, ascribe the E text to Levites who traced their ancestry to Moses. These two Levite priestly houses, the Aaronids and the Mushites, were engaged in struggles for leadership and in polemic against each other.[22] The E (Mushite) source took pains, as we have seen, to connect Moses' Midianite family back to Abraham. That is understandable. E was justifying the Mushite Levites' line in Israel's history. And it is equally understandable why their opponents, the Aaronids, cast aspersions on any Midianite background. That put a cloud over any Levites, or any text, that claimed a Midianite genealogy. We all could easily think of parallel examples in politics and religion in history and in our day.

Midian Was Important

So this much can be clear: one of our main sources has Moses first appear in Midian, one has him move to Midian, and one buries any connection between him and Midian by treating Midian horribly. Together they say: Midian must have been important. Midian could not be ignored. Yahweh, Moses, and Midian were linked in too intimate a way for anyone to disregard. Indeed, all three of the sources, whatever their view of Moses' origins and/ his marriage, have this much in common in their stories: after the exodus, Moses and the people do not go directly to the promised land (Canaan/Israel/Judah). They go to a mountain called Horeb or Sinai, which was somewhere in proximity to Midian. The fourth source (D) never mentions Midian, but it also has them go to Mount Horeb and also says in its very first verses that this mountain is adjacent to Edom (Mount Seir, which is in the region of Midian).[23] That is, our sources all have the entire people, not just Moses, spending time in the vicinity of Midian.

As we asked in Chapter 2, why would anybody make this up? George Mendenhall, of the University of Michigan, wrote:

> The connections between Moses and the Midianites are manifold, detailed, and remarkable (Exodus 2–4; 18; Numbers 25; 31) and can hardly be explained on any basis other than historical fact.[24]

The English scholar Graham Davies wrote:

> The Midianite connections of Moses are scarcely likely to have been invented, and the association of Yahweh with a mountain to the south of Canaan is both strongly supported and unlikely to have arisen from a population that was solely derived from the Canaanite city-states.[25]

And the French scholar Thomas Römer wrote:

> In sum, what we know about Moses and Midian con-
> firms the evidence provided by the biblical texts that
> suggest a provenance of Yhwh from the south, and
> possibly a connection with the Shasu, the group of
> semi-nomadic tribes that may include the Midianites
> and Kenites.
>
> It is more difficult to know what degree of historical
> plausibility we should attribute to the narratives about
> Moses and Midian. Moses was perhaps the leader of
> a group of 'apiru who, when they had left Egypt, en-
> countered Yhwh in Midian and passed on the knowl-
> edge of him to other tribes in the south.[26]

And so, as I said above, many scholars have arrived at various
formulations of the Midianite hypothesis.[27] Almost all of them
cite the passages in the Bible that say outright that Yahweh came
from that region where Edom and Midian lay, from Seir, a
mountain associated with Edom. The old Song of Deborah says:

> Yahweh, in your coming out from Seir
> In your marching from a field of Edom
>
> (Judges 5:4)

And the old song called the Blessing of Moses begins:

> Yahweh came from Sinai
> And rose from Seir for them.
>
> (Deuteronomy 33:2)

The Song of Deborah and the Blessing of Moses are two of
those oldest poems in the Bible that we cited earlier. What starts

in those lines continues in the prose and poetry texts for centuries that followed.[28] Yahweh came by way of the south: Sinai, Seir, Edom, Midian.[29]

Moses the Midianite: Two Questions

Still, I see two problems with the idea of a Midianite origin of Moses. (1) Why then does he have an Egyptian name?! And (2) if he is a Midianite, how did he come to be in Egypt at the head of a group of people leaving there?

We might simply answer that people sometimes have names that derive from foreign languages. Or maybe his original Midianite name was something other than Moses, but he was merged in the story with a hero who led the people to Midian from Egypt. Or maybe his name was Reuel, and the name Jethro belonged to his father-in-law the priest, or vice versa, and that is how we came to have a confusion of two different names for the father-in-law in two different sources. Maybe he was a Midianite who made a trip to Egypt and encountered an oppressed group of aliens who were distant, Semite, kin of his. He sees their oppression in Egypt and rallies them to follow him to freedom. Coming from Egypt, they call him by an Egyptian name: Moses. But these are speculations—interesting, intriguing, tantalizing—but not evidence. So for now let us just take note of the Midianite possibility. Other possibilities exist, and they are tantalizing as well.

2. MOSES THE EGYPTIAN

Why does he have an Egyptian name? We recognized that the name Moses is Egyptian practically at the very beginning of the trail that we have been following. Egyptologists and Bible scholars have been aware of this for a long time. Its most famous, exciting treatment, though, did not come from a Bible scholar or an Egyptologist. It is Sigmund Freud's. It was the subject of his last book before he died, *Moses and Monotheism*.[30] Scholars of past generations in my field, including William Foxwell Albright, treated Freud's work with disdain. They saw it as coming from a man from another field, who had no sense of how to do history. Albright wrote that Freud's book "is totally devoid of serious historical method and deals with historical data even more cavalierly than with the data of introspective and experimental psychology."[31] (It was ironic that, while Albright criticized Freud for venturing into a field in which he was not trained, Albright felt himself to be qualified to so "cavalierly" add judgments about Freud's work in psychology.[32]) But intellectual pendulums swing back and forth. Lately, a number of my colleagues have begun to take Freud seriously, including Propp, Ronald Hendel, and Jan Assman. Some parts persuade them, some parts they reject as mistaken. But, unlike the generation of our academic grandparents, we do not simply dismiss it. We address it.

Freud questioned the fact that, though everyone seemed to know that the name Moses was Egyptian, no one had raised the natural, logical explanation of this fact: namely, that Moses *was* Egyptian. Freud:

> Now, we should have expected that one of the many people who have recognized that "Moses" is an Egyptian name would also have drawn the conclusion or would at least have considered the possibility that the person who bore this Egyptian name may himself have been an Egyptian. . . . Nevertheless, so far as I

know, no historian has drawn this conclusion in the case of Moses.[33]

Freud was right that this was indeed strange. One would think that practically everyone who wrote about Moses and the exodus would have brought this point up—even to reject it. But instead, practically no one had raised it. So Freud did. Now what did Freud have besides Moses' name to support the possibility that, if Moses was historical, he was an Egyptian? Freud zeroed in on the story of Moses' birth, the story we have seen that starts with the baby in the basket. Born to a family of slaves, the infant floats along the river to the king's daughter, he grows up among royalty, but eventually he comes to be back leading his enslaved people. Freud noted that we have many stories like this in world folklore and literature. We know them from the legend of Sargon to the stories of Oedipus and King Arthur.[34] These stories have a common, three-step pattern:

1. The hero is born into a royal or noble family.

2. Because of some crisis or threat, the hero is separated from his family and is raised by some other family, usually a family from a lower class.

3. Through the hero's gifts of strength or wisdom, the hero arrives back at his rightful place in royalty or nobility.

There are many variations on this pattern. (Oedipus, for example, is raised by a different royal family from his own, rather than by a poor family.) But the essential pattern is so common that most of us have encountered it at least once or twice.

From where do such stories come? At least some of them must reflect the realities of history: that individuals of a lower class occasionally do rise to very high stations in life, even making it all the way to king. Now, some countries might take pride in such a rags-to-riches story: look, our king was born a pauper, but he was so wise and strong that he deserved to become our king. Other countries, however, might not be so proud, especially in the face of their neighbor kingdoms, that their king had no royal blood. So the hero myth is born. You thought our king came from a lower-class family? Oh no. Our king came from a royal family, but he was torn from them when he was an infant. His nobility came out, however, and he earned his way back to the royal place that he rightfully occupies today.

In such a scenario, the three-step hero myth is formed to promote and defend the king. But which step in the pattern is the historical reality? Answer: step 2. The royal person in question really was from the lower class. People invented the story to veil that fact.

But, Freud pointed out, the Moses story reverses the usual pattern. Moses starts in the lower class, moves to royalty, and then comes back to the lower class. The pattern here is inside out. But the question is still: which step is the historical reality? And the answer is still: step 2. Moses was an Egyptian, possibly of the royal house. The slave people who left Egypt would be uncomfortable with the idea that their leader was an Egyptian, as uncomfortable as those other cultures would be with the idea that their king was a pauper. The baby-in-the-basket story has all the earmarks of these folktales. They are etiologies: stories that people fashioned to deal with and explain an embarrassing reality. The Egyptologist Jan Assman referred to Freud's treatment of the reversal of the usual pattern as "Freud's ingenious observation."[35] It is not a proof. It is a serious possibility. The hero of the exodus story has an Egyptian name, and the story seems designed possibly to camouflage his Egyptian roots. Even as we acknowledge that the Bible story about his early life may be invented, we are bound to consider the possibility that the story behind it—the story that made it necessary—was real. Freud's treatment was not cavalier. It was a sober and ingenious defense of the possibility that Moses was an Egyptian.

Moses and Akhenaten

Moses an Egyptian: that was Freud's step one. His second step was no less sensational. He confronted the question: if Moses, the founding teacher of what became Israelite religion, was an Egyptian, how do we explain the fact that Israel's religion was so obviously and profoundly different from Egyptian religion? Israelite religion was monotheistic, it was far less concerned with the afterlife, it rejected magic, it was against idols. What we know of ancient Israel's religion does not look like it came out of an Egyptian source. This was more than just a good question. It would appear to be a deal-breaker for Freud's hypothesis.

But an archaeological discovery changed all that. This time it was not a goat. It was a woman in Egypt digging up material to use for fertilizer. This was in 1887, during Freud's lifetime, about fifty years before he wrote about Moses and monotheism. What that woman found was more than fertilizer. It was some three hundred tablets that we now know as the Amarna Letters. The discovery of the Amarna Letters also led to archaeological excavations of that site. Amarna now is a region about 190 miles south of Cairo. But around thirty-four hundred years ago it was not called Amarna. It was Akhetaten, and it was the capital of Egypt. It was built by King Akhenaten. The similarity of his name and the name of his royal city is not coincidental. They both reflect the name Aten, the name of his god, who was symbolized by the sun. The king's name had been Amenophis IV, but he changed it to Akhenaten to incorporate his god's name in a new religion. That religion is widely identified as the first known monotheism. The literature on Akhenaten and monotheism is now vast.[36] I recall being introduced to the subject already as a child when I saw the Hollywood extravaganza *The Egyptian* in 1954—two years before *The Ten Commandments*. As in the movie version, so in history: Akhenaten's monotheism ended soon after he died. With his monuments effaced and his name erased, his religious revolution was practically lost to history until the Amarna discoveries gave it back to us.

Akhenaten and Amarna were becoming known in the late nineteenth and early twentieth centuries. Freud made the connection: if Moses was an Egyptian, the problem was that the religion that we associate with him had next to nothing to do with Egyptian religion. But, Freud saw, it was much more like Akhenaten's religion! Was it coincidence that the first two known monotheisms on earth both came out of Egypt? And within a couple of centuries of each other? Assman wrote: "Akhenaten must have appeared to Freud as the ultimate solution to the riddle."[37] Freud speculated that Moses was a follower of Akhenaten, perhaps a noble in that king's court. With the demise of Akhenaten and his religious revolution, this Moses took a band of followers from among Egypt's slaves, and he led them to a new life in a new faith. Not only did connecting Moses to Akhenaten provide an answer to a deal-breaking problem. It bolstered the case that Moses was historical and was an Egyptian. Moses as an Egyptian offered a link in a chain from one monotheism to the other.

There were other elements as well. (1) Freud admitted that he was no linguist of ancient languages, but he wondered if there might be a link between the god's name Aten and the Hebrew word for lord: *'ădōnay*. Actually, they are not linked linguistically. (2) Many scholars after Freud perceived a similarity between a prayer praising Aten and a prayer in the Bible praising Yahweh. They claimed that a number of parallels of ideas and wording occur between the Amarna text known as the Hymn to the Aten and the biblical text Psalm 104. To many, including me, those parallels are not compelling enough to prove a connection, and the hymn and the psalm are, after all, centuries apart.[38] (The two texts are readily available for anyone to examine.[39]) So I would not include them or the Aten/*'ădōnāy* terms as proofs in the mix of evidence.

I should acknowledge here that scholars have argued over whether Akhenaten's religion was truly monotheistic.[40] It may have been henotheistic: recognizing the existence of other gods but focusing worship on just one. And scholars have long argued over when Israel's religion became truly monotheistic as well.[41] We shall see the evidence in Chapter 5 for when Israel's religion was monotheistic. But for now we can say that to whatever degree each religion approached what we mean by monotheism, and whether or not each religion was "pure" monotheism, still, at minimum, practically everyone has recognized the conceptual similarity of the two.

Timing: From Akhenaten to Israel

So more people today take Freud's proposal seriously and respond to it, but still its essential point—the connection between Akhenaten's religion and the religion of Moses or Israel—has not been persuasive. And that is not because of a bias against Freud. The main argument against this connecting of Akhenaten's religion and Israel's is the timing.[42] Akhenaten lived in the mid-fourteenth century BCE. The earliest known reference to Israel as a people, as we have seen, is not until over a hundred years later, in the Merneptah stele around 1205 BCE. So where were Moses' people for nearly two centuries? That is a fair question, and I have raised it myself whenever I was asked about Freud's idea over the years. This argument about timing, however, was responding to a picture of Moses' and the original Israelites' having been in Egypt around Akhenaten's time. So, yes, that leaves a nearly two-hundred-year gap until they show up in Israel. But that is not our picture of the history any longer. Once we think in terms of the Levites and the establishment of Israel as two separate things, the dating argument evaporates—just as we saw it evaporate in the entire matter of the exodus in Chapter 2. If Moses and the Levites arrived at monotheism sometime after Akhenaten, it could have been soon after his reign, or it could have been some generations later if the memory of Akhenaten's religious adventure was still in the air in ancient Egypt. Their departure—the exodus—could have been for religious freedom or for liberation from slavery or for some other political or social reason. Their route could have included a brief stop in the region of Midian-Edom-Seir, or it could have been a period of residence for years, decades, or centuries. Whatever they called their god when they left Egypt, they knew Him as Yahweh—a name we know from that region—by the time they came to Israel.

We can speculate about whether events followed these or other steps, just as we speculated about the possible steps of a Midianite origin. The point is that, like a Midianite origin, an Egyptian origin of Israel's religion is possible historically. Both are possible, and both have some points of substance to be considered in making a historical judgment. Indeed the most likely historical possibility may be that it is both: Moses and his people, the Levites, learned their monotheism from Akhenaten's Egypt, and then they identified that monotheism with the God named Yahweh during their residence in Midian. In fact, Freud went so far as to formulate a two-Moses model, with two leaders at two stages: both Moses the Egyptian and Moses the Midianite. That is further than most scholars (and I) are prepared to go, but at minimum it means that Freud shared an instinct that some scholars (and I) have that the trail includes time in both Egypt and Midian.

The Levites may have acquired the worship of Yahweh from Midian. They may have acquired it from Egypt. They may have formed it through the influence of both. But we should consider at least one more possibility. They may not have learned it from anybody. They may have come to their religion themselves.

3. MOSES THE LEVITE

Could it not be that Moses and/or the Levites just came to it on their own?! Scholars have a tendency to take any parallel between ancient Israel's culture and other cultures and assume that Israel took it from the others.[43] Why? I see no good reason at all. Did Moses get this religion from the Midianites? All right then, where did the Midianites get it? Did Moses get it from Akhenaten? All right then, where did Akhenaten get it? If Akhenaten thought of it on his own, why could an Israelite not have done it on his (or her) own as well? Is it a far-out thought that sometimes more than one person thinks of an idea—without influencing each other, without knowing each other?

And we have another crucial consideration. The difference between Israel's monotheism and whatever preceded it is more than arithmetic. It is not just one god versus many. Biblical religion involves a different conception of what this one God *is*. In pagan religion, the gods and goddesses were identified with forces in nature: the sun, the sky, the sea, death, fertility, the storm wind.[44] Even in Akhenaten's religion, whether it was fully monotheistic or not, Aten was identified closely with the sun. In Israelite religion, no force in nature can tell you more about God than any other. Yahweh is above nature and beyond it. One cannot learn more about this God's essence by contemplating the sky than by contemplating the sun or anything else. Yahweh is not a god who is known through nature. Yahweh is known through His acts (and words) in history. Possibly some event that the people experienced and perceived to be extraordinary—for example, the exodus—gave birth to such a view of God. Or possibly it was an insight by an extraordinary individual—for example, Moses—which this person then taught to his people. But it need not have come from some other, preexisting people or individual. We simply do not know of any people or any individual—Midianites or Akhenaten—who had such an idea of who and what God was. As my teacher George Ernest Wright put it:

> We can never be certain of the true reason for this particular Israelite view of nature and history. It is the one primary, irreducible datum of Biblical theology, without antecedents in the environment whence it might have evolved.[45]

Wright favored the event of the exodus as most probably the impetus. The Israeli scholar Yehezkel Kaufmann favored the insight of an exceptional individual. He wrote:

The spiritual revolution, that gave historic moment to these ideas, must have been, like all similar events in history, the working of a creative genius and leader of men. Following the biblical saga, we call this pioneer creative spirit by the name Moses.[46]

It may have been some of both: an event and an individual with the insight to interpret it. We are all part of chains of events, persons, and ideas that precede and surround us. I can testify to this from my own experience. One of the first convergences of evidence that I brought in this book was that the Song of Deborah does not mention Levi, and the Song of the Sea does not mention Israel. I was proud when I thought of that, but then, when I was going through some old notes, I found that my colleague David Noel Freedman had said it in a seminar back when I was at the University of California, San Diego, years earlier. If Noel had not made the Song of Sea and Song of Deborah distinction, I might not have landed on any of this. I want to acknowledge David Noel Freedman's important contribution, and I also want to make a broader point. If one looks back at the evidence assembled above that the exodus was historical and involved the Levites, one finds an array of scholars from several fields and several continents. Each contributed a piece of the puzzle. We are all links in chains of a tradition of knowledge. We take our place in the sequence and add what we can. If that doesn't teach us humility, I don't know what can.

4. MOSES THE LEVITE ISRAELITE

I suppose we should at least consider the possibility that the Israelites themselves came to the worship of Yahweh back in Israel without the help of the Levites. But then we are left back at the question of why it is the Levite sources that tell the story of God telling Moses that His name is Yahweh though He used to be called El. That fits too well with a history of Levites who arrive and identify Yahweh with the Israelites' god El. And there are the two earliest references to the name Yahweh, and they are both from Egypt and both refer to the land of the *Shasu* of Yahweh.

True, there is still the Song of Deborah, which comes from Israel and does not mention the Levites. It calls God by the name Yahweh. So does that argue that Israel had come to Yahweh on its own, before the Levites showed up? How can we explain the presence of Yahweh's name in the song? (1) The appearance of the name Yahweh in the song could be an editor's later change or addition, though I do not like to resort to such arguments. We must be very circumspect about when we solve a problem by imagining that an unknown editor changed a text. Sometimes editors do that, and we are right to consider it as a possibility, but we should do so with caution and preferably where there is evidence that such editorial emending actually took place. (2) The Levites' arrival in Israel and the merger of El and Yahweh could have already taken place before the time of the Song of Deborah. One might ask, then, why the Levites are not included among the tribes in the song. But that may be because they were the clergy, not a tribe. We had recognized that this was one of the possibilities back in Chapter 2. (3) The two references to Yahweh in the Egyptian texts, identifying Yahweh with the region of Midian/Edom, are from long before the time of the Song of Deborah. And the song itself says, "Yahweh, in your coming out from Seir, in your marching from a field of Edom" (Judges 5:4). So it seems that the Israelites themselves understood their acquaintance with Yahweh to have come from that region—the region where Moses and the Levites had been. So, in the end, I think we still have to see the merger of El and Yahweh as directly related to the merger of Israel and the arriving Levites.[47]

THE LORD IS ONE

Whether it was the Levites first, as suggested here, or the Israelites or their ancestors in the land first, then that still leaves the question of where this people got their idea of monotheism. Their own story is that Yahweh Himself revealed it to them: to Abraham, to Isaac, to Jacob, to Joseph, to Moses. That is the Bible's story, and it is a matter of faith, not to be proven by archaeology and scholarship. What the evidence has shown us is that historically it started with the Levites, probably with a leader named Moses. They may have gotten it from Midian. They may have gotten it from Egypt. They may have gotten it on their own. But, whatever their source, we know this much: they got it.

So with around thirty-four hundred years of perspective we have our pick of possibilities of where the Levite group from Egypt may have gotten Yahweh as their deity. For all we know, it could have been a combination of all or some of the above. After all, even if the Levites did learn of Yahweh in Midian, that does not mean that they came by the idea there that only Yahweh existed. The idea of monotheism may have been in the air in Egypt after the demise of Pharaoh Akhenaten's religion of Aten. The majority of Egypt's population may have rejected that idea. A minority may have been attracted to it. The Levite community that left Egypt may have been led by an Egyptian man, Moses, who was attracted to that one-God idea, and when they arrived at Midian he married a priest's daughter and learned of the God Yahweh, whom he identified as the one God. Or the Levites may have left Egypt and then met a Midianite man, Moses, and were attracted to identify his God Yahweh as the one God. Or maybe Moses and/or the Levites found the idea of one God on their own, and they were then influenced either by the Egyptian monotheism in the air or by the Midianite faith of Yahweh. We can arrange these puzzle pieces in a number of possible ways. The bottom line, though, one way or another, is that the Levites had spent time in both Egypt and Midian, their God was Yahweh, and then they came to Israel.

CHAPTER FIVE

THE MYSTERIES
OF BABYLON

I am God, and there is not another.

(Isaiah 45:22)

1. THE EMERGENCE OF ONE GOD

How do we get from the exodus to monotheism? The probability that we have raised is: the Levites left Egypt, they spent some period of time in the region of Midian, they came to Israel and became part of it, and they became its priests. And their deity Yahweh and the land's deity El came to be seen as one God. In Chapter 2, I cited Professor Noegel, who wrote of the gradual fusion of the god El with Yahweh; and Professor Cross, who wrote of there being no conscious distinction between El and Yahweh in ancient Israel; and Professor Smith, who wrote that at an early point Israelite tradition identified El with Yahweh. And I added the significance of the doctrine that two Levite authors developed in the Bible's story: that God revealed to Moses that El and Yahweh were one and the same. I said there in Chapter 2 that we would definitely return to this fusion of El and Yahweh because its implications are potentially tremendous.

Tremendous indeed. The implications of this consolidating of El and Yahweh are of historic significance:

Literary: it was the main clue that led to working out the documentary hypothesis. Even in this present period of scores of proposals and struggles over consensus, this remains the single most viable and accepted explanation for the composition of the Bible's first books.

History: it joins the other evidence pointing to the exodus of a Levite group of Yahweh-worshippers who came to Israel and integrated with its population.

But perhaps most civilization-changing of all: it means an early birth of monotheism in Israel (and, at some point, in Judah). From wherever it came, this impulse toward one God was present in this very early stage of Israel's history, before Israel and Judah even had their first kings. Both the biblical text and archaeology testify that monotheism took a long time to win, by which we mean: to catch on with the masses. That is why the scholarly debate over when Israel became monotheistic has gone on for so long and has been so difficult. We have been looking for at least two things: when the idea emerged, and when it caught on. The historical development of monotheism is hard to get at because we have so many texts from so many periods, so we argue over when someone first had the idea, when it became the view of the priests, or the prophets, or the kings, or the population. So scholars have rightly looked at a number of passages in the Bible, and many have concluded that Israel was not monotheistic until a very late stage in the biblical world. To name a few examples of what the scholars saw:

The Song of the Sea says, "Who is like you *among the gods, Yahweh!*"[1]

Sometimes in the Bible God speaks in the plural. ("Let *us* make a human in *our* image."[2])

The book of Job has an assembly of the gods meeting with Yahweh: "And the sons of the gods [Hebrew *běnê 'ĕlōhîm*] came to assemble upon God."[3]

Even the Ten Commandments say, "You shall have no other gods before me,"[4] which, many people have observed, seems to acknowledge that other gods do, in fact, exist.

Now, every one of these passages could be interpreted in some other way that still leaves the door open to a monotheistic possibility. But we can plainly see why people read these lines and a fair number of others like them and had reasonable doubts about whether the Bible was entirely monotheistic.

Exile in Babylon

A common view among Bible scholars for a long time has been that this idea—one God—was a late development in Judaism. They say that it was a product of exile: the Jews had no monotheism until after the Babylonians drove them out of their country in 587 BCE and deported thousands of them to Babylon. Until then, not only the masses, but the leaders, the priests, the writers, maybe even the prophets, all still had the gods. They were polytheists, or at most henotheists, meaning they followed one god but still believed that the other deities existed too. So, for example, a law in an early[5] text known as the Covenant Code says:

One who sacrifices to gods shall be completely destroyed—except to Yahweh alone.

(Exodus 22:19)

It does not say that other gods do not exist. It just says that one should not sacrifice to them. So, the scholars said, as in the four passages I quoted above, this was not monotheism. Monotheism was not native, not homegrown. It was not a product of Israel nor of Judah. It was born in exile, in Babylonia. This is an understandable view: As long as the people were in their homeland, Yahweh was their chief god, their national god; but once they were out in the world they had to explain how Yahweh could be in power and watching over them there. As their psalmist asked in a famous psalm that begins "By the rivers of Babylon,"

How shall we sing a song of Yahweh on foreign soil?

(Psalm 137:4)

And they also had to answer the question of how the Babylonians had defeated them. Were the Babylonian gods more powerful than Yahweh?! So they promoted Yahweh in their theology to being the one and only God, the God of all the earth: of Judah, Babylon, everywhere. In the biblical scholarship of recent centuries, Babylon is the great equator of the Hebrew Bible. Everything is before Babylon or after Babylon. Pre-exilic or post-exilic. Everything, including monotheism. Yes, this is understandable, a reasonable speculation. After all, many things really did change then. The monarchy was over. The Temple was destroyed. But our contemplation of the fusion of Yahweh and El in the wake of the exodus already suggests that this common view of when monotheism started must at least be modified. So does our observation of the distribution of the element "Yahweh" or "Yahu" in people's names in pre-exilic inscriptions from Israel and Judah that we saw in Chapter 3. The names overwhelmingly specify Yahweh and sometimes El as their God, but rarely any other deity's name. Monotheism was early, and it was present in Israel and Judah for centuries before the Babylonians showed up, not born in exile on foreign soil. We still have all those passages that refer to the gods. But at the same time an array of texts from the Bible are blatantly monotheistic long before the Babylonian exile. We have to explain this.

Second Isaiah

If you ask my colleagues among Bible scholars when and where monotheism started, most (not all) will say Second Isaiah. That will be confusing to some readers because there is no such book as Second Isaiah in the Bible. The book of Isaiah says in its first verse that it contains the vision of Isaiah son of Amoz, a prophet in Jerusalem in the eighth century BCE. People observed long ago that these prophecies appear in the first thirty-four chapters of the book of Isaiah but that then the book suddenly changes. Chapters 35 to 39 are no longer the words attributed to Isaiah. They are instead a history about events in Isaiah's lifetime. And then, after this history, the rest of the book, chapters 40 to 66, returns to containing prophecies, except now they appear to be the words of a different prophet. This "second Isaiah" is writing two centuries later, and he is speaking to Jews in exile in Babylon, not in Jerusalem. Instead of the eighth century, it is the sixth. Instead of Judah, it is Babylonia. It appears that two prophetic works are combined into one book. So we call them First Isaiah and Second Isaiah. We also call the latter work Deutero-Isaiah (which is Greek for Second Isaiah).

That is the short version. Scholars have proposed multiple theories about why someone combined these two into one book. And some scholars divide the second Isaiah into two works, making both a Second Isaiah and a Third Isaiah. Don't get scholars started.[6]

The existence of this Second Isaiah and its location in the Babylonian exile are very widely accepted conclusions in biblical scholarship. I too find the case for this persuasive. But what does it have to do with monotheism?

In Second Isaiah, God says:

> I am Yahweh, and there is not another.
> Except for me there is no God.
>
> (Isaiah 45:5)

And:

> I am first, and I am last, and outside of me
> (Hebrew *mibbal'āday*) there is no God.
>
> (Isaiah 44:6)

And:

> Who has made this heard from antiquity?
> Who has told it from then?
> Is it not I, Yahweh?
> And there is not another god outside of me
> (Hebrew *mibbal'āday*).
> A righteous and saving god: there is none except me.
> Look to me and be saved, all the ends of the earth,
> For I am God, and there is not another.
>
> (Isaiah 45:21–22)[7]

And:

> Before me no god was formed,
> And after me there will not be.

> I, I am Yahweh,
> And outside of me (Hebrew *mibbal'āday*) there is no
>   savior.
>
> (Isaiah 43:10–12)[8]

And:

> I am God (Hebrew *El*), and there is not another,
> God (Hebrew *Elohim*) and there is none like me.
>
> (Isaiah 46:9)

My colleagues whom I have mentioned look at these verses, and they say, "Now that is monotheistic." To them these are the first clear-cut, properly monotheistic statements in the Bible.[9] I put on a conference about twenty years ago, to which I invited some twenty-five of the best scholars I knew in the United States, Europe, and Israel. I questioned this idea that monotheism starts with Second Isaiah and the Babylonian exile, and I soon found that I was swimming upstream. A lot of very smart people were absolutely persuaded: Look to Babylon. Look to Second Isaiah. I did not believe it then, and I am even more certain now. We have also looked to Egypt, to Midian, and to earliest Israel. We have seen that at least the monotheistic impulse ignited from that very early stage when the Levites arrived from Egypt, and Israel identified Yahweh and El as one and the same God. And this evolved from an impulse into a religious doctrine.

Early Poetry

When Cross and Freedman identified the earliest texts in the Bible, which were all in poetry, they included "A Royal Song of Thanksgiving." This poem appears in two different places in the Bible: in 2 Samuel 22 and again in Psalm 18. Cross and Freedman held that it was written down not later than the ninth to eighth centuries BCE, and they added that a tenth-century date is not at all improbable.[10] According to this text, which comes from early in Israel's history:

> Who is a god outside (*mibbal'ădê*) of Yahweh,
> And who is a rock outside (*mibbal'ădê*) of our God.
>
> (2 Samuel 22:32 = Psalm 18:32)

This wording is incredibly close to the wording above from Isaiah 44:6—"outside of me (Hebrew *mibbal'āday*) there is no God"—the passage that so many people were saying is fully monotheistic. Yet those words in the Royal Song of Thanksgiving were written hundreds of years earlier—certainly long before the Babylonian exile.

Another early composition is the Song of Moses (Deuteronomy 32). Some scholars have dated it to the eleventh or tenth century BCE.[11] Noel Freedman wrote that "the dating of this poem has proved a difficult problem to scholars, who have tested an assortment of dates from Moses to the exile and beyond." But he went on to list considerable evidence that it was archaic, and he concluded that he would date it to the latter tenth century BCE at the earliest or in the ninth century.[12] Others have shown that the song is quoted by the prophets Hosea and Jeremiah.[13] That is, the Song of Moses had to be an earlier work, already written in an archaic Hebrew before the Babylonian exile. And here is what God says in this song:

> I, I am He, and there are no gods with me.
>
> (Deuteronomy 32:39)

How different is that from the passages in Second Isaiah? If we were given this text and the lines from Isaiah without being told from where they all came, we might even guess that they were all from the same work. If we are looking for monotheistic passages in the Bible, we do not need to wait for the Babylonians to show up.

Early Prose

These have all been examples from the early poetry of Israel, from the eleventh through the ninth centuries BCE. Prose texts that others and I trace to the seventh century BCE are just as explicit about there being no god other than Yahweh.[14] Here is what the texts say:

> Yahweh: He is God. There is no other outside of Him.
> (Deuteronomy 4:35)

And:

> And you shall know today and store it in your heart that Yahweh: *He* is God in the skies above and on the earth below. There is not another.
> (Deuteronomy 4:39)

And perhaps the most famous line of all from this text:

> Hear, O Israel. Yahweh is our God. Yahweh is one.
> (Deuteronomy 6:4)

"Yahweh (or: the LORD) is one." For many, this is the ultimate biblical declaration of the unity of God. For Judaism, it appears in the prayer book to be said every day. For Christianity, in the New Testament Jesus declares it to be the first among commandments (Mark 12:29). Yet we frequently hear denials that the verse means this. Some translate it rather as "Yahweh is our God. Yahweh *alone*." By this rendering it does not necessarily mean that God is one but rather that Yahweh alone is Israel's God—while not denying that other gods may exist. There is a problem with this rendering, however: There is no basis for it at all in the Hebrew Bible. The word is Hebrew *'eḥād,* which every school child would know to mean "one." It occurs in 546 verses in the Hebrew Bible, and there is not a single one in which it would clearly mean "alone." Those who translate *'eḥād* as "one" everywhere else it occurs in the Bible and then suddenly take it to mean "alone" in this single case appear to be resisting the verse's patent meaning. That is its meaning especially in its context following the other two passages we have seen from this same author just two chapters earlier, which are visibly monotheistic.

We attribute passages in other biblical books to this same historian. We call this person the Deuteronomistic historian because his work starts with Deuteronomy—which we have just read—and he writes his history from the perspective of the laws and views in Deuteronomy. But we see his hand, editing and collecting sources, through the next six books as well: Joshua, Judges, 1 and 2 Samuel, and 1 and 2 Kings.[15] I attribute all of the texts that I am citing here either to this historian himself in the seventh century BCE or to his sources—which are even older. Thus in 2 Samuel the historian attributes a prayer to King David, and David says there:

> For there is none like you,
> and there is no God except for you.

> (2 Samuel 7:22)

Is this really less monotheistic than those passages we read from Second Isaiah? Recall the passage in Isaiah 46:9:

> there is none like me

and the passage in Isaiah 45:5:

> Except for me there is no God.[16]

Likewise in 1 Kings, King Solomon blesses the people at his Temple dedication, saying:

> So that all the peoples of the earth will know that Yahweh He is God. There is not another.
>
> (1 Kings 8:60)

How different is that from what we read in Isaiah 45:21–22:

> For I am God, and there is not another.

Farther on in the Deuteronomistic history comes the story of the prophet Elijah's duel with prophets of the Baal on Mount Carmel (in present-day Haifa). Elijah introduces the duel with these words to the people:

> If Yahweh is the God, follow him; and if the Baal [is], follow him.
>
> (1 Kings 18:21)

They prepare two sacrificial altars, one for Yahweh and one for the Baal. (The word *Baal* is preceded by the definite article: *the* Baal. It is not a god's name. It is a standard term for a male pagan deity.) But they do not light fires. Rather, Elijah says, "The god who will respond with the fire, he is the God" (18:24).

The prophets of the Baal get no response to their prayers. Elijah gets fire. The people fall on their faces and say, "Yahweh, He is the God! Yahweh, He is the God!" (18:38f.). The story does not leave room for two gods. The declared point of its duel is not whether Yahweh is *greater* than the Baal; it is which one *is* God. And this story must be even older than the last few passages we considered, because it is not traced to the Deuteronomistic historian himself. It is part of an older work that the historian used as one of several sources for his history.[17]

Prophets

How many more examples of monotheistic texts prior to Second Isaiah do we need? We can also turn to prophets who precede Second Isaiah. Hosea precedes Second Isaiah by a couple of centuries. In the book of Hosea, God is quoted as saying:

> I am Yahweh your God from the land of Egypt,
> and you shall know no god except me,
> there is no savior but me.
>
> (Hosea 13:4)

Again, this is reminiscent of words that we read above in Second Isaiah:

> A righteous and saving god: there is none except me.
>
> (Isaiah 45:21)

Jeremiah as well, preceding Second Isaiah, chides his people over and over for still worshipping other gods. At minimum Jeremiah is assuming an uncompromising henotheism, not allowing the worship of any other gods even if they exist. And at maximum, he is assuming monotheism. Propp writes, comparing Jeremiah to Second Isaiah:

> But even Second Isaiah does not compare monotheism and polytheism as systems. Jeremiah, on the other hand, mocks the Judeans for the multitude of their gods (Jer 2:28; 11:13) and so has a better claim as Israel's first self-conscious monotheist.[18]

We might say that Hosea's and Jeremiah's criticism of the people shows that at least some of those people (a minority? a majority? all? the leaders?) were not in fact practicing monotheism. That is true. But it also means that Jeremiah himself and Hosea himself were monotheistic. And it means that monotheism was out there enough that these prophets could imagine criticizing the people for doing anything else.

Some scholars attribute some of these passages of history and narrative and prophecy to later periods, after the Babylonian exile. But these texts cannot all be that late. They cannot all be archaizing that successfully. And we shall see even more of such texts below.

Monotheism had arrived. It had been preached. It was the way the story was told.[19] The battle was on. The fight over monotheism was in play. Its biggest victory may have come in the wake of the Babylonian exile, but that is just geography and politics. The idea and the texts and persons who championed it: all of these were in place before the Babylonians arrived.

The Ten Commandments

One more item to clear up: at the beginning of this chapter, we acknowledged that even the Ten Commandments say: "You shall have no other gods before me,"[20] and that some say that this commandment is not monotheistic. They say that its words in fact prove the opposite: it recognizes that other gods exist, but it just forbids Israel from worshipping them. That is called henotheism or monolatry, not monotheism. We must admit it: the commandment does indeed say "other gods." But we must also be cautious of what we derive from that. For years I have been telling my students, as an exercise, to think of five ways to command people to be monotheistic without mentioning those gods in whom they are not supposed to believe. Try it. It is possible but really hard. We should simply recognize a fact of linguistics that it is difficult to formulate a command against doing something without mentioning the something that is not supposed to be done. The issue is more likely to be linguistic than theological. The command against having "other gods" is just an example of this linguistic phenomenon, probably the most famous example of it in all literature.

Another point: the text says "before me." The Hebrew is 'al pānāy, which, more carefully, means "in my presence." Literally, it translates as "in my face." The old, usual English translation "before me" in fact originally meant just this: "in my presence." It became misunderstood when the phrase "before me" came to be taken also as meaning "ahead of me." That meaning is not present in the original Hebrew for this word. So, since it means "in my presence," then the question is: where exactly is not in God's presence? The implied answer is: nowhere.

Now if an early text like the Ten Commandments did in fact imply henotheism, that would not be a crisis. The original meaning of "Who is like you among the gods" in the Song of the Sea might be the same. This would just reflect the stages that we have been tracing on the stairway to monotheism. It need not ruin anyone's day. But still, we should recognize that the words of the Commandment may very well be genuinely monotheistic in the light of these linguistic considerations.

Centralization

Finding signs of monotheism before the exile to Babylon is not just a matter of the text's words. It is also a matter of what is *happening* in the text. The words themselves, like "The LORD is one" and "He is God; there is no other outside of Him" appear to reflect and promote a monotheism in Deuteronomy. But we should look at the *content* of Deuteronomy as well. The book contains a code of laws. They appear in Deuteronomy 12 to 26. The Deuteronomic Law Code begins, in its very first chapter, with a commandment that all sacrifices must occur at one place, and only one place, out of all Israel's tribes. This central place is called "the place where Yahweh tents His name." (Older, less literal translations make it "The place where Yahweh causes His name to dwell.") In the Deuteronomistic history, this place is always where the ark is, a place originally located in a tent or Tabernacle and later located in the Temple. All kinds of sacrifices and ceremonies are limited to this single location. One cannot offer a sacrifice in Beth-El or Beer Sheba or Bethlehem or Dan. The law code says:

> the place that Yahweh, your God, will choose to tent
> His name there: there you shall bring everything that
> I command you, your burnt offerings and your sacri-
> fices, your tithes and your hand's donation and every
> choice one of your vows that you'll make to Yahweh.
>
> (Deuteronomy 12:11)

It repeats this with a strong caution:

> Watch yourself in case you would make your burnt
> offerings in any place that you'll see. But, rather, in the
> place that Yahweh will choose in one of your tribes:
> there you shall make your burnt offerings, and there
> you shall do everything that I command you.
>
> (Deuteronomy 12:13–14)

The book of Leviticus contains a code (or codes) of laws as well. It comes from a different group of priests from those who wrote the Deuteronomic Law Code, and the two codes have different histories and sometimes have different laws. But not on this point. They both require centralization of worship. The commandment in Leviticus phrases the rule differently. It focuses the commandment on the Tabernacle itself, not on the divine name that it houses. But the bottom line is the same— and even more emphatic:

> Any man from the house of Israel who slaughters an
> ox or a sheep or a goat in the camp or who slaughters
> outside the camp and has not brought it to the entrance
> of the Tent of Meeting to bring forward an offering to
> Yahweh in front of Yahweh's Tabernacle: blood will
> be counted to that man. He has spilled blood. And
> that man will be cut off from among his people.
>
> (Leviticus 17:3–4)

The idiom "to spill blood" refers elsewhere in the Bible to murder.[21] According to this law, if someone kills an animal anywhere and does not bring it as an offering at the Tabernacle, this act is as if that person had murdered a human being.

This commandment is taken so seriously that, since the last Temple was destroyed by the Romans and never rebuilt, leaving no more central place, Jews have not offered sacrifices for nearly two thousand years. Why was this commandment so prominent, its penalty so severe? Why could one not offer a sacrifice anywhere but one place on earth? We might be cynical and say that writing this commandment was a move by the central priests to bring all the wealth and authority to themselves. But I think that centralization of worship was about more than money. Today, when we see Christians go to thousands or perhaps millions of churches in the world, we do not imagine that they worship different gods in those different buildings: the Jesus of Paris versus the Jesus of London or Sydney. Likewise, when we see Jews go to thousands of synagogues we do not think that some are worshipping the Yahweh of Haifa and others are worshipping the Yahweh of New York or Toronto. But the reason why this is so obvious and that these examples are so preposterous is that monotheism has won. Monotheism triumphed in the Western world and much of the Eastern world long ago, solidly, decisively, over polytheism. But when the law codes of the Bible were being written, this was not the case. The battle was still on. Multiple temples at multiple locations could mean multiple respective gods. The Levitical priests of Israel and Judah were vigilant not to leave room for that possibility. One Temple. One central altar. One God. Do anything else, and "that man will be cut off from among his people." Centralization to a single nucleus expressed monotheism as much as the words "I am God, and there is not another."

And all of this preceded the Babylonian exile. Others and I have collected the evidence that the law codes of both Deuteronomy and Leviticus were pre-exilic. But even for those who disagree about those dates, there is also the report of the books of Kings and Chronicles. Those histories report that two kings of Judah in particular promulgated the centralization of worship. They were Hezekiah and Josiah.[22] Hezekiah ruled at the end of the eighth century BCE. Josiah ruled at the end of the seventh. So if we are right about centralization being connected to the implementation of monotheism, this too was well before the Babylonians arrived in 587 BCE.

Postscript

I wrote in Chapter 2 about the strange state of the field of Hebrew Bible studies at present. It sometimes feels as if everyone has his or her own theory, and, worse, it seems that many scholars are not addressing one another's evidence, evidence that challenges their own theories. This is not entirely their fault. It is partly the result of an explosion of information—and *publication*—on our subject. It is happening in other fields as well. There are simply so many books and articles coming out all the time that no one can read them all. I admit that I too have sometimes missed published works, some that challenged me and some that would have supported me. On the question that we are addressing here, though, the question of when various texts were written, this state of the field has been particularly vexing. People date more and more of the Bible later and later. For every text that I have quoted from the early centuries of ancient Israel, one can find scholars who date them late. There are some who date practically everything past the time of the Babylonian empire. Forty years of research on the Hebrew language (a biblical number) has gone against their late dates. We can distinguish between the Classical Biblical Hebrew of the kingdoms of Israel and Judah, on the one hand, and the Late Biblical

Hebrew of Judah after the exile, on the other. The dividing line is essentially pre-exile versus post-exile Hebrew. Just as the English of Shakespeare's time is different from the English that I am writing right now, so Hebrew went through the natural development that all languages do over centuries. I have written about the challenge of getting the late-daters even to address all this evidence.[23] If it is right, they are wrong. So one would think that they would have pounced all over it to challenge it. And one would think that they would have addressed it *before* they published their books and articles claiming that so many of the biblical texts were late—when those texts have been shown to be written in Classical Biblical Hebrew. It would be as if they claimed that a Valley girl wrote Hamlet. I have described sessions at international conferences in which they simply refused to discuss it. I have compared their dating of the Bible without taking *Hebrew* into account to someone writing about diabetes without mentioning *sugar*. I have listed a major sampling of unrefuted research on Biblical Hebrew here in earlier chapters.[24]

Besides being poorly defended—actually *un*defended—these works as a whole paint a surreal history. Israel and Judah existed as nations in a land from at least 1205 BCE until 587 BCE. These works picture those nations producing almost nothing significant during the 618 years of their existence in their land. They picture the Jews producing practically everything important—monotheism, history-writing, nearly all of their literature—only after they were thrown out of their land. I recognize that crises can give birth to innovations and creativity in human history. But this attribution of so many texts to the centuries after the crisis, and so little to the centuries before it, is extreme by any standard. As Professor Hendel wrote in reviewing some of these works: "It seems arbitrary to define 'Israel' as a Persian period phenomenon and to leave the tenth–sixth centuries as a blank, with no memories or literate thinkers to be found."[25] And, again, the evidence of the stage of the Hebrew language of the texts goes completely against it.

So, yes, there is a big debate over when Israel became monotheistic. Was it early or late in the biblical world? But what we have found about the exodus gave us a starting point. What we have said thus far is, first, that the impulse, the *idea,* was early. The merger of El and Yahweh was a first step, a very early first step, on that stairway. That merger is what the Levite priests taught all of Israel and Judah from some of the earliest known texts, and it never went away: one God. And it continued to surface in texts that we have seen from before, during, and after the Babylonian exile—from the eleventh century to the end of the biblical period.

2. THE DEATH OF THE GODS

So monotheism arrived. One won. How did that work? How did some priests and teachers and prophets and kings gradually persuade the people to embrace this belief? One God. When there had always been many gods. How must that have felt? We have seen signs that Israel, Judah, and the Levites kindled the flame of monotheism in the era following the exodus. That energy persisted through centuries. And *whenever* most of the community became monotheistic, whenever there was the first generation to which we could point and say now that is properly monotheistic, what did people think of their parents or grandparents who had worshipped the gods? What did they think happened to the gods—and the goddesses? What did they tell their children? How did their writers depict it in the Bible?

We do have the answer to this. What they did was: they said that the gods used to exist, *but they died.*

The Song of Moses

Near the end of the Torah comes a song. The text attributes it to Moses. It may not in fact be by Moses, but it is in fact very old. It says:

> When the Highest gave nations legacies,
> when He dispersed humankind,
> He set the peoples' borders
> to the number of the children of Israel.
>
> (Deuteronomy 32:8)

What in the world is that supposed to mean? When God created the nations with their respective borders, He set them according to the number of Israelites? That is a lot of nations! People already were puzzled by this passage two millennia ago. One proposal was that it refers to the story at the beginning of the book of Exodus. There the patriarch Jacob is said to have gone down to Egypt with seventy (male) persons in his family.[26] Since Jacob's other name in the Bible is Israel, the "children of Israel" in the Song of Moses was interpreted to refer to these seventy people. And, these interpreters said, there were seventy nations in antiquity.[27] There are three things wrong with this. First, the phrase "children of Israel" occurs 593 times in the Hebrew Bible. Why pick out this one line in Exodus and decide that that is the meaning of the passage in Deuteronomy 32? Second, we do not know of any time in the history of the world when there were exactly seventy nations. The interpreters were just referring to a list of names of individuals, families, and nations in Genesis 10.

Mixing and matching those names and counting all of them as nations, they arrived at seventy. But the list comes from another source (or sources) than either the song in Deuteronomy 32 or the text about the seventy people who went down to Egypt in Exodus.[28] And third, the wording of that text in Exodus is uncertain anyway. One Hebrew manuscript says seventy persons, but other ancient manuscripts say seventy-five.[29]

So we did not know what the passage meant. And then this goat made the greatest archaeological discovery of the twentieth century: the Dead Sea Scrolls. Among these scrolls at Qumran we found portions of every book of the Hebrew Bible (except Esther). They are in bad condition. Only the book of Isaiah is complete. If you have ever seen photographs of them, you know that they are often just fragments, shreds. But before that goat, our oldest complete manuscript of the Hebrew Bible was the Leningrad Codex. It is now a little over a thousand years old (1008 or 1009 CE).[30] The Dead Sea Scrolls had been sitting in those caves for two thousand years, so they gave us texts that are a thousand years older than the Leningrad Codex.

I have to stop a moment and take in the irony: With the end of the Soviet era, the Russians changed the name of the city of Leningrad back to its old name, Saint Petersburg. So now the most prominent thing that retains the communist name of the city is: the Bible. (The Lord moves in strange ways.)

So do we have our passage (Deuteronomy 32:8) in the Scrolls? We do. And instead of "the children of Israel" (Hebrew *běnê yiśrā'ēl*), it says, "the children of the gods" (Hebrew *běnê 'ĕlōhîm*).[31] (This can also mean "the children of God" because Elohim, the Hebrew word for God, can have a singular or plural meaning, depending on the context.) This phrase, *běnê 'ĕlōhîm,* is a term for the gods in the Bible.[32] So the passage in the Song of Moses would mean that when God created the nations, He set them according to the number of the gods. That is, He made Greece and gave it to Zeus, He made Babylon and gave it to Marduk, He made Assyria and gave it to Ashur, and so on. Each people had its god. But, the next verse of the Song of Moses says, "Yahweh's portion is His people. Jacob is the share of His legacy." So Yahweh, the Highest God, assigned countries to the various gods, but He kept Israel for Himself. This makes a good deal more sense than making one country for every person in Israel.[33]

Can we refine this any further? There is a third ancient witness to the original text of the Hebrew Bible. It is the Septuagint, the ancient Greek translation. It is important because it is not a translation of the Hebrew that we have in the Leningrad Codex, and it is not a translation of the Hebrew that we have in the Dead Sea Scrolls. It is a translation of a third Hebrew text that is now lost. So we have to read the Greek, figure out what Hebrew it is translating, and then compare that to the other two Hebrew texts. For this passage in the Song of Moses, the Septuagint says that when the Highest gave the nations their legacies, He set their borders according to the number of the *angels* of Elohim rather than the *children* of Elohim. There is no way that the Greek translator would have mistaken the word for "children" and written "angels." We generally understand, therefore, that the translator was uncomfortable with a reference to gods in Moses' song, and so he changed the word to "angels," which may well be what he thought these children of Elohim might be. The Greek translation has the exact same thing in two other places, where the Hebrew text had *children* of Elohim but the translator made it *angels* of Elohim (Job 1:6; 2:1). But, whatever the translator's motives were, he apparently had a Hebrew text that was like the Dead Sea Scrolls text. It had gods, not Israelites.

Now, that is two out of three texts, but this is not math, and it is not something that one settles by a democratic vote. We are trying to get at the original meaning of a text.[34] The meaning of "gods" makes vastly more sense than the meaning of "Israelites." What makes the former meaning even more likely, though, is that we have other passages in the Bible that confirm this, passages that refer to the existence of the gods.

When we dealt with the Exodus, we looked at the Song of Sea, which is one of the two earliest things in the Bible. We have witnessed that one of the famous lines of that song is:

> Who is like you among the gods, Yahweh!
>
> (Exodus 15:11)

That seems pretty clear. Most English translations correctly translate the Hebrew that way. A few have made it "Who is like you among the mighty?" or "Who is like you among the celestials?" or "Who is like you among the gods who are worshipped?" But all of these translators are just plain struggling not to translate the words that they see in front of them: "Who is like you among the *gods*!" Their discomfort, and their attempts to translate their way out of it, just highlights how significant this is.

The same thing happens with Psalm 29. The first verse says:

> Give to Yahweh you children of the gods (Hebrew
> *běnê ʾēlîm*)

That is a literal translation. But look at the range of English translations rather than "children of the gods":

King James Version: "ye mighty"

Jewish Publication Society: "sons of might"

New Jewish Publication Society: "divine beings"

New International Version: "heavenly beings"

Revised Standard Version: "heavenly beings"

   but with a footnote saying, "Hebrew *sons of gods*"

New English Bible: "you gods"

Revised English Bible: "you angelic powers"

New American Standard: "sons of the mighty"

   but with a footnote saying, "or *sons of gods*"

No two the same. Just as with the Song of the Sea, the translators are struggling with the plain meaning of their text. Their problem is not linguistic. They know Hebrew. Their problem is theological. They are struggling over what to do with a psalm in the Bible that addresses the gods and tells them to give something to Yahweh.

The same thing happens with the famous opening chapters of the book of Job:

> And the children of God (or children of the gods) came to stand before Yahweh.
>
> (Job 1:6; 2:1)[35]

Again, some translators have made it "the divine beings," which is not necessarily wrong, but their meaning is uncertain.[36] Most have left it as the sons of God. As I said above, the Greek translator in the Septuagint again changed it to "angels of God." But there is honestly no way around what it says. The Hebrew is *běnê 'ělōhîm,* which is a standard term for the gods. The eminent Yale scholar Marvin Pope, in his commentary, which has been a particularly respected one on Job, just translated it as what it means: "the gods."[37] The book of Job clearly and unapologetically begins with an assembly of the gods presenting themselves before Yahweh. Yahweh is the highest, but the gods exist.

The sons of God (or sons of the gods) come up very near the Bible's beginning in the book of Genesis as well. It is one of the strangest stories in the Bible. Here is the whole thing:

> And it was when humankind began to multiply on the face of the ground and daughters were born to them: and the sons of God saw the daughters of humankind, that they were attractive, and they took women, from all they chose. And Yahweh said, "My spirit won't stay in humankind forever, since they're also flesh. And their days shall be a hundred twenty years." The Nephilim were in the earth in those days and after that as well, when the sons of God came to the daughters of humankind, and they gave birth by them. They were the heroes who were of old, people of renown.
>
> (Genesis 6:1–4)

Here gods have sex with human women and give birth to some sort of superior humans, the Nephilim. Much later, in the book of Numbers, Moses sends scouts into the land of Canaan, and the scouts come back with a report that terrifies everyone. They say:

> We saw the Nephilim there, sons of giants from the Nephilim, and we were like grasshoppers in our eyes, and so were we in their eyes.
>
> (Numbers 13:33)

The sex between deities and humans has apparently produced giants. God limits the divine element in humans by decreeing that humans are not to live more than a hundred twenty years. (And so the text notes later that Moses lives to be a hundred twenty. That is, he gets the maximum.[38]) Now all of this would be right at home in Greek or ancient Near Eastern myths, where there are stories about gods and goddesses having sex with humans and producing superhumans like Achilles and Gilgamesh. But it is not what we expect in the Bible. We know that there are plenty of passages in the Bible where the people of Israel are forbidden to worship other gods. And there are passages that deny that the gods exist. We have seen several of them. So what are we to do with these passages that say the opposite? How can the Bible have these other gods? And: where did they go?

Psalm 82—
The Myth of the Death of the Gods

Here is the text of Psalm 82 with commentary. It is not some obscure little chapter of the Bible. As a song in the book of Psalms, it was probably sung at the Temple in Jerusalem in biblical times. And to this day it is read every Tuesday in the traditional Jewish prayers as the "Psalm of the Day." It says:

> 1 God is standing in the divine assembly
> He judges among the gods.

That is about as explicit as you can get. There are gods. They meet in a divine assembly, as in Job. And one God, the highest of them, has the authority to judge them. Here is what He says to them:

2 "How long will you judge falsely
and favor the wicked?
3 Judge the weak and the orphan.
Justify the humble and the poor.
4 Adjudicate the weak and the needy,
Save them from the hand of the wicked."

The highest God criticizes them for failing to act correctly as gods. They should defend the weak, but they favor the wicked. He concludes:

5 They don't know.
They don't understand.
They walk in darkness.
All the foundations of the earth melt!

The gods pervert justice, and the very foundations of the earth are dissolving. And so He renders a terrible judgment on them:

6 I had said, "You are gods
and children of the Highest, all of you."
7 But: like a human you will die,
and like one of the rulers you will fall.

The judgment is: death. The gods, His children, are to lose their immortality. They will die just like humans. The psalmist then concludes:

8 Arise, God. Judge the earth.
Because *you* give legacies among all the nations.

Notice the final verses, identifying God as "the Highest" (Hebrew *Elyon*) and saying that He is the one who "gives the legacies among all the nations." These are the very words of the passage in the Song of Moses (Deuteronomy 32:8–9) where we started: "When the Highest gave nations legacies." The American biblical scholar Peter Machinist, Hancock Professor of Hebrew at Harvard, wrote that "every interpreter of Psalm 82" has made some connection between Psalm 82 and that passage in the Song of Moses.[39]

Now what if we could walk up and ask ancient Jews singing this at the Temple in Jerusalem, or even ask the poet who composed the psalm, "Do you mean this literally? Do you think that there really used to be gods but they were condemned to death? Or do you mean this as a metaphor, that we used to believe in such things, but now we reject them?" It is hard to know what their answer would be. But, literally or figuratively, Psalm 82 contains their myth of the death of the gods.

3. WHY DOES GOD SPEAK IN THE PLURAL?

There is more. It is one of the classic mysteries of the Bible, and it turns out to relate directly to this idea that there used to be gods and goddesses who died. The mystery is: why, in the Bible's monotheism, does God sometimes speak in the plural? For example, in the creation story in the Bible's first chapter, God says:

> Let *us* make a human, in *our* image, according to *our* likeness.

> (Genesis 1:26)

And in the story of the garden of Eden two chapters later, after the humans have eaten fruit from the tree of knowledge of good and bad, Yahweh says:

> Here, the human has become like one of *us,* to know good and bad.
>
> (Genesis 3:22)

And in the story of the tower of Babylon (also called Babel; it is the same word in the Hebrew, *bābel,* the Hebrew for Babylon), Yahweh says:

> Come on, let *us* go down and babble their language there . . .
>
> (Genesis 11:7)

If the Bible is monotheistic, why picture the one God talking like this? People have proposed various answers over the years. Some have suggested that it might be that God is pictured as using the "Royal We" like kings and queens and popes. Thus a popular attribution to the Queen of England is the line, "We are not amused." We scholars have our own special version of this. A scholar never says, "I don't know." A scholar says, "*We* don't know"—graciously sharing the ignorance with our colleagues. Another suggestion is that God speaks in the plural because God is addressing the angels or some other heavenly creatures in the divine court.[40] But the problem for all of these answers is that the three examples I gave here of God's speaking in the plural are *the only three examples in the Hebrew Bible!*

Some say that God speaks in the plural one time in the book of Isaiah as well, but that is not clear at all. In that passage God says:

> Whom shall I send?
> And who will go for us?
>
> (Isaiah 6:8)

"Whom shall *I* send?" Definitely singular, not plural. The reason people misunderstand the verse to be a plural is that God then says, "And who will go for us?" There is no way that the "us" refers to God Himself. He has clearly already said "I." When He asks, "And who will go for us?" He is talking to heavenly creatures (only to creatures called *seraphim,* not to gods) who are present and who have already been referred to explicitly twice in this passage. It is as if I needed to send one of the students in my class to get something at the office and I said, "Whom shall I send? Who will go for us?" No one would have thought that by "us" I meant for myself alone. And no one would have read the Isaiah passage and thought that God was referring to Himself there in the plural except under the influence in their minds of those three passages in Genesis where God does so.

So God is pictured as speaking in the plural only at creation, the garden of Eden, and the tower of Babylon. Then it is over. And we are only at the eleventh chapter of the first book of the Hebrew Bible. There are still thirty-nine more chapters to go in Genesis and then thirty-eight more books of the Hebrew Bible after that. Why stop using the plural at the tower of Babylon? Interpreters have not addressed this question—why does the plural occur only three times, why are all three at the beginning of the earth's story, and why stop at, of all possible places, the story of the tower of Babylon? I think that we have been missing the crux of the whole thing. We need to ask: what happens in the story of the tower of Babylon? What happens there is: God *disperses* humankind. At the beginning of the story, all humans are together, and all speak the same language. But God creates different languages, so humans scatter and cluster into different nations. Professor Theodore Hiebert of McCormick Theological Seminary makes a particularly clear and strong case for seeing the dispersal of humankind into separate cultures as the primary point of the story of Babel in Genesis 11, more than as a narrative of pride and punishment, as it has often been seen.[41] The text just before the Babel story says:

> The nations were dispersed from these in the earth.
>
> (Genesis 10:32)

And the text at the end of the story says:

> Yahweh scattered them from there over the face of all the earth.
>
> (Genesis 11:9)[42]

What happens there in Genesis 11 is what we saw happen in the Song of Moses:

> When the Highest gave nations legacies,
> when He dispersed humankind.

What happens there in Genesis 11 is also what we saw in Psalm 82:

> Arise, God. Judge the earth.
> Because *you* give legacies in all the nations.

God speaks in the plural in these three primordial stories because there are still others to whom to speak. Thus the German biblical scholar Gerhard von Rad, commenting on the plural in the story of Babel, wrote, "The 'we' in God's mouth presupposes the idea at one time of a pantheon, a council of the gods." But von Rad did not make the next step, to deal with the fact that the "we" ends here.[43] There are gods, children of the Highest. But sometime after the event at the tower of Babylon these others start to die off. The disappearance of the divine plural occurs right there, 100 percent consistent with the demise of the gods.

Thus the story of the sons of the gods (or sons of God) having sex with human women comes in Genesis 6, which is in the middle of that primordial age when the gods still exist. It comes five chapters before the tower of Babylon.

And thus it is immediately after the tower of Babylon story that Yahweh is first said to appear to a human: "And Yahweh appeared to Abram" (Genesis 12:7). That is the beginning of Yahweh's defined relationship with Abraham and his descendants, to be their God. And that too is consistent with the picture in the Song of Moses. There, as we read above, God distributes the peoples' borders according to the various gods, but in the very next verse He keeps Jacob/Israel, Abraham's descendants, as His people:

> When the Highest gave nations legacies,
> when He dispersed humankind,
> He set the peoples' borders
> to the number of the children of the gods.
> But Yahweh's portion is His people.
> Jacob is the lot of His inheritance.
>
> (Deuteronomy 32:9)

And thus God later says to Moses in the exodus story:

> I shall make judgments on all the gods of Egypt.
>
> (Exodus 12:12)

People have struggled with this verse as well. It seems to be recognizing that Egypt's gods exist. So some have interpreted it to mean that God is saying that He will show that they are not really gods. But the wording there in the book of Exodus is the same as in Psalm 82. That psalm said, "He *judges* among the gods" and "Arise God. *Judge* the earth." And Exodus now says, "I shall make *judgments* on all the gods of Egypt."[44] Like the other gods and goddesses, Egypt's deities now die as well. The Levite authors of the account of the plagues were consistent with what comes before that account, at the beginning of Genesis. Thus the most prominent god of Egypt, the sun, is blacked out for three days in the last plague before the slaying of the firstborn. That is more than an eclipse. Eclipses do not last three days. It is a defeat of the sun god, a removal of the sun's divinity. It becomes just an object, not a god. And so the other plagues produce the gods' demise, with Yahweh defeating the divinities of nature: turning the waters to blood, controlling disease and storm. And so the Song of the Sea, coming just a few chapters later, is right to say, "Who is like you among the gods!" At the time that this song was composed, its poet may have really believed in the existence of those other gods. But as the song stands now in the context of Genesis and Exodus that precedes it, this line takes on a new meaning: it now refers to the failure of those gods and to their demise. Their time has come to an end. Indeed, the point of the explicit reference to "judgments on all the gods of Egypt" may be that, in our texts, the Egyptian gods are the last to go. That fits with everything else we have seen in the texts that connects the arrival and merger of Yahweh and El with the period following the exodus from Egypt.

People have also struggled with the verse "Let us make humans in our image" in another way. Does it mean that humans are created in the physical image of God, with faces and hands and feet? Or the spiritual image, or the intellectual image? If it did in fact refer to the physical image, then this raised the question of how both male and female humans were created in the divine image. But if Genesis 1 pictures an age when the gods and goddesses are still alive, then this answers that classic question as well. The text says that God created humans in the image of *'ĕlōhîm,* which can mean "in the image of God" or "in the image of gods," and that He created them male and female. This could simply mean that he created the females in the image of the goddesses and created the males in the image of the male gods.

Now who wrote these things? In the study of the sources of the Bible, we attribute the creation story in Genesis 1 to the Priestly source (P). This story is where God says "Let *us* make a human, in *our* image." And we attribute the stories of the Garden of Eden and the tower of Babylon to the source called J. These stories are where God says "The human has become like one of *us*" and "Let *us* go down and babble their language." The point is that two different authors, two of the major authors of the Bible's first books, both had this idea that God speaks in the plural only at the beginning of their story and then never again.[45] In the past, when people read those authors' divine plurals, they concluded that these authors were not monotheistic. And when they read the story of the male gods having sex with human women, this seemed to confirm that these authors were not monotheistic. But all of those things end after the tower of Babylon story. The author of J and the author of P and the poets of Psalm 82 and the Song of Moses all reflect this idea that there used to be gods, but no more. That is why that Song of Moses could say that God apportioned the nations to the gods in verse 8, but the very same song could say "I, I am He, and there are no gods with me" in verse 39. The theology is consistent: Once there were gods. Now there are not.

This is consistent with the book of Job as well. There we saw the assembly of the gods. Scholars debate the date of when the book of Job was written. But whenever it was written, the fact remains that the story that it tells is understood to take place early in human history. The prophet Ezekiel groups Noah, Daniel, and Job as three righteous men of old.[46] Noah of course comes early in the flood generation. And the Daniel whom Ezekiel mentions is not the person in the book of Daniel. He is rather another Daniel (Dan'il) known in Ugaritic myth as an ancient righteous man. Job is not an Israelite. Like Noah and Daniel, he is a man of high antiquity.[47] In his day, as in Noah's day, there are still gods.

My point is that the death of the gods is not a remote, hypothetical little phenomenon. It plays a crucial role in the works of several of the major authors of the Bible. Professor Machinist wrote about Psalm 82 that there is a "legion of scholarly studies of it."[48] And, as I said above, people have recited it regularly for centuries. These passages have been there for all to see for millennia. Yet most people, even fairly knowledgeable people with regard to the Bible, have not heard about this matter of the death of the gods. And now we can add how the passages all fit together: how exquisitely the connection between the death of the gods and the distribution of the nations coincides with the end of God's use of the plural after that distribution of the nations at the story of the tower of Babylon in Genesis.[49] All of these biblical authors knew it. Maybe everyone in ancient Israel who read these stories and sang these songs knew it. The gods had died.

How Do Gods Die?

Why did they come up with this concept? Gods dying. How did it get started? How did people come to accept it? In part the grounds were already set for it in the ancient Near East because in pagan religion there were known myths of gods dying. Professor Machinist at Harvard and Professor Mark Smith at Princeton have addressed this. Machinist, in an article titled "How Gods Die, Biblically and Otherwise," summarized:

> In Ugarit itself, to restrict ourselves to some examples from the ancient Near East, the Ba'al cycle of texts depicts the death, the violent death, of three of its divine principals: Yamm/Nahar; then his killer, Ba'al; who, in turn, is masticated by his killer, Mot; who himself is later dismembered. The Mesopotamian mythic text of *Enuma Elish,* likewise, treats the death and, at points, dismemberment of the deities Apsu, Tiamat, and Qingu. And in Mesopotamia as well, dead gods can be referred to as a category.[50]

Smith titled an article "The Death of 'Dying and Rising Gods' in the Biblical World,"[51] which is just one treatment out of a collection of publications of Smith's on the relationship of Israel's religion and the pagan religion of the ancient Near East.

My point: the stage was set. When monotheism began to catch

on in Israel, when the prophets no longer had to browbeat people to stop worshipping all those other gods, when the Israelite moms and dads and Sunday (or Saturday) school teachers were teaching their children that there is only one God—whenever things reached that point—they had to explain what had happened to the gods. The idea of the death of the gods was already a known concept in the ancient Near East. I think that the answer to the question of why they were drawn to that idea in Israel lies in the questions with which I began this chapter: What did people think of their parents and grandparents who had worshipped the gods? What did they think happened to the gods—and the goddesses? What did they tell their children? When the children were taught that there is only one God, and they asked, "But Grandma worshipped lots of gods. Was Grandma bad?" the parent could answer, "No, dear. Grandma wasn't bad. There used to be those gods, but *they* were bad, and they died. And now there is only one God." What I have simplified here as a little conversation between a parent and child must have existed as a real theological issue that needed an answer. And, actually, it may well have occurred in numerous family and school conversations like this as well. Religious changes require religious explanations. And the mythological background of gods dying in the ancient Near Eastern pagan religions made this religious explanation fit right in.[52] It was not even necessarily a radical idea. Gods die. What was radical was getting the number down to one.

The Mystery of Babylon

The story of the tower of Babylon has been the missing piece of the puzzle all along.[53] It is the culminating story of the Primeval

History (Genesis 1–11, also known to scholars by its German name, the *Urgeschichte*). Why? Because, from the biblical author's point of view, it is the end of the old world of the gods. What follows is not the beginning of monotheism in history. It is the beginning of the monotheistic *story*. It is the story of the relations between Yahweh and humankind. It will take up the entire rest of the Bible.

In Jewish, Christian, and Muslim traditions, that story starts with Abraham. There is a traditional story (a midrash), not found in the Bible, that Abraham's father was an idol maker, that Abraham arrived at monotheism on his own, and that Abraham smashed the idols in his father's house. Why does the monotheism story start with Abraham and not with Adam, Eve, Cain, Lamech, Enosh, Isaac, Jacob, Joseph, Moses, or anyone else? The instincts of the three religions were precisely right. Abraham comes after—immediately after—the story of the tower of Babylon. The tower of Babylon tale comes in Genesis 11, and the first words of Genesis 12 are: "And Yahweh [or: the LORD] said to Abraham . . ." From the time of Babylon, the gods are condemned to death. And, instead of the gods, the one highest God now makes humans His companions to whom He speaks.[54]

The logical progression between these two chapters is even stronger than that. In the tower of Babylon story in Genesis 11, separate languages and lands are formed. In the Abraham story in Genesis 12, God's first words to Abraham are a direction to leave his land and go to a new land:

> And Yahweh said to Abram, "Go from your land and
> from your birthplace and from your father's house to
> the land that I'll show you."

Everything else in the story, all the adventures of this man, his family, and their descendants, will follow from this move. And, as we know well from our previous observations, the longest and largest of their adventures will be their stay in Egypt and their exodus from it and their return to the land. Languages, geography, and history are all intimately, intricately tied to theology. Choose the metaphor you prefer: a network, a tapestry, a lentil stew. But the bottom line is: arrival at belief in one God.

So, many scholars among my colleagues and my teachers attributed monotheism to the Babylonian exile. We can understand that. They naturally saw great revolutions in thought coming as a result of great, catastrophic events in human history. That is often the case. Of course big events have big consequences in a culture. But in this case, the exodus from Egypt and the uniting of the Levites with the rest of Israel was at least as monumental an event as the Babylonian defeat of Judah.

The scholarly attraction to Babylon is not exactly wrong. The biblical authors did connect the gods' demise to Babylon, but to the ancient Babylon of mythology, not to the Babylonian empire of history that would conquer the Jews centuries later.

The Queen of the Heavens

We are not quite done. Until now we have spoken of either one god or many gods. But there is another possibility that rounds out this picture: two gods.

In the English-speaking culture in which I grew up, when we learned grammar—I mean in the good old days when they still taught grammar in school—we learned that the grammatical number of a word was either singular or plural. That is how we think: one or many. But not all languages work that way.

In Hebrew—both Biblical and Modern—there are three forms to indicate number: singular, plural, and dual. The dual is used when there are two of something. It is formed by adding the syllables -*ayim* to the end of a word. It is especially useful for body parts that come in twos. Thus an arm in Hebrew is a *yad*. A person's arms are *yadayim*. A leg in Hebrew is a *regel*. A person's legs are *raglayim*. If you own two Cadillacs, I guess you have Cadillacayim. Now the point is not just about grammar. It is about a different concept of number. Two of something is as different from nine or ten as it is from one. Now I bring this just as an example, not to prove anything. I mean to convey that this conceptual difference of number can apply to grammar, but it can also apply to theology. In other words: to gods. We know from both text and archaeology that Israelites and Jews in the biblical period conceived of Yahweh as male, and they sometimes worshipped a goddess alongside Yahweh. She was apparently His consort, His wife. In the text, the prophet Jeremiah criticizes the people because they worship "the Queen of the Heavens." The text is ironic. Jeremiah reprimands the people for worshipping her and predicts terrible things to come.[55] Later, when all the terrible things that Jeremiah prophesied have come true, the people declare the opposite: that they were fine as long as they worshipped the Queen of the Heavens but that things turned bad only when they listened to Jeremiah and stopped worshipping her:

> The thing that you spoke to us in the name of Yahweh: we're not listening to you. But we *shall* do everything that has proceeded from our mouth: to burn incense to the Queen of the Heavens and to pour libations to her, as we've done, we and our fathers, our

kings, and our officials in Judah's cities and in Jerusalem's streets, so we had plenty of bread and were well
and saw no bad. But since we stopped burning incense
to the Queen of Heaven and pouring libations to her,
we've been lacking everything, and we've been consumed by the sword and by the famine.

(Jeremiah 44:16–18)

In archaeology, too, we have found direct evidence of a female
consort along with Yahweh. At a location called Kuntillet 'Ajrud
along Judah's border, the archaeologist Z. Meshel of Tel Aviv
University found inscriptions in the 1970s that refer to "Yahweh
of Samaria and His Asherah."[56] An Asherah is a goddess. Some
have taken it to be the goddess' name, Asherah, but actually it is
simply the word for a goddess. It normally is preceded by the Hebrew definite article—*the* Asherah, like *the* Baal—indicating that
it is the general term for a goddess, not any particular goddess'
name.[57] The inscription "Yahweh of Samaria and His Asherah"
on the side of a giant jar from Kuntillet 'Ajrud is consistent with
the picture in Jeremiah: the people worshipped Yahweh, but
they also worshipped a queen goddess alongside Him.

Back to the text: One of the relevant Bible stories that we
considered earlier was the account of the prophet Elijah and the
prophets of the Baal at Mount Carmel. There Elijah challenges
450 prophets of the Baal to the duel. The prophets of the Baal
pray fervently, but nothing happens. Elijah prays to Yahweh,
and the fire falls and consumes the sacrifice. But I left out the
next part of the story there. Elijah has the people slaughter
the 450 prophets of the Baal. Now, an interesting thing is that
people often leave out a significant detail when they retell this
story. There are not just the 450 prophets of the Baal present.

There are also 400 prophets of the Asherah.[58] But the prophets of the Asherah do not have an altar or an offering and do not pray. And the prophets of the Baal all get killed, but nothing at all happens to the prophets of the Asherah. Why not? Because, as the great biblical scholar David Noel Freedman put it, "The winner gets the girl." The duel was between the two male deities. The female deity was not challenged and was not, like the Baal, shown not to be a true deity. She was the spouse of the triumphant God. The story is set in the kingdom of Israel, and its capital at this time was the city of Samaria. Recall that the inscription at Kuntillet 'Ajrud refers to "Yahweh of Samaria and His Asherah."[59]

It appears that even when the struggle was going on between monotheism and polytheism, that revolution was going to take an extra step to get people to give up the goddess. Human males had wives. Why would they not expect their God to have a divine wife as well? Now you might say, "What about Psalm 82 and the whole matter of the death of the gods?" Did not all the goddesses die too? Why would this one queen goddess live? But in Psalm 82 the Highest God, Yahweh, condemns all the *children* of the Highest (the *běnê 'elyôn*) to die like humans. But the Queen of the Heavens, the Asherah, is not one of His children. She is His wife. So, the fact is, we do not ever really find out what became of her. We have no mythic text that addresses it. What we can say is that people continued to feel a need for a female presence somewhere in their religious picture, even if it was not a goddess. Mariology developed in Catholicism. And Biblical Judaism at one point identified the nation itself as God's wife.[60] Later Judaism developed the idea of the *shechinah,* a term for the divine presence. The word *shechinah* never occurs in the Hebrew Bible, but in the Jewish mystical system known as Kabbalah it acquired a status of its own. The word is grammatically feminine, and perhaps because of this it is treated as a feminine aspect of the deity. These and other terms and persons are not the equivalent of a divine wife, but they reflect a perfectly understandable feeling among some that both masculine and feminine must exist in the divine world just as they do in the human world. In the pagan world, this was not a problem. There were both gods and goddesses. And in Israel the Asherah was the last one to go.[61]

The biblical accounts of the kings of Israel and Judah convey the struggle over her exit. They refer to Israel's tenth-century BCE king Ahab, who ruled in Samaria, making an Asherah, which stood in Samaria through several kings' reigns.[62] That fits with the archaeological discovery of the "Yahweh of Samaria and His Asherah" inscription. They report that King Asa of Judah (c. 918–873 BCE), whose reign may have overlapped near its end with Ahab's, removed his mother from her royal status because she had made a "monstrosity" (some sort of idol?) to the Asherah. He burned the Asherah.[63] If that report is correct, the Asherah must have been reestablished, however, because around two hundred years later, King Hezekiah of Judah destroys it again.[64] But that is not the end of the Asherah. The book of 2 Kings reports that Hezekiah's son, King Manasseh, put a statue of the Asherah in the Temple![65] But then Manasseh's grandson, King Josiah, took it out of the Temple and burned it at the same place where King Asa had burned one about three hundred years earlier.[66] And still, as we saw above, the prophet Jeremiah continues to struggle against those who wanted to continue burning incense to her.

Those references in Jeremiah are the last ones to the Asherah or the Queen of the Heavens. There are none in the books that tell the later destiny of the Jews: the books of Ezra, Nehemiah, Esther, Daniel, and the prophets Haggai and Zechariah. So at some point after Jeremiah, the acceptance of monotheism also came to include the demise of the last goddess. When, where, and why: we just do not know. The text does not say. What the people believed to have come of her is a mystery.

When Monotheism Won

By the end of the biblical period, monotheism had won.

Monotheism had won so much so that on the whole we have forgotten what pagan religion was about. Most people could not tell you what the word "pagan" means.

Monotheism had won so much so that even educated people think that pagan religion involved idol worship.

Monotheism had won so much so that college Departments of Religion today usually do not offer a course on pagan religion. Departments and programs of religious studies commonly offer Judaism, Christianity, Islam, Buddhism, Daoism, Confucianism, and Hinduism. Only Hinduism might come close insofar as it involves multiple gods, but a course on it would not aim to shed light on pagan religion as such. If you want a course on Greek or Roman pagan religion, go to the Classics Department. If you want a course on ancient Near Eastern pagan religion, go to the Near Eastern Studies Department or the Oriental Institute. But to find this in a Religion Department would be rare, even though pagan religion is the longest-lasting religion on earth.

Monotheism had won so much so that rabbis in antiquity turned to a new sort of explanation for why the Second Jerusalem Temple was destroyed. When the first Jerusalem Temple had been destroyed in the wake of the Babylonian conquest in

587 BCE, the biblical interpretation of that catastrophe was that the people had worshipped other gods. But when the second Jerusalem Temple fell to the Romans in 70 CE, the rabbis' interpretation of the catastrophe was moral rather than worship of other gods. The people had accepted monotheism enough by that time that one could not trace the disaster to apostasy. So the rabbis taught that it was because of "pointless hatred" (Hebrew śin'āt ḥinām). Monotheism was no longer the issue.

The triumph of monotheism has changed everything, probably even the nature of atheism. Today more people than ever believe in God. And more people than ever don't. How different would this be if the difference were not between atheists and those who believe in God, but instead were between atheists and those who believe in *the gods and goddesses*? Would books like those of Richard Dawkins (*The God Delusion*) and Christopher Hitchens (*God Is Not Great*), for example, look different if they had had to frame the argument this way?[67] Would the evidence on both sides be different? We shall never know. Monotheism won.

The Exodus and Monotheism

We have seen a movement from many deities to two to one. Whether you take that movement to be fact, mythology, or theology, it is the story of how we got to where most (Western) religions are now. And, as I said, it even defines where atheism is at. Have you heard the old joke about the Jewish man who was left on a desert island for years? When a ship found him, they saw two large huts that he had built on a hill. They asked him what they were. He said, "That one's my synagogue. I go there and pray and celebrate holidays." And they asked him what the other hut was. He said, "That's the synagogue I *don't* go to!" (You can change this to churches or any house of worship you like when you tell the joke.) So we hear people say, "Do you believe in God?" But we do not generally hear people say, "Do you believe in the gods?" The religion that atheists don't go to is monotheism—by default. Or, better: by history. Is the idea of one God *higher* than the idea of many? Is it more logical? More attractive? The idea of many gods—polytheism—served humankind for about three or four millennia before monotheism came along. Pagan religion was the most successful religion of all time (in terms of how long it lasted; Christianity is the most successful in the number of adherents). I have read and heard it said many times that monotheism has done more harm than polytheism. The claim is that monotheism is exclusive—"If my belief is right, then everybody else's beliefs must be wrong"—so monotheists are more likely than polytheists or atheists to exclude, persecute, and purge others. We can admit that there is some logic to that claim, but still the evidence of history goes both ways. Polytheist and atheist nations and empires have done their share of atrocities. I would not want to take a side in a depressing debate over which has done more horrible things. My task here has not been to argue that monotheism is higher or lower than other ideas. It has just been to track how it came about and to recognize that it succeeded. Monotheism won. One won.

Which brings us back to the point about why the exodus matters to the emergence of monotheism: Monotheism prevailed, but if the exodus had not happened, monotheism would have developed either (1) later, or (2) completely differently, or (3) it might never have happened at all.

CHAPTER SIX

THE MYSTERY OF JUDAH

Love Your Neighbor as Yourself

THE EXODUS:
ETHICAL CONSEQUENCES

So: if there was an exodus from Egypt, just of Levites, who later merged with the Israelites, this was a crucial event in the formation of monotheism. But there is more. Much more, I think. The exodus not only gave birth to theological consequences. It also had ethical consequences.

"Love your neighbor as yourself."[1] One of the most famous lines from the Bible. Impressive. Fascinating. Inspiring. Capable of a thousand interpretations and raising ten thousand questions. It appears in a text from the kingdom of Judah. I trace this text to the time of King Hezekiah of Judah, around 700 BCE. Many of my colleagues in biblical scholarship ascribe it to a later period, the post-exile period of the fifth century or later.[2] We differ on the time but not on the geography. It is a product of Judah, written after the Assyrians had conquered and eliminated the other kingdom, Israel, from the map. As we shall see, though, the idea in Judah comes down from a long chain of texts and events. It was a remarkable proposition to come out of ancient Judah, which was embedded in the ancient Near Eastern world of wars, slavery, class and ethnic divisions, discriminations of all kinds. In the Christian New Testament it was clear enough to Jesus that he made it one of the two essential commandments.

Together with loving one's God, he said, "There is no other commandment greater than these."[3]

But:

There has been a claim for a while now that turns this famous idea on its head. The claim is that the verse means only to love one's fellow Jews or Israelites as oneself, that the word for "neighbor" there means only a member of one's own group. Inclusive? No. It is actually *ex*clusive. Is there anything to this claim? Come with me back to ancient Egypt and Israel.

EQUAL TREATMENT OF ALIENS

We have examined the likelihood that the exodus from Egypt was historical but that it involved only the Levites. The Levites were the ones with the Egyptian names, Egyptian cultural elements in their ark, their Tabernacle, and circumcision. Only the Levite sources develop the idea that the world did not know Yahweh's name until He first revealed it to Moses. The Levites are not mentioned among the people of Israel in the Song of Deborah, and all of Israel is not mentioned among those leaving Egypt in the Song of Miriam. In that song, the people who leave Egypt come to the sacred mountain where the sanctuary is located.

And we saw one more thing: all three Levite sources of the Torah (known in critical Bible scholarship as E, P, and D) command fair treatment of aliens. Just, equal treatment of aliens. Foreigners. Outsiders. Not members of the group. It is not a small point. In these Levite sources it comes up fifty-two times. And how often does the non-Levite source, J, mention it? None. The first occurrence of the word "torah" in the Torah is: "There shall be one torah for the citizen and for the alien who resides among you" (Exodus 12:49, from the Levite source P). According to the Levites, in Israel every week was Be Kind to Aliens Week.

One of the things that has impressed me through my years of study of the Hebrew Bible was this repeated concern for aliens. Fifty-two times? How many things are mentioned in the Five Books of Moses fifty-two times?[4] What was the reason for this? We might say that it was a matter of geography. We observed earlier that Israel lay at the point where Africa, Asia, and Europe meet. People of all backgrounds regularly passed through there. So we can imagine a nation at that fulcrum of the trade route having a policy of welcome to all those valuable aliens. Still, not all countries that have wanted trade in history have made this emphasis. There had to be something more. Israel's own witness, over and over, in all three Levite sources, rather gives this reason:

> And you shall not persecute an alien, and you shall not oppress him, *because you were aliens in the land of Egypt.*
>
> (Exodus 22:20)

> And you shall not oppress an alien—since you know the alien's *soul, because you were aliens in the land of Egypt.*
>
> (Exodus 23:9)

> . . . you shall not persecute him. The alien who resides with you shall be to you like a citizen of yours, *and you shall love him as yourself, because you were aliens in the land of Egypt.*
>
> (Leviticus 19:33–34)

So you shall *love* the alien, *because you were aliens in the land of Egypt.*

(Deuteronomy 10:19)

You shall not abhor an Egyptian, *because you were an alien in his land.*

(Deuteronomy 23:8)

You shall not bend judgment of an alien. . . . You shall remember that *you were a slave in Egypt,* and Yahweh, your God, redeemed you from there. *On account of this,* I command you to do this thing.

(Deuteronomy 24:17–18)

Why, according to these sources, should we be good to aliens? Because we know how it feels. We know the alien's soul. So we shall not persecute foreigners, we shall not abhor them, we shall not oppress them, we shall not judge them unfairly, we shall treat them the same as we treat ourselves, we shall *love* them.

Indeed, one of the possible meanings of the word Levi itself in Hebrew is "alien." As I said in Chapter 2, William Propp makes a strong case on the etymology of the word *levi* in his commentary on Exodus, that its most probable meaning is an "attached person" in the sense of resident alien.[5] The Levites were attached resident aliens during their stay in Egypt, and they were attached resident aliens after their arrival among the Israelite population. There they were not one of the original union of tribes. Thus the Song of Deborah does not include them. But after they were adopted and assimilated into Israel and Judah, the Bible's authors added them into their national history. They were seen as kin, descended from a man named Levi, who was the brother of the ancestors of the tribes. But the Levites' experience as aliens was deeply embedded in them. Hence the concentration on aliens in every Levite source. And—remember this—we do not find it anywhere else in the laws of the ancient Near Eastern world. As we quoted in Chapter 2:

> *This is an emphasis unique to the Hebrew law codes.*[6]

In the whole ancient Near East, in all those lands, through several millennia, we have found fifty-two references to equal treatment of aliens, and all fifty-two are in the first five books of the Bible—and only in the Levite sources of those five books!

Now the point of the textual and archaeological evidence that I gave was not just whether the exodus was historical or not. I argued that the merger of Yahweh, the God of the Levites, with El, the God of the Israelites back in the land, was crucial to the very formation of monotheism. If Israel had chosen to worship them as two separate gods, the history of Judaism and Christianity and Islam would be entirely different. And the point that I want to make now is likewise broader than just that the exodus, in some form, was historical. In addition to the theological consequences, I now want to recognize that there were also these *ethical* consequences. The experience of being aliens, of being oppressed, apparently led Israel's clergy and teachers, the Levite priests, to say, "You must never do that."

WAR

We all know that there are harsh passages toward others in the Bible as well: dispossess the Canaanites, destroy Jericho, etc. But, as I said earlier, the evidence in the ground indicates that most of that (the Conquest) never happened. Likewise in the case of the destruction of the Midianites, as I described in Chapter 4, this was a story in the Priestly (P) source written as a polemic against any connection between Moses and Midian. It is a polemical story in literature, not a history of anything that actually happened. At the time that the Priestly author wrote the instruction to kill the Midianites, there were not any Midianites in the region. The Midianite league had disappeared at least four hundred years earlier.[7] As we saw in Chapter 2, it was an attested practice in that ancient world to claim to have wiped out one's enemies when no such massacre had actually occurred. King Merneptah of Egypt did it. King Mesha of Moab did it. And, so there is no misunderstanding, the purpose of bringing up those parallels is not to say that it was all right to do it. It is rather to recognize that, even in what are possibly the worst passages about warfare in the Bible, the stories do not correspond to any facts of history. They are the words of an author writing about imagined events of a period centuries before his own time. And, even then, they are laws of war only against specific peoples: Canaanites, Amalekites, and Midianites, none of whom exist anymore. So they do not apply to anyone on earth. The biblical laws concerning war in general, against all other nations, for all the usual political and economic reasons that nations go to war, such as wars of defense or territory, do not include the elements that we find shocking about those specific cases. (See examples below.)

Now one can respond that even if these are just fictional stories they are still in the Bible, after all, and can therefore be regarded as approving of such devastating warfare. That is a fair point to raise. I would just add this caution: when people cherry-pick the most offensive passages in the Bible in order to show that it is bad, they have every right to point to those passages, but they should acknowledge that they are cherry-picking, and they should pay due recognition to the larger—vastly larger—ongoing attitude toward aliens and foreigners. In far more laws and cases, the principle of treatment of aliens is positive. Besides the outright cases above, it is expressed in specific rules of how to relate to others in general: Do not rape a captured woman in war (Deuteronomy 21:10ff). Do not abhor an Edomite (Deuteronomy 23:8). If you happen upon your enemy's ox or donkey straying, *bring it back* to him. If you see the donkey of someone who hates you sagging under its burden, and you would hold back from helping him: you shall *help* him (Exodus 23:4–5). The Bible permits a violent response to those who threaten Israel's existence, but it still requires that in a siege during war Israel must offer the besieged city peace first, and it forbids a massacre if they surrender. And if they do not surrender, women and children can be captured but may not be killed.[8] It is still war, the worst thing in the world, and one cannot deny its presence in some of the texts, but we should at minimum recognize that the biblical laws of conventional war are different from the horrible scenes of the fictional holy wars that people often cite in criticism of the Bible's story. Remarkably, the biblical texts do not advocate persecution of pagans *for being pagans*. Pagan worship is forbidden only to the Israelites and Jews themselves. Biblical texts taught that pagans were wrong, that their beliefs in the gods and goddesses were mistaken, that Israel's Canaanite predecessors in the land had committed moral offenses that, the texts claimed, had polluted the land in earlier times.[9] But at the same time biblical religion was remarkably ecumenical in respecting others' rights to their continued beliefs in the gods. A Greek could worship

Zeus, and a Canaanite could worship the Baal, as long as they did not try to convert the Israelites or Jews to that worship. The story of Elijah and the execution of the 450 prophets of Baal at Carmel, for example, does not require or advocate going out and killing all prophets of the Baal. The story presents this episode as a singular event in a context of a struggle to stop Queen Jezebel's effort to bring the Baal worship into Israel. We do not have to like, agree with, or make up excuses for a story that has blood spilled in an early battle of miracles for monotheism. We have to understand why the author of such a story presented that moment as so dire that he there, and only there, in his writings could conceive of a massacre in that revolution.[10] Our world literature is filled with such stories. What we can do, hopefully, is to learn from them—and change.

ALL THE FAMILIES OF THE EARTH WILL BE BLESSED

People sometimes have thought that monotheism promoted exclusivism, prejudice: if there is only one God, and it is *our* God, then others must be wrong, foolish, in need of correction. But there is another side to this as well: the birth of monotheism was paralleled with the birth of love of neighbors, even alien neighbors. The exodus led both to monotheism and to the exceptional attitude toward others. Still, as I said at the beginning, some have claimed that the famous verse "Love your neighbor as yourself" means only to love one's fellow Jews or Israelites as oneself. Not all-inclusive, they say. It is actually narrowly selective. These writers not only misunderstand the Hebrew word for "neighbor." They miss the entire context of fifty-two references to love and treat even aliens as oneself.

The very fact that the Bible's sources start off with the creation of the earth and all of humankind instead of starting with
Israel itself is also part of this context. As I asked in Chapter 3,
if any of us were asked to write a history of the United States,
would we start by saying, "Well, first there was the Big Bang,
and then . . ."? The biblical authors saw Israel's destiny as being
to bring good to all those foreign nations and peoples—to the
earth. This is not a minor point. It appears in God's first words
to Abraham, and again in God's first words to Isaac, and again
in God's first words to Jacob: your descendants' purpose is to be
that

> *all* the families of the earth will be blessed through
> you.
>
> (Genesis 12:3; 26:2–4; 28:10–14)

It appears again in God's words to Abraham following the
near-sacrifice of his son Isaac (Genesis 22:18). In some of these
verses the text says all the *families* of the earth will be blessed,
and in some it says all the *nations* of the earth will be blessed.
So both on the large scale and the small, the message is explicit
that the purpose of the divine relationship with Abraham is, in
some way, to benefit everyone. That fact is all the more unusual
because in the Bible the deity is rarely depicted as giving reasons
for His actions or His commandments. (When you are an om-
nipotent being, you should not have to explain yourself all the
time.) But this case is a most notable exception. Right from the
beginning, God tells Abraham and Isaac and Jacob what this is
going to be all about. Their descendants' task is to care about
everyone and to try to bring blessings to them.

Because of a quirk of Biblical Hebrew grammar, some readers
have taken these words to mean that all the nations or families

"will bless themselves" through Abraham's descendants rather than "be blessed" through them. So they understand the passages to mean that people from many families and nations will bless their children saying, "May you be like Abraham."[11] This understanding is not necessarily wrong. The Hebrew verb occurs in these verses in two different conjugations.[12] Both of these conjugations in Biblical Hebrew can be sometimes passive and sometimes reflexive. If we take them as passives in these particular verses, then they mean "the nations (or families) of the earth will be blessed through you." If we take them as reflexives, then they mean "may the nations (or families) of the earth bless themselves through you." The grammar allows for either, but to my mind the former is more profound, and it fits better with the context: it follows upon the creation of all humans, and then, most especially, it comes immediately after the story of the tower of Babylon. As we recall, that story, in Genesis 11, culminates in the formation of the different nations, spread around the earth according to their different languages. And then the very next chapter begins with God's first appearance to Abraham and expressing the aim that Abraham's descendants' destiny is to be a source of blessing to all of those many peoples. The Bible's message, repeated all those times, seems direct: you are not in this just for yourself.

YOU SHALL LOVE HIM
(THE ALIEN) AS YOURSELF

Which brings us back to our opening question. Does "Love your neighbor as yourself" refer only to loving your fellow Jews/Israelites? When the text already directs every Israelite to love aliens as oneself, what would be the point of saying to love *only* Israelites—and in the very same chapter![13] My friend the biblical scholar Jacob Milgrom, of blessed memory, wrote that it is precisely because the love of the alien is specifically mentioned there that love of "neighbor" must mean just a fellow Israelite.[14] I see his point, but it would have been more likely if the verse about love of aliens came first in the text. But it comes after we have already had the instruction to love the neighbor as oneself, so it can just as well be a specification for anyone who would have thought that love of neighbor did not include loving others as well. Did the authors think that such specifications were necessary? We *know* that they did because they added it fifty-two times in the Torah! And, in any case, Milgrom and I would both recognize that the bottom line is that one is supposed to love both, alien and neighbor, whether they overlap or not.

So from where did that idea come, that the Hebrew word for neighbor in this verse, means only a member of one's own group? As we saw in the case of Moses' "heavy mouth" in Chapter 4, when we want to check the meaning of a biblical term, the first step is to look at other places where it occurs in the Hebrew Bible. The Hebrew word for neighbor here is *rē'a*. Now the first occurrence of *rē'a* is in the story of the tower of Babel (Babylon), the Bible's story of the origin of different nations and languages. It involves every person on earth:

> and they said each to his *rē'a* . . .
>
> (Genesis 11:3)

That is, the term refers to every human, without any distinctions by group. Now one might say, though, that the word might still refer only to members of one's own group because, at this point in this story, all humans are in fact still members of a single group. So let us go to the next occurrence of the word. In the story of Judah and Tamar in Genesis, Judah has a *rē'a* named Hirah the Adullamite.[15] Hirah is a Canaanite! He comes from the (then) Canaanite city of Adullam. He cannot be a member of Judah's clan because, at this point in the story, that clan, the Israelites, consists only of Jacob and his children and any grandchildren.

In the exodus story the word appears in both the masculine and feminine in the account of how Moses instructs the Israelites to ask their Egyptian neighbors for silver and gold items before their exodus from Egypt.[16] The word there refers precisely to non-Israelites. On the other hand, in the story of Moses' early life in Egypt, when he intervenes between two "Hebrews" who are fighting, he says to the one at fault, "Why do you strike your *rē'a*?"[17] So in that episode it refers to an Israelite.

In short, the word *rē'a* is used to refer to an Israelite, a Canaanite, an Egyptian, or to everyone on earth. And still people say that "Love your *rē'a* as yourself" means just your fellow Israelite. When the Ten Commandments include one that says: "You shall not bear false witness against your *rē'a*" (Exodus 20:16; Deuteronomy 5:17), do they think that this meant that it was okay to lie in a trial if the defendant was a foreigner—even though elsewhere, as we saw, the law forbids Israel to "bend the judgment of an alien"? When another of the Ten Commandments says not to covet your *rē'a*'s wife (Exodus 20:17; Deuteronomy 5:20), do they think that this meant that it was okay to covet a Hittite's wife—even though elsewhere the Bible condemns King David for doing just that? David desires Bathsheba, who is the wife of Uriah the Hittite, and the prophet Nathan brings God's condemnation for David's behavior.[18]

AN ERROR OF CONTEXT

So, again, from where did this idea come that one is supposed to love only one's own group? Some get it from context. When we read it with the preceding line, it says:

> You shall not take revenge, and you shall not keep on
>   at the children of your people.
> And you shall love your neighbor as yourself.

Since the line before it is about "the children of your people," and the two lines were put together into a single verse when verse numbers were added to the Bible, some have assumed that the "love your neighbor as yourself" line must also be just about "the children of your people." Why? No reason at all. In fact, read the chapter, Leviticus 19, carefully. Coming near the very center of the Torah, it is a remarkable mixture of laws of all kinds. It goes back and forth between ethical laws and ritual laws: sacrifice, heresy, injustice, mixing seeds, wearing mixed fabrics (*shaatnez*), consulting the dead, gossip, robbing, molten idols, caring for the poor. It has everything! I tell my students: if you are on a desert island and can have only one chapter of the Bible with you, take Leviticus 19. And its laws all come mixed in between each other. No line can be judged by what comes before it or after it. And remember, there are no verse numbers or periods or commas in the original. And people want to use *context* to judge the meaning of this line?! That is baseless.

The biblical scholar Harry Orlinsky made the context argument in 1974.[19] He said, "Alas," he could not see any way around it. As he was a respected biblical scholar, he was followed by others. Robert Wright cited him in *The Evolution of God*.[20] (Wright had consulted with me on the matter of loving the alien, but unfortunately we did not discuss the neighbor verse, so I did not get to caution him about this.) Hector Avalos also followed Orlinsky, saying, "as Orlinsky has deftly noted . . ."[21] Look at the Internet and you will find numerous sites quoting his "deftly noted" remark. It was not deft. It actually was not defended at all.

Indeed, there is context and there is *context*. As we saw, in the full context of the first books of the Bible, starting with creation and with caring for all the families of the earth, we would not imagine the verse about loving your neighbor to apply only to one's own people. And in the full context of the occurrences of the word *rē‘a,* too, we would never take the verse about loving your neighbor to mean: now that is just if your neighbor has the same religion as you. These people who have been reading the verse as meaning just-your-own-kind were both misreading the *immediate* context of the passage and completely missing its *total* context in the Bible.

The same undefended mistake of context was made by John Hartung, a professor of anesthesiology.[22] He in turn was trusted by Richard Dawkins in his bestselling *The God Delusion,* saying,

> "Love thy neighbour" didn't mean what we now think
> it means. It meant only "Love another Jew." The point
> is devastatingly made by the American physician and
> evolutionary anthropologist John Hartung.[23]

It was not devastating. Hartung emphasized the importance of context, but he then used only the one verse (quoted above), even though he was aware that the joining of its two statements was done by those who created numbered verses centuries after the Bible was written. And, reading the Bible only in translation, he did not understand the meaning of the word *rē'a*. Regarding the debates between atheists and theists, if Dawkins thinks he knows better about the question of the existence of a God than theologians and religious people, then that is between him and them. But when he presents himself as knowing something better about a Hebrew term in the Bible, a book that he cannot read unless someone translates it for him, now that is something else. When he denigrates the Bible and the Jews by saying that one of their very greatest gifts—"love your neighbor as yourself"—was no gift but was a piece of ethnic superiority, then it is my job as a Bible scholar to set the record straight. It would be one thing if Hartung and Dawkins made some little mistake about the meaning of a verse in the Bible. People do that all the time. But they picked a *big* verse, a verse that makes all the difference in the world, a verse with a tremendous context. And then they used their uninformed view of that verse to disparage the Bible and the persons who wrote it. That is irresponsible in a scholar. The bottom line is simply that they were incorrect in claiming that "love your neighbor" meant anything limited or negative. In this book we have seen the fruits of two revolutions that are still taking place in biblical studies: archaeology and critical biblical scholarship: literary, historical, linguistic, and anthropological. We can be generous and say that Dawkins and others did not know the extent to which these revolutions have enriched our understanding. Many people did not know. Let us grant the maximum: that they made an honest mistake because they did not know of the tremendous leaps that have been made in the lifetimes of all of us living now. Fair enough. But now we know. So let us just not repeat this mistake again. Something extraordinary happened in ancient Israel. The writers of the Bible who came from the stock of those who had experienced the exodus bequeathed to us all something tremendous: Treat the alien the same. Love your neighbor as yourself. This piece of wisdom has reached us from a text written over two millennia ago. And if we are right in our analysis, it derived from an event over three millennia ago. Now we no longer need to argue over whether love of neighbor really means what we thought. It does. Perhaps now we can use our time on trying more than ever to live it.

I shall say it again: I recognize that the Bible also contains well-known passages that involve violence or cruelty or unequal treatment. Not only do I not want to smooth over such things; I have tried to present both sides of such things. One does not need to deny what is troubling in order to pay respect to what is heartening.

IN THE END: "ETHICAL MONOTHEISM"

The exodus led both to monotheism and to the exceptional attitude toward others. The two great consequences of this really early stage of religion were a theological one, namely monotheism, and an ethical one, namely love of both one's fellow and the alien. The two—ethics and monotheism—went hand in hand from the beginning. And this we call: ethical monotheism. This is funny coming from me of all people. I never liked the term "ethical monotheism," and I have never used it in my teaching or writing. Did it not imply that people who were not monotheists were *un*ethical? Are pagans on average less ethical than monotheists? Are atheists or agnostics less ethical than monotheists? Was the whole world really unethical until the monotheists came along? Was Hammurapi unethical? Was Socrates unethical? With such thoughts as these I rejected the claim that we were superior in ethics if we were monotheistic. But I have changed my thinking—or more accurately: I have nuanced it—in light of this new picture of the exodus, the merger of Yahweh and El, the rejection of the gods and of the goddess, and the parallel development of the love of aliens and the insistence on treating them equally. Not everyone has to be a monotheist. But perhaps nearly everyone can treat his or her neighbors with kindness. In the last chapter I declined to argue that monotheism is higher or lower than other ideas. Monotheists are not necessarily superior to others morally. But monotheism and ethical treatment of all humans, whether they are members of the group or not, were both by-products of a common historical development. And that historical development was: the Exodus from Egypt. It did not have two million people who experienced it. But millions of us have been its heirs.

We still are asking what "Love your neighbor as yourself" means. What does it mean to command a feeling? Can you really command someone to feel love? And what does it mean to love others *as yourself*? What, exactly, does that mean that we are supposed to do? Here is what it means to me. To try to feel inside me what another human being is feeling. Empathy. Sympathy. Compassion.

That feeling is foreshadowed near the beginning of the Bible's story. Abraham's seed are to act in a way that will bring blessing to all the earth's families. Can we not all take on the role of Abraham's seed? Not just Jews. Not just Christians. Not just Muslims.

That feeling is expressed in the reason for treating the alien right: "because you know the alien's soul." So we are commanded to love him or her. The last of the Ten Commandments is: you shall not covet. So the Decalogue too ends in a command about a feeling. And, for the record, let us not forget how the Ten Commandments begin: "I am the LORD your God who brought you out of the land of Egypt." *They premise the whole thing on the exodus from Egypt!* Then the first commandment that follows is "no other gods," and the tenth is not to covet. The Ten Commandments make a perfect finale for the path we have been following. They go from (1) being brought out of Egypt to (2) monotheism to (3) not coveting what belongs to someone else, your *rē'a,* your neighbor.

It has been over three thousand years. Why does anybody care all that much whether the exodus happened or not? Why care whether it happened "the way it is told in the Bible"? Why? Because history matters. What happened matters. Understanding how ideas got started and why people hang on to them matters. The exodus of a group of people from Egypt happened. It made a difference. It still makes a difference.

FROM EGYPT TO MIDIAN

The Oppression in Egypt and the Revelation in Midian

I have distinguished the sources, thus:

The E text is in *italics*.

The J text is in standard typeface.

The P source is in SMALL CAPS.

One can read each source separately or read the whole text together.[1]

EXODUS 1:7–3:12

1:7. AND THE CHILDREN OF ISRAEL WERE FRUITFUL AND TEEMED AND MULTIPLIED AND BECAME VERY, VERY POWERFUL, AND THE LAND WAS FILLED WITH THEM.

8. And a new king rose over Egypt—who did not know Joseph. 9. And he said to his people, "Here, the people of the children of Israel is more numerous and powerful than we. 10. Come on, let's be wise toward it or else it will increase; and it will be, when war will happen, that it, too, will be added to our enemies and will war against us and go up from the land."

11. And they set commanders of work-companies over it in order to degrade it with their burdens. And they built storage cities for Pharaoh: Pithom and Raamses. 12. And the more they degraded it, the more it increased, and the more it expanded; and they felt a disgust at the children of Israel. 13. AND EGYPT MADE THE CHILDREN OF ISRAEL SERVE WITH HARSHNESS; 14. AND THEY MADE THEIR LIVES BITTER WITH HARD WORK, WITH MORTAR AND WITH BRICKS AND WITH ALL WORK IN THE FIELD—ALL THEIR WORK THAT THEY DID FOR THEM—WITH HARSHNESS.

15. *And the King of Egypt said to the Hebrew midwives—of whom the name of one was Shiphrah and the name of the second was Puah—* 16. *and he said, "When you deliver the Hebrew women, and you look at the two stones, if it's a boy then kill him, and if it's a girl then she'll live." 17. And the midwives feared God and did not do what the King of Egypt had spoken to them, and they kept the children alive. 18. And the King of Egypt called the midwives and said to them, "Why have you done this thing and kept the children alive?"*

19. *And the midwives said to Pharaoh, "Because the Hebrews aren't like the Egyptian women, because they're animals! Before the midwife comes to them, they've given birth!"*

20. *And God was good to the midwives. And the people increased, and they became very powerful,* 21. *and it was because the midwives feared God, and He made them households.*

22. And Pharaoh commanded all of his people, saying, "Every son who is born: you shall throw him into the Nile. And every daughter you shall keep alive."

2:1. And a man from the house of Levi went and took a daughter of Levi. 2. And the woman became pregnant and gave birth to a son. And she saw him, that he was good, and she concealed him for three months. 3. And she was not able to conceal him anymore, and she took an ark made of bulrushes for him and smeared it with bitumen and with pitch and put the boy in it and put it in the reeds by the bank of the Nile. 4. And his sister stood still at a distance to know what would be done to him. 5. And the Pharaoh's daughter went down to bathe at the Nile, and her girls were going alongside the Nile, and she saw the ark among the reeds and sent her maid, and she took it. 6. And she opened it and saw him, the child: and here was a boy crying, and she had compassion on him, and she said, "This is one of the Hebrews' children."

7. And his sister said to Pharaoh's daughter, "Shall I go and call a nursing woman from the Hebrews for you, and she'll nurse the child for you?"

8. And Pharaoh's daughter said to her, "Go." And the girl went and called the child's mother. 9. And Pharaoh's daughter said to her, "Take this child and nurse him for me, and I'll give your pay." And the woman took the boy and nursed him. 10. And the boy grew older, and she brought him to Pharaoh's daughter, and he became her son. And she called his name Moses, and she said, "Because I drew him from the water."

11. And it was in those days, and Moses grew older, and he went out to his brothers and saw their burdens, and he saw an Egyptian man striking a Hebrew man, one of his brothers. 12. And he turned this way and that way and saw that there was no man, and he struck the Egyptian and hid him in the sand. 13. And he went out on the second day, and here were two Hebrew men fighting. And he said to the one who was in the wrong, "Why do you strike your companion?"

14. And he said, "Who made you a commander and judge over us? Are you saying you'd kill me—the way you killed the Egyptian?!"

And Moses was afraid and said, "The thing is known for sure." 15. And Pharaoh heard this thing and sought to kill Moses, and Moses fled from Pharaoh's presence and lived in the land of Midian.

And he sat by a well. 16. And a priest of Midian had seven daughters, and they came and drew water and filled the troughs to water their father's flock, 17. and the shepherds came and drove them away. And Moses got up and saved them and watered their flock. 18. And they came to Reuel, their father, and he said, "Why were you so quick to come today?"

19. And they said, "An Egyptian man rescued us from the shepherds' hand, and he drew water for us and watered the flock, too."

20. And he said to his daughters, "And where is he? Why is this that you've left the man? Call him, and let him eat bread."

21. And Moses was content to live with the man. And he gave Zipporah, his daughter, to Moses, 22. and she gave birth to a son, and he called his name Gershom, "Because," he said, "I was an alien in a foreign land."

23. And it was after those many days, and the king of Egypt died.

AND THE CHILDREN OF ISRAEL GROANED FROM THE WORK, AND THEY CRIED OUT, AND THEIR WAIL WENT UP TO GOD FROM THE WORK. 24. AND GOD HEARD THEIR MOANING, AND GOD REMEMBERED HIS COVENANT WITH ABRAHAM, WITH ISAAC, AND WITH JACOB. 25. AND GOD SAW THE CHILDREN OF ISRAEL. AND GOD KNEW!

3:1. And Moses had been shepherding the flock of Jethro, his father-in-law, priest of Midian. And he drove the flock at the far side of the wilderness, and he came to the Mountain of God, to Horeb.

2. And an angel of Yahweh appeared to him in a fire's flame from inside a bush. And he looked, and here: the bush was burning in the fire, and the bush was not consumed! 3. And Moses said, "Let me turn and see this great sight. Why doesn't the bush burn?"

4. And Yahweh saw that he turned to see. *And God called to him from inside a bush, and He said, "Moses, Moses."*

And he said, "I'm here."

5. And He said, "Don't come close here. Take off your shoes from your feet, because the place on which you're standing: it's holy ground." 6. *And He said, "I'm your father's God, Abraham's God, Isaac's God, and Jacob's God." And Moses hid his face, because he was afraid of looking at God.* 7. And Yahweh said, "I've seen the degradation of my people who are in Egypt, and I've heard their wail on account of their taskmasters, because I know their pains. 8. And I've come down to rescue them from Egypt's hand and to bring them up from that land to a good and widespread land, to a land flowing with milk and honey, to the place of the Canaanite and the Hittite and the Amorite and the Perizzite and the Hivite and the Jebusite.

9. *"And now, here, the cry of the children of Israel has come to me, and also I've seen the oppression that Egypt is causing them. 10. And now go, and I'll send you to Pharaoh, and you shall bring out my people, the children of Israel, from Egypt."*

11. *And Moses said to God, "Who am I that I should go to Pharaoh and that I should bring out the children of Israel from Egypt?"*

12. *And He said, "Because I'll be with you. And this is the sign for you that I have sent you. When you bring out the people from Egypt you shall serve God on this mountain."*

THE STORY ACCORDING TO EACH OF THE MAIN SOURCES OF THE PENTATEUCH

THE STORY ACCORDING
TO THE E SOURCE

1. Before the Exodus

Abraham in Gerar, says his wife Sarah is his sister: Genesis 20:1–18

Abraham's son Isaac is born: 21:6

Abraham's concubine Hagar and their son Ishmael are sent away: 21:8–21

Abraham makes a treaty with King Abimelek: 21:22–34

The binding of Isaac: 22:1–10, 16b–19

Abraham and Keturah have six sons, including Midian: 25:1–4

Jacob has a dream of angels and a celestial ladder at Beth-El: 28:11b–12, 17–18, 20–22

Jacob's wives give birth to sons: 30:1b–3, 4b–24a

Jacob and Laban: 31:1–2, 4–16, 19–48, 50–54; 32:1–3

Jacob returns from Aram: 32:14b–24

Jacob struggles with God, is named Israel: 32:25–33

Jacob meets with Esau: 33:1–17

Jacob buys land at Shechem, sets up an altar to "El, God of Israel": 33:18a, 18:c–20

Jacob returns to Beth-El: 35:1–8

Rachel dies at Bethlehem giving birth to Benjamin: 35:16b–20

Joseph and his brothers: 37:3a, 4, 12–18, 21–22, 24–25a, 28a, 29–30, 36

Joseph in Egypt: 40:1–23; 41:1–45, 47–57; 42:5, 7, 21–25, 35–37; 43:14, 23b; 45:3

Jacob comes to Egypt: 46:1–5a; 47:13–26; 48:1–2, 8–22; 50:15–21, 23–26

2. The Exodus

Egypt oppresses Israelites: Exodus 1:8–12, 15–21

Moses, in Midian, summoned by God; Yahweh reveals His name: 3:1, 4b, 6, 9–18; 4:1–18, 20b, 21a, 22–23

Aaron speaks for Moses to Israel's elders in Egypt: 27–31

Moses, Pharaoh, and the plagues: 5:3–6:1; 7:14–18, 20b, 21, 23–29; 8:3b–11a, 16–28; 9:1–7, 13–34; 10:1–19, 21–26, 28–29; 11:1–8

The exodus: 12:21–27, 29–36, 37b–39; 13:1–16

The Red Sea: 13:17–19; 14:5b, 7, 11–12, 19a, 20a, 25a

Miriam sings the (incipit of the) song of the sea: 15:20–21

3. The Journey After the Exodus

Yahweh sets laws: 15:25b–26

Water in the wilderness, Moses strikes a crag, water flows from Horeb to Meribah: 17:2–7

Attack by Amalek: 17:8–16

Jethro, priest of Midian, Moses' father-in-law: 18:1–27

Mass revelation at mountain: 19:2b–9, 16b–17, 19; 20:18–26

The Covenant Code: 21:1–27; 22:1–30; 23:1–33

Vision of Moses, Aaron, Nadab, Abihu, and seventy elders at mountain: 24:1–15a

The golden calf: 32:1–33

Theophany to Moses: 33:1–23

Rebellion at Taberah: Numbers 11:1–3

Rebellion over food: 11:4–35

Moses' Cushite wife: 12:1–16

Rebellion over food, Moses' bronze snake: 21:4b–9

Moab and Balaam: 22:3–41; 23:1–30; 24:1–25

Joshua succeeds Moses: Deuteronomy 31:14–15, 23

THE STORY ACCORDING
TO THE J SOURCE

1. Before the Exodus

Creation: Genesis 2:4b–25

Garden of Eden: 3:1–24

Cain and Abel: 4:1–16

Cain genealogy: 4:17–24

Sons of God and human women: 6:1–4

The flood: 6:5–8; 7:1–5, 7, 12, 16b–20, 22–23; 8:2b–3a, 6, 8–12, 13b, 20–22

Noah's drunkenness: 9:18–27

Generations of Noah's sons: 10:8–19, 21, 24–30

The tower of Babel: 11:1–9

Promise to Abraham: 12:1–4a

Abraham's migration: 12:6–9

Abraham in Egypt, says his wife Sarah is his sister: 12:10–20

Abraham and Lot: 13:1–5, 7–11a, 12b–18

Abraham and Hagar give birth to Ishmael: 16:1–2, 4–14

Yahweh appears to Abraham, the three visitors: 18:1–33

Sodom and Gomorrah: 19:1–28, 30–38

Birth of Isaac: 21:1a, 2a, 7

Rebekah: 22:20–24; 24:1–67

The death of Abraham: 25:8a

Jacob and Esau: 25:11b, 21–34; 27:1–45

Isaac says his wife Rebekah is his sister: 26:1–11

Isaac and Abimelek: 26:12–33

Jacob at Beth-El: 28:10–11a, 13–16, 19

Jacob, Leah, and Rachel: 29:1–30

Jacob's children: 29:31–35; 30:1a, 4a, 24b

Jacob and Laban: 30:25–43; 31:49

Jacob's return: 31:3, 17; 32:4–13

Dinah and Shechem: 34:1–31

Reuben takes Jacob's concubine: 35:21–22a

Kings and chiefs of Edom: 36:31–43

Joseph and his brothers: 37:2b, 3b, 5–11, 19–20, 23, 25b–27, 28b, 31–35

Judah and Tamar: 38:1–30

Joseph in Egypt: 39:1–23; 42:1–4, 6, 8–20, 26–34, 38; 43:1–13, 15–23a, 24–34; 44:1–34; 45:1–2, 4–28

Jacob in Egypt: 46:5b, 28–34; 47:1–4, 27a, 29–31; 50:1–11, 14, 22

2. The Exodus

Egypt oppresses Israelites: Exodus 1:6, 22

Baby Moses in the basket: 2:1–10

Moses from Egypt to Midian: 2:11–23a

Moses summoned by Yahweh at burning bush: 3:2–4a, 5, 7–8, 19–22; 4:19–20a, 24–26

Moses and Pharaoh: 5:1–2

The Red Sea: 13:21–22; 14:5a, 6a, 9a, 10b, 13–14, 19b, 20b, 21b, 24, 25b, 27b, 30–31

3. The Journey After the Exodus

Water in the wilderness: 15:22b–25

Food in the wilderness, manna: 16:4–5, 35b

Mass revelation at Mount Sinai: 19:10–16a, 18, 20–25

Theophany to Moses: 34:1a, 2–13

The Ten Commandments: 34:14–28

Departure from Mount Sinai: Numbers 10:29–36

Moses sends scouts into the land: 13:17b–24, 27–31, 33; 14:4, 11–25, 39–45

Rebellion led by Dathan and Abiram: 16:1b–2a, 12–14, 25, 27b–32a, 33–34

Edom refuses to let Israel pass through its border: 20:14–21

King of Arad attacks but is defeated by Israel: 21:1–3

Israel fights the Amorites: 21:12–35

Apostasy to Baal Peor with Moabite women: 25:1–5

Trans-Jordan tribal inheritances: 32:1, 3, 5a, 5c, 7–12, 25–27, 33–42

The death of Moses: Deuteronomy 34:5–7

THE STORY ACCORDING TO THE P SOURCE

1. Before the Exodus

Creation: Genesis 1:1–2:3

The Flood: 6:9b–22; 7:8–11, 13–16a, 21, 24; 8:1–2a, 3b–5, 7, 13a, 14–19; 9:1–17

Noah's descendants: 10:1b–7, 20, 22–23, 31, 32

Abraham migrates to Canaan: 11:27b–31a; 12:4b–5

Abraham and his nephew Lot: 13:6, 11b–12a

Abraham and Hagar give birth to Ishmael: 16:3, 15–16

Covenant with Abraham: 17:1–27

Destruction of cities of the plain: 19:29

Abraham and Sarah give birth to Isaac: 21:1b, 2b–5

Abraham buys the cave of Machpelah as a family tomb: 23:1–20

Death of and burial of Abraham: 25:7, 8b–11a

Ishmael's descendants: 25:13–18

Isaac marries Rebekah: 25:20

Esau's wives and Jacob's departure to Aram: 26:34–35; 27:46; 28:1–9

Jacob's return to Canaan: 31:18

Jacob's name changed to Israel at Beth-El: 35:9a, 9c–15

Jacob's wives and his sons: 35:22b–26

Death and burial of Isaac: 35:27–29

Esau's wives and descendants: 36:2–30

Jacob lives in Canaan: 37:1

Joseph in Egypt: 41:46a

Jacob in Egypt: 46:6–27; 47:5–12, 27b–28; 48:3–7; 49:29–33; 50:12–13

2. The Exodus

Egypt oppresses Israelites: Exodus 1:7, 13–14; 2:23b–25

Moses, in Egypt, summoned by God; Yahweh reveals His name: 6:2–11, 30; 7:1–9

Moses, Pharaoh, and the plagues: 7:10–13, 19–20a, 22; 8:1–3a, 12–15; 9:8–12

The exodus: 12:1–20, 28, 40–50

The Red Sea: 14:1–4, 8, 9b, 10a, 10c, 15–18, 21a, 21c, 22–23, 26–27a, 28–29

3. The Journey After the Exodus

Food in the wilderness, manna: 16:2–3, 6–35a, 36

Mass revelation at Mount Sinai: 19:1; 24:15b–18a

Tabernacle instruction: 25:1–31:11

Sabbath instruction: 31:12–17

The tablets of the testimony: 31:18[*]

The skin of Moses' face: 34:29–35

Tabernacle construction: 35–40

Priestly law code: Leviticus 1–27[**]

Census, last days at Mount Sinai: Numbers 1:1–2:34; 3:2–9:14; 10:1–12, 14–27

Moses sends scouts into the land: 13:1–16, 25–26, 32; 14:1–3, 5–10, 26–38

A Sabbath violation: 15:32–36

Law of fringes on clothes: 15:37–41

Rebellion led by Korah: 16:1a, 2b–11, 15–24, 27a, 32b, 35; 17:1–28

---

[*]The P text does not say what the tablets of the testimony contained. There is no mention of the Ten Commandments, and several of them are contained elsewhere in the Priestly law codes.

[**]The Priestly law code does not include Leviticus 23:39–43 or 26:39–45.

The tithe and the division of the Aaronid priests from the other Levites: 18:1–32

Law of the red cow: 19:1–22

Water in the wilderness, Moses strikes a rock at Meribah: 20:1b–13

The death of Aaron: 20:23–29

Apostasy at Peor with Midianite women: 25:6–19

Census: 26:1–7, 12–65

Law of women's inheritance: 27:1–11

Appointment of Joshua to succeed Moses: 27:12–23

Laws of women's vows: 30:2–17

War against Midian over Peor, Midianite women: 31:1–54

Tribal inheritances: 32:2, 4, 6, 13–24, 28–32; 33:50–56; 34:1–29; 35:1–34; 36:1–13

The death of Moses: Deuteronomy 34:8–9

THE STORY ACCORDING TO THE D SOURCE

Moses reviews his experience with the people: Deuteronomy 1–11

The Deuteronomic law code (called Dtn): 12:1–26:15

Moses encourages the people: 26:16–19; 27:1–10

Covenant ceremony: 27:11–26

Blessings and curses: 28:1–69

Moses concludes: 29:1–28; 30:1–20; 31:1–6

Moses charges Joshua to succeed him: 31:7–8

Moses writes a torah and entrusts it to the "Levitical priests": 31:9–13, 16–22, 24–29

Moses gives a song to the people: 31:30; 32:44–47

Moses gives a poetic blessing to the people: 33:1

Moses sees the promised land from a mountain in Moab before he dies: 34:1–4, 10–12

OTHER SOURCE TEXTS

Genesis 14: This story is from an independent source.

Genesis 15: Identification of this text by sources is uncertain. Verses 13 to 16 can be identified as coming from the Redactor, not from any of the sources.

Genesis 49:1–27: The Blessing of Jacob is an old poem, now embedded in the J text.

Exodus 15:1–18: The Song of the Sea is an old poem, now embedded in the J text.

Exodus 20:1–17: The Ten Commandments, an independent source. Verses 1 and 11 can be identified as coming from the Redactor.

Deuteronomy 32:1–43: The Song of Moses, an old poem

Deuteronomy 33:2–29: The Blessing of Moses, an old poem

NOTES

Chapter and verse numbers were inserted into the biblical text long after it was written. They sometimes merge lines from separate sources into a single verse. When that happens, we identify the parts of the verse with a lowercase *a* or *b* to show that the verse as now numbered contains more than one source text. People sometimes misunderstand and mistakenly accuse scholars of splitting verses, when in fact it is the opposite: it was the persons who put the verse numbers into the text who created the confusion.

The process of identifying the sources is a continuing task. Some of the source identifications of verses in my *The Bible with Sources Revealed* (2003) are different from those I made in *Who Wrote the Bible?*, which first appeared in 1987, and which were modified in a second edition in 1997. Where these differences occur, readers should regard the identifications in *The Bible with Sources Revealed* as representing my more recent thinking.

Many scholars have eliminated portions of the Priestly (P) source, of all different sizes, and ascribed them to a separate source called the Holiness (H) text. Some claim that there was an entire Holiness school of persons who produced the H text(s). As I have said in *Who Wrote the Bible?* on p. 172, *The Bible with Sources Revealed* on pp. 218 and 296–297, and here in Chapter 6 in note 2, I do not think that this claim of a Holiness text or school has ever been adequately defended, and I do not think that it is correct.

❧ NOTES ❧

Introduction

1. William Propp, *Exodus 19–40*, The Anchor Bible (New York: Doubleday, 2006), p. 795.

2. On the "King of the House of David" (*mlk byt dwd*) inscription, see Avraham Biran and Joseph Naveh, "An Aramaic Stele Fragment from Tel Dan," *Israel Exploration Journal* (1993): 81–98; and "The Tel Dan Inscription: A New Fragment," *Israel Exploration Journal* (1995): 1–18. On the Moabite inscription, see André Lemaire, "'House of David' Restored in Moabite Inscription," *Biblical Archaeology Review* 20 (1994): 30–37. See also Emile Puech, "La stele araméenne de Dan," *Revue Biblique* 101 (1994): 215–41.

3. Yigal Shiloh, *Excavations at the City of David I 1978–1982: Interim Report of the First Five Seasons;* and *Excavations at the City of David 1978–1985,* vol. 5, ed. D. T. Ariel, Qedem Monographs of the Institute of Archaeology (Institute of Archaeology, Hebrew University of Jerusalem, 2000); Eilat Mazar, "Did I Find King David's Palace?" *Biblical Archaeology Review* (January/February 2006); A. Faust, "Did Eilat Mazar Find David's Palace?" *Biblical Archaeology Review* (September/October 2012); see also Mazar, "Excavate King David's Palace!" *Biblical Archaeology Review* 23 (January/February 1997). See also Mazar, "The Undiscovered Palace of King David in Jerusalem—A Study in Biblical Archaeology," in Avi Faust, ed., *New Studies on Jerusalem* (Ramat Gan, Israel: Bar-Ilan University, 1996), pp. 9–20 (Hebrew).

4. Most highly recommended is Baruch Halpern's *David's Secret Demons: Messiah, Murderer, Traitor, King* (Grand Rapids, MI: Eerdmans, 2001), which is recognized and praised in the books published subsequently about David. Others include Jonathan Kirsch, *King David: The Real Life of the Man Who Ruled Israel;* Steven McKenzie, *King David: A Biography;* Robert Alter, *The David Story;* Joel Baden, *The Historical David: The Real Life of an Invented Hero;* Jacob Wright, *David, King of Israel, and Caleb in Biblical Memory;* David Wolpe, *David: The Divided Heart;* and R. E. Friedman, *The Hidden Book in the Bible.*

CHAPTER ONE
History Recaptured

1. Numbers 2:32.

2. See Thomas E. Levy and David Noel Freedman, *William Foxwell Albright, 1891–1971: A Biographical Memoir* (Washington, DC: The National Academies of Sciences, 2008), pp. 1–29.

3. John van Seters, *Abraham in History and Tradition* (New Haven, CT: Yale University Press, 1987); T. L. Thompson, *The Historicity of the Patriarchal Narratives: The Quest for the Historical Abraham* (New York: De Gruyter,1974); Israel Finkelstein and Neil Asher Silberman, *The Bible Unearthed: Archaeology's New Vision of Ancient Israel and the Origin of Its Sacred Texts* (New York: Free Press, 2001); and even the Albrightians, including my teachers and colleagues and myself, took a more critical approach.

4. Donald Redford, *Egypt, Canaan, and Israel in Ancient Times* (Princeton, NJ: Princeton University Press, 1992), p. 422.

5. David Sperling, *The Original Torah* (New York: New York University Press, 1998).

6. Lee Levine, "Biblical Archaeology," in David Lieber and Jules Harlow, eds., *Etz Chayim: Torah and Commentary* (New York: Rabbinical Assembly, Jewish Publication Society, 2001), pp. 1341–42.

7. Finkelstein and Silberman, *The Bible Unearthed* (New York: Free Press, 2001).

8. Finkelstein and Silberman, *The Bible Unearthed*, p. 58.

9. Finkelstein and Silberman, *The Bible Unearthed*, p. 61.

10. William Dever, *What Did the Biblical Writers Know and When Did They Know It?* (Grand Rapids, MI: Eerdmans, 2001), p. 99.

11. Some think that the name Palestine for that land goes back to earlier times because Herodotus used it. But if one looks at all the references in Herodotus, one sees that they refer only to the region where the Philistines lived, not to all of Israel or Judah. That is presumably why Herodotus called it Philistia/Palestine.

12. This was published later in Abraham Malamat, *The History of Biblical Israel* (Leiden: Brill, 2001).

13. Johannes de Moor, "Egypt, Ugarit, and Exodus," in N. Wyatt et al., eds., *Ugarit, Religion and Culture* (Münster: Ugarti-Verlag, 1996), pp. 213–47.

14. James K. Hoffmeier, *Israel in Egypt: The Evidence for the Authenticity of the Exodus Tradition* (New York: Oxford University Press, 1997); K. A. Kitchen, *On the Reliability of the Old Testament* (Grand Rapids, MI: Eerdmans, 2003).

15. Thomas E. Levy, Thomas Schneider, and William H. C. Propp, eds., *Israel's Exodus in Transdisciplinary Perspective: Text, Archaeology, Culture, and Geoscience* (hereafter: *IETP*), Quantitative Methods in the Humanities and Social Science (New York: Springer, 2015), http://exodus.calit2.net/.

16. William H. Propp, *Exodus 1–18*, The Anchor Bible (New York: Doubleday, 1998); and Propp, *Exodus 19–40*, The Anchor Bible (New York: Doubleday, 2006).

17. Reported in *Who Wrote the Bible?* (hereafter: *WWTB*), *The Bible with Sources Revealed, The Hidden Book in the Bible,* and *The Exile and Biblical Narrative.* See the bibliographies in these for works by other scholars. I shall also cite some more recent works as we go on here. For better or worse, the bibliography on this subject is now so extensive that no one work can list it all.

18. Bernard Batto, "The Reed Sea: Requiescat in Pace," *Journal of Biblical Literature* 102 (1983): 27–35; "Red Sea or Reed Sea? How the Mistake Was Made and What *Yam Sûp* Really Means," *Biblical Archaeology Review* (July/August, 1984); R. E. Friedman, *Commentary on the Torah*, pp. 214–15; Propp, *Exodus 1–18*, pp. 486–87; John Huddlestun summarizes the varieties of views in "Red Sea," *Anchor Bible Dictionary* (hereafter: *ABD*) (New York: Doubleday, 1992), vol. 5, pp. 633–42.

19. Eric Cline, *From Eden to Exile: Unraveling Mysteries of the Bible* (Washington, DC: National Geographic Society, 2012), p. 90.

20. E.g., G. E. Mendenhall, "The Census Lists of Numbers 1 and 26," *Journal of Biblical Literature* 77 (1958): 52–66.

21. Friedman, *Commentary on the Torah*, comment on Numbers 3:43, p. 432. There are no cases at all in the Torah in which *'eleph* means "clan." Baruch Halpern finds two cases elsewhere in the Hebrew Bible where the term means "clan": Judges 6:15 and 1 Samuel 10:19–21, but he too shows that this term cannot be applied to the lists in Numbers arithmetically. Halpern, *The Emergence of Israel in Canaan* (Chico, CA: Scholars Press, 1983), pp. 114–16.

22. Mark Harris, "The Thera Theories: Science and the Modern Reception History of the Exodus," in *IETP*, p. 97.

23. The same applies to other attempts to propose possible natural explanations for the Red Sea episode. Such an attempt to explain it in terms of winds appears in Doron Nof and Nathan Paldor, "Are There Oceanographic Explanations for the Israelites' Crossing of the Red Sea?" *Bulletin of the American Meteorological Society* 73 (1992): 305–14; and see citations there. Much more cautious is the approach of A. Salomon, S. Ward, F. McCoy, J. Hall, and T. Levy, who go so far as to examine only what possible natural occurrences such as tsunamis could have "inspired" the biblical story; "Inspired by a Tsunami? An Earth Sciences Perspective of the Exodus Narrative, *IETP*, pp. 109–29; and see citations there.

24. Harris, "The Thera Theories," p. 91. See recently Sturt W. Manning, *A Test of Time and A Test of Time Revisited: The Volcano of Thera and the Chronology and History of the Aegean and East Mediterranean in the Mid-second Millennium BC*, 2nd ed. (first edition 1999), (Oxford: Oxbow, 2014), and the review by Manfred Bietak in *Bryn Mawr Classical Review* (2016) online, http://bmcr.brynmawr.edu/2016/2016-04-06.html.

25. G. Ernest Wright, *Biblical Archaeology*, 2nd ed. (Philadelphia: Westminster, 1962); *The Challenge of Israel's Faith* (Chicago: University of Chicago Press, 1944); *God Who Acts* (London: SCM, 1952); *The Old Testament and Theology* (New York: Harper & Row, 1969).

CHAPTER TWO
The Mystery of Egypt

1. Baruch Halpern wrote, "Semites always swarmed in the Delta." *IETP*, p. 294 (and see the following note). John Collins wrote, "The existence of Semitic slaves in Egypt in the late second millennium is well attested." Collins, *Introduction to the Hebrew Bible*, 2nd ed. (Minneapolis: Fortress Press, 2014), p. 111. William Propp wrote, "Multitudes of Asiatics were continually entering Egypt both voluntarily and involuntarily throughout the New Kingdom." Propp, *Exodus 19–40*, p. 765. Thomas

Römer wrote, "Egyptian texts mention several cases of 'Asiatics' ('*3mw*) who had successful careers in Egypt, often attaining high office." Römer, *The Invention of God* (Cambridge, MA: Harvard University Press, 2015), p. 52. See, for instance, David Srour et al., *IETP*, p. 180; and the chapters by Manfred Bietak and James Hoffmeier in *IETP*. Carol Meyers, *Nova* interview, posted November 18, 2008; Jeffrey Tigay, "Exodus," in *The Jewish Study Bible*, 2nd ed., A. Berlin and M. Brettler, eds. (New York: Oxford University Press, 2014), pp. 103–4; and Iain Provan, V. P. Long, and T. Longman, in *A Biblical History of Israel* (Louisville, KY: Westminster John Knox, 2003), pp. 125–26.

2. For example, my colleague the archaeologist Thomas Levy excavated evidence of Shasu migration to Egypt. See T. Levy, R. B. Adams, and A. Muniz, "Archaeology and the Shasu Nomads: Recent Excavations in the Jabal Hamrat Fidan, Jordan," in R. E. Friedman and W. Propp, eds., *Le-David Maskil, A Birthday Tribute for David Noel Freedman* (Winona Lake, IN: Eisenbrauns, 2004), pp. 63–89. And Halpern notes that "a report that 'Shasu of Edom' passed the Wadi Tumeilat (Pap. Anastasi VI 4.11–5.5) or that two slaves escaped past Migdol (Pap. Anastasi V 19.2–20.6; both *ANET* 259) may be routine police blotter material. Or, the Exodus." *IETP*, p. 294. Volkmar Fritz, *The Emergence of Israel in the Twelfth and Eleventh Centuries* BCE (Atlanta: Society of Biblical Literature, 2011), pp. 126–30. Thomas E. Levy, Mohammad Najjar, and Erez Ben-Yosef, *New Insights into the Iron Age Archaeology of Edom, Southern Jordan: Surveys, Excavations and Research from the Edom Lowlands Regional Archaeology Project (ELRAP)* (Los Angeles: UCLA Cotsen Institute of Archaeology Press, 2014).

3. Avraham Faust, "The Emergence of Iron Age Israel," in *IETP*, p. 476. One could also add archaeologist Jodi Magness, who wrote of the many scholars who view the early Israelites "who joined with new arrivals (including perhaps a small group from Egypt—hence the story of the Exodus) to form a new group unified by their worship of a patron deity known as YHWH (Yahweh)," in Magness, *The Archaeology of the Holy Land* (Cambridge: Cambridge University Press, 2012), p. 25.

4. Finkelstein and Silberman, *The Bible Unearthed*: "Was a *Mass* Exodus even possible in the time of Ramesses II?" (p. 58). "The escape of more *than a tiny group* from Egyptian control . . . seems highly unlikely" (p. 60). "One can hardly accept the idea of a flight of a *large group* of slaves from Egypt" (p. 61). "The text describes the survival of a *great number* of people. . . . Some archaeological traces of their *generation-long* wandering in the Sinai should be apparent" (p. 62).

5. Finkelstein and Silberman, *The Bible Unearthed*, p. 52.

6. Lee Levine, "Biblical Archaeology," in David Lieber and Jules Harlow, eds., *Etz Hayim: Torah and Commentary* (New York: Rabbinical Assembly, Jewish Publication Society, 2001), p. 1341.

7. David Wolpe, "Did the Exodus Really Happen?" http://www.beliefnet.com /Faiths/Judaism/2004/12/Did-The-Exodus-Really-Happen.aspx.

8. James Hoffmeier in *IETP*, p. 205. Hoffmeier noted that in answer to the question "Do you think the early Israelites lived in Egypt and that there was some sort of Exodus? Nineteen answered YES. None said NO." (The other six expressed various forms of uncertainty.)

9. *WWTB*, pp. 82–83.

10. Exodus 2:1–10; Numbers 26:59.

11. Baruch Halpern, *The Emergence of Israel in Canaan* (Chico, CA: Society of Biblical Literature, 1983), p. 250.

12. On Merari and Mushi, see William Propp, *Exodus 1–18,* The Anchor Bible (New York: Doubleday, 1998), p. 276. On Moses, Hophni, and Phinehas, see Donald Redford, *Egypt, Canaan, and Israel in Ancient Times* (Princeton, NJ: Princeton University Press), pp. 417–19. On Hur, see Ernst Axel Knauf, "Hur," *ABD,* vol. 3, p. 334. The name Miriam may also be Egyptian; see Propp, *Exodus 1–18,* p. 546.

13. The name Hur, connected with the Egyptian god Horus, never occurs among any of the ten tribes of Israel. Outside of its occurrence among the Levites (Exodus 17:10, 12; 24:14) it occurs only in Judah (Exodus 31:2). At the time that the Levites would have arrived in the region, Judah (with Simeon) was a separate entity from Israel.

14. The Egyptian names occur in the sources and editors J; E; P; Dtr; R; Joshua 24; Samuel (A and B); Isaiah; Jeremiah; Micah; Malachi; Psalms 77; 90; 99; 103; 105; 106; Daniel; Chronicles; and Ezra/Nehemiah.

15. Frank Moore Cross and David Noel Freedman, *Studies in Ancient Yahwistic Poetry,* 2nd ed. (Grand Rapids, MI: Eerdmans, 1997).

16. Their case was further supported in Cross's *Canaanite Myth and Hebrew Epic* (Cambridge, MA: Harvard University Press, 1973), pp. 112–44; in Freedman's, "Early Israelite Poetry and Historical Reconstructions," in *Pottery, Poetry, and Prophecy* (Winona Lake, IN: Eisenbrauns, 1980), pp. 167–78; and in Baruch Halpern's *The First Historians* (San Francisco: Harper & Row, 1988). See also Ronald Hendel, "The Exodus as Cultural Memory: Egyptian Bondage and the Song of the Sea," in *IETP,* p. 71. On the other side, Konrad Schmid of the University of Zurich says in "Distinguishing the World of the Exodus Narrative from the World of Its Narrators: The Question of the Priestly Exodus Account in Its Historical Setting," *IETP,* p. 333, that viewing the song as a very ancient piece of literature "is probably untenable, given the links in Exodus 15 to the preceding narrative in Exodus 14 (including its Priestly portions)." But the links to those narratives are precisely that the narratives have the song as their source, not the other way around. Halpern's demonstration that the narratives depend on the song, which Schmid does not cite, disproves that claim, as does the original work of Cross and Freedman showing the antiquity of the language of the song, further reinforced in Brian D. Russell, *The Song of the Sea: The Date of Composition and Influence of Exodus 15:1–21,* Studies in Biblical Literature, vol. 101 (New York: Peter Lang, 2007).

17. Cross and Freedman, *Studies in Ancient Yahwistic Poetry,* p. x.

18. The Song of the Sea is used by the author of J. The Song of Deborah is used by the author of Judges 1–4; 6–8. These are discussed in Halpern, *The First Historians* (San Francisco: Harper & Row, 1988), pp. 76–97; Cross, *Canaanite Myth and Hebrew Epic,* pp. 112–44.

19. R. E. Friedman and Shawna Dolansky, *The Bible Now* (New York: Oxford University Press, 2011), pp. 68–72.

20. Freedman, *Pottery, Poetry, and Prophets,* p. 146. Some readers mistakenly think that the word Israel appears in the song in the first line, which says, "Then Moses and the children of *Israel* sang this song" (Exodus 15:1). But that line (which is prose, not poetry) is visibly the prose introduction to the song, not part of the song

itself. It is as if someone would say, "And then Frank Sinatra sang, 'My kind of town, Chicago is . . .'" and someone thought that the words "And then Frank Sinatra sang" were part of the song.

21. In King Solomon's Temple dedication speech (1 Kings 8:13; 2 Chronicles 6:2).

22. In Exodus 25:8; Leviticus 12:4 plus five more occurrences; Numbers 3:38; 10:21; 18:1; 19:20; Joshua 24:26; Isaiah 63:18; Jeremiah 17:12; Ezekiel 5:11 plus twenty-two more occurrences; Amos 7:13; Psalms 74:7; 78:69; 96:6; Lamentations 1:10; 2:7, 20; Nehemiah 10:40; 1 Chronicles 22:19; 28:10; 2 Chronicles 20:8; 26:18; 29:21; 30:8; 36:17.

23. Freedman, *Pottery, Poetry, and Prophecy*, p. 136 and notes; Baruch Halpern, *The Emergence of Israel in Canaan*, p. 33n.; Cross, *Canaanite Myth and Hebrew Epic*, p. 142.

24. Ephraim, Benjamin, Machir (=Manassesh?), Zebulun, Issachar, Reuben, Gilead (=Gad?), Dan, Asher, Naphtali. It does not include Judah or Simeon, which were in the south and were a separate geographic and political entity from Israel.

25. So Halpern, *The Emergence of Israel in Canaan*, pp. 120–21.

26. Freedman, *Pottery, Poetry, and Prophecy*, p. 175.

27. Reported in *WWTB*, *The Bible with Sources Revealed*, *The Hidden Book in the Bible*, and *The Exile and Biblical Narrative*. See the bibliographies in these for works by other scholars. As noted above, the bibliography on this subject is now so extensive that no one work can list it all.

28. The Tel Dan Inscription and the Mesha Stele. See Chapter 3.

29. 2 Kings 18 and 19; Isaiah 36 and 37. Text from Sennacherib in James B. Pritchard, ed., *Ancient Near Eastern Texts Relating to the Old Testament* (Princeton, NJ: Princeton University Press, 1969), hereafter *ANET*, p. 288. See also G. E. Wright, *Biblical Archaeology*, rev. ed. (Philadelphia: Westminster, 1962), pp. 167–74; Victor H. Matthews and Don C. Benjamin, eds., *Old Testament Parallels* (New York: Paulist Press, 2006), pp. 190–92; Friedman, *WWTB*, pp. 93–95.

30. See, for example, the website TheTorah.com; also see such works by orthodox scholars as Louis Jacobs, *We Have Reason to Believe* (Elstree, UK: Vallentine Mitchell, 2004); Shalom Carmy, ed., *Modern Scholarship in the Study of Torah*, The Orthodox Forum Series (New York: Jason Aronson, 1996); Marc Brettler, *How to Read the Bible* (Philadelphia: Jewish Publication Society, 2005); James Kugel, *How to Read the Bible* (New York: Free Press, 2007).

31. The Swiss scholar Konrad Schmid summarized these divergences in current Pentateuchal scholarship in "Distinguishing the World of the Exodus Narrative from the World of Its Narrators: The Question of the Priestly Exodus Account in Its Historical Setting," *IETP*, pp. 331–33. Carol Meyers at Duke University confirms that "the documentary hypothesis may no longer dominate biblical studies, but recent overviews show that little consensus has emerged about the formation of the Pentateuch," in Meyers, *Exodus*, New Cambridge Bible Commentary (Cambridge: Cambridge University Press, 2005), p. 17.

32. I have diagnosed this strange condition of my field as a failure of method. But recently a colleague told me that he thinks it is rather a failure of memory. And I think that he is right. People keep coming up with new models and new variations on the old model. That is fine. But they do not pay sufficient respect to the evidence and arguments of the models that they are casting off. The documentary hypothesis

once held (and maybe still holds) the agreement of the majority of scholars. But that is not what made it right. We do not determine truth by a majority vote. The hypothesis held us because its evidence was (and is) strong. None of the new alternatives has replaced it, not only because they have not won over a majority of the field, but because they remain insufficiently defended and because they have not dealt with the evidence that made the documentary hypothesis the standard for a century.

33. They were not (*could* not have been) composed by one author. (1) They are written in the Hebrew of several different periods, more widespread than the distance from Shakespeare's English to mine. (2) They can be separated into sections that each use distinct terminology: words that the other sections rarely or never use. There are some five hundred of these unique occurrences of words. (3) The sections with the different terminology also each consistently have their own particular depictions of the revelation of the name Yahweh, of the role of priests and of Levites, and of various sacred objects such as the ark, the Tabernacle, and the cherubs. (4) There are stories that are told twice, called doublets. (5) There are texts that contradict each other on events, on numbers, and on names of persons and places. (6) When we separate the texts according to their distinct terminology, the doublets and contradictions "disappear." That is, they comfortably and *consistently* fit into one section or another. (7) When we separate the texts along the lines of all these consistent points of evidence, the sections each flow naturally. That is: if one section interrupts another, then the next time that we find the one that was interrupted, it picks up naturally where it left off before the intrusion. (8) Each of these continuous, consistently worded, consistently depicted, noncontradicting, nonrepeated texts, which relate to the specific periods of Hebrew in which they are respectively written, also have unique connections to other parts of the Bible. One of them has over seventy-five connections with the book of the prophet Jeremiah. Another has about as many with the book of the prophet Ezekiel. Another of the texts is disproportionately connected with a group of sections of the Bible's history of Israel's monarchy in later books. It has over a hundred occurrences of words that occur only in this section of the Torah and in those history texts. (9) We can trace each of these sections to particular times and events in Israel's history. We can see how those particular times and events influenced the respective authors to tell the story as they did.

The most important point of all is that these many types of different evidence *converge*. When we separate the texts from one another, the doublets all resolve, the contradictions turn out to be in distinct texts, the terms do not slip into other sections, the texts each flow continuously, and they fit their respective histories and their respective periods of Hebrew.

34. Friedman, *The Bible with Sources Revealed*.

35. Antony Campbell and Mark O'Brien, *Sources of the Pentateuch: Texts, Introductions, Annotations* (Philadelphia: Fortress, 1993); J. E. Carpenter and G. Harford-Battersby, *The Hexateuch* (London: Longmans, Greens, 1902).

36. The online Hebrew text is the Westminster Leningrad Codex, at http://tanach.us/Tanach.xml.

37. *WWTB*, pp. 54–59.

38. The very obvious Levite connections of E, P, and D but not J are treated in most introductions to the Hebrew Bible/Old Testament. My treatment is in *WWTB*.

39. Called variously Mushite, Aaronid, Shilonite, Zadokite, and others. See F. M. Cross, "The Priestly Houses of Early Israel," in *Canaanite Myth and Hebrew Epic,* pp. 195–215.

40. *WWTB,* pp. 85–86; *The Hidden Book in the Bible,* pp. 51–52.

41. Genesis 4:1. The Greek text has *Theou* here, which translates Hebrew Elohim rather than Yahweh. So if the Greek text is original, and the woman does not say the name Yahweh here, then the first person to say the name Yahweh in J is Lamech. See Friedman, *The Bible with Sources Revealed,* p. 40.

42. Scholars sometimes refer to "the names of God" imprecisely when we first introduce people to the history of the subject. I admit that I did this myself in *Who Wrote the Bible?* In my later work, *The Bible with Sources Revealed,* I took care to emphasize that it is more accurate to speak of the question of when the divine name was revealed, not a question of different divine names.

A second mistake that people commonly make is that they imagine that we just circularly call any verse with the name Yahweh in it J and any verse with El or Elohim in it E or P, and then we claim, "See: it's consistent." But that is not how it works at all. The passages in which the words Yahweh, El, and Elohim occur have to come out consistent with all of the other evidence for identifying passages as J or E or P, namely: the unbroken continuity of narrative texts (you can separate them and read a continuous story in each, with few gaps); the consistent use of the five hundred other characteristic terms in each text; the division of twice-told stories (doublets) with the terms Yahweh or Elohim appearing *consistently* in one or the other of the two stories; the links between the stories in each source with the era in history that each reflects; the connections between the respective sources with other parts of the Bible (for example, J with the Court History of David in 2 Samuel, and P with the prophet Ezekiel); and the multiple connections of the source J to the Southern Kingdom of Judah, and the source E to the Northern Kingdom of Israel—which were two separate countries for two hundred years. No scholar is clever enough to make all of that work consistently and still have the name of God always in the right place.

43. Genesis 22:14 has Elohim *yir'eh* (4QGen-Exod^a) for MT Yahweh *yir'eh.* But we attribute this verse to RJE, which can use either term. Numbers 23:3 has Elohim (so does Greek) for MT Yahweh (4QNum^b). But we attribute this verse to E, which could use either word at this point in any case.

44. Thomas Römer, "The Name Israel," in *The Invention of God* (Cambridge, MA: Harvard University Press, 2015), pp. 72–73; originally published in French as *L'Invention de Dieu,* Éditions de Seuil, 2014.

45. David Noel Freedman, "The Name of the God of Moses," in Freedman, *Divine Commitment and Human Obligation* (Grand Rapids, MI: Eerdmans, 1997), p. 87; Norman Gottwald, *The Hebrew Bible: A SocioLiterary Introduction* (Philadelphia: Fortress, 1985), p. 224.

46. See F. M. Cross, "Yahweh and El," in *Canaanite Myth and Hebrew Epic,* pp. 44–75.

47. W. Randall Garr, "The Grammar and Interpretation of Exodus 6:3," *Journal of Biblical Literature* 111 (1992): 385–408.

48. That, too, may be why the Song of Deborah includes the name of Yahweh and twice identifies Him as "God of Israel" even though the Song of Deborah does

not mention the Levites. (It also calls him "the one of Sinai," which may share whatever history lies behind calling him Yahweh, or it may refer to someplace other than the place where the Levites had converged, which in their earliest source [E] is called Horeb, not Sinai. See Chapter 4, pp. 132–33.) Perhaps the Levites were still in Egypt, and our text of the song is an adaptation of a song that originally did not name Yahweh, just as J telescoped the name back in its prose accounts. Or perhaps the Levites had arrived and had taken up their priestly rather than tribal identity, teaching that Yahweh is Israel's God, but as priests they were not subject to the tribal military muster. Or perhaps it is precisely the Levites who are the singers of the Song of Deborah. The prose narrator attributes it to Deborah and Barak themselves, but that has always been recognized to conflict with the fact that the song speaks to Deborah and Barak in second person (Judges 5:7, 12). I formulated my thinking on the appearance of the name of Yahweh in the Song of Deborah through illuminating conversations with Alexa J. Friedman.

49. Scott B. Noegel, "The Egyptian Origin of the Ark of the Covenant," *IETP*, p. 236.

50. Frank Cross, "Yahweh and 'El," in *Canaanite Myth and Hebrew Epic*, p. 44.

51. Mark Smith, *The Early History of God*, 2nd ed. (Grand Rapids, MI: Eerdmans, 2002), p. 33.

52. Ziony Zevit, *The Religions of Ancient Israel* (London: Continuum, 2001), pp. 687–88, writes: "In Israel, the major participants in YHWH cults and the disseminators of its myths may have been groups of manics and clans of Levites." See also p. 657.

53. Michael Homan, *To Your Tents, O Israel!* (Leiden: Brill, 2002), pp. 111–15.

54. A photograph of the carved image of Rameses' tent appears together with a parallel artist's rendering of the Tabernacle in "The Exodus Is Not Fiction: Interview with Richard Elliott Friedman," in *Reform Judaism* (Spring 2014): 6. My rendering of the Tabernacle appears in *WWTB*, pp. 174–82; in "The Tabernacle in the Temple," *Biblical Archaeologist* 43 (1980); and in the "Tabernacle" entry in the *ABD*, vol. 6, pp. 292–300.

55. Scott B. Noegel, "The Egyptian Origin of the Ark of the Covenant," *IETP*, pp. 223–42. Cf. Exodus 25:10–22.

56. Genesis 17:10–14, 23–27; 21:4; Leviticus 12:1–3.

57. Jeremiah 1:1; Ezekiel 1:3. Their connections to the Levite priestly houses and to the D and P texts is laid out in *WWTB*, pp. 125–27, 146–49, 168–70. See also *The Bible with Sources Revealed*, pp. 14–17.

58. See Propp, *Exodus 1–18*, pp. 218–20, 233–38; and Friedman, *Commentary on the Torah* (San Francisco: HarperSanFrancisco, 2001), comment on Exodus 4:24 (pp. 184–85); Martin Noth, *Exodus* (Philadelphia: Westminster, 1962, translated from the German *Das zweite Buch Mose, Exodus*, 1959), pp. 49–50; Moshe Greenberg, *Understanding Exodus*, 2nd ed. (Eugene, OR: Cascade, 2013), pp. 94–96; and the interpretations of the rabbinic commentators Rashi, Ibn Ezra, and Sforno on these verses.

59. See the discussion in Friedman and Dolansky, *The Bible Now*, pp. 93–95.

60. Judges 18:30.

61. Joshua 5 also tells the story of a circumcision of the Israelites when they arrive at the promised land. Joshua 5:9, worded like the Dinah episode, says, "Today

I've rolled the disgrace of Egypt off of you." I understand this section of the book of Joshua to be part of the J source. This was also the understanding of earlier generations of biblical scholars. Today, most scholars no longer identify this or other Joshua accounts as J. I disagree with them, and I gave the evidence for this in *The Hidden Book in the Bible* (San Francisco: HarperCollins, 1998). For here, though, we need only agree that, whether this story is J or some other source, nothing in it points to a Levite author, as opposed to most of Joshua 14–22, which has visible priestly language and concerns.

62. R. G. Hall, "Circumcision," *ABD*, vol. 1, p. 1025; Jack Sasson, "Circumcision in the Ancient Near East," *Journal of Biblical Literature* 85 (1966): 473–76.

63. Gary Rendsburg, "Moses the Magician," in *IETP*, pp. 243–56.

64. Except the "drowning," which is in the Song of the Sea. Even in this case, P has the sea "covering" the Egyptian army in the middle of the sea and "not one of them was left," which certainly indicates drowning all of them, while J has them fleeing toward the sea and God "overthrows" them in the midst of the sea, and then Israel sees Egypt dead on the shore," which is less specific.

65. Exodus 1:11. Graham Davies, "Was There an Exodus?" in John Day, ed., *In Search of Pre-exilic Israel* (London: Clark, 2004), pp. 28–30; Baruch Halpern, "The Exodus and the Israelite Historians," *Eretz Israel* 24 (1993): 92; Redford, *Egypt, Canaan, and Israel in Ancient Times,* p. 451; Manfred Bietak, "On the Historicity of the Exodus: What Egyptology Today Can Contribute to Assessing the Biblical Account of the Sojourn in Egypt," *IETP,* pp. 24–25, 31; James Hoffmeier, "Which Way out of Egypt? Physical Geography Related to the Exodus Itinerary," *IETP,* pp. 105–6; William Dever, "The Exodus and the Bible: What Was Known; What Was Remembered; What Was Forgotten?" *IETP,* p. 403.

66. Exodus 1:14.

67. Exodus 5:6–16.

68. Exodus 5:18–19.

69. Halpern, "The Exodus and the Israelite Historians," p. 92.

70. Pithom and Rameses in 1:11 is E in my reckoning, though I recognize that others have identified it as J. Propp weighs the evidence in this passage for making either a J or an E identification (*Exodus 1–18,* pp. 126–27). Brickmaking in 1:14 is P in practically everyone's reckoning (Driver, Noth, Propp, Baden, and myself). Straw for bricks in 5:6–16 and imposed quotas in 5:18–19 are E. Here, too, I recognize that many scholars have seen Exodus 5 as J. Again, Propp weighs the evidence for both J and E (pp. 250–51); in the end he favors E, as I do. So to summarize: for those who identify some of these items as J, this shows the plausibility of the biblical account; and for those who, like me, have seen them all as E or P, they also add to the evidence of the Levite connection in the exodus.

71. James Hoffmeier, *Akhenaten and the Origins of Monotheism* (New York: Oxford University Press, 2015), p. 245. Even more cautiously, we should distinguish that Halpern's formulation of the point was more properly about historiography, that is, the forces that affected the writers, than about history, that is, the proofs of what happened. See Halpern, "The Exodus and the Israelite Historians," p. 93.

72. In both my identification of the sources and William Propp's, at which we arrived independently, these accounts in Exodus are from E and P (Propp, *Exodus 1–18;* Friedman, *WWTB,* p. 250; *The Bible with Sources Revealed,* pp. 126–33). The D source refers to it too in Deuteronomy 4:34; 6:21–23; 7:18–19; 21:2; 26:8; 29:1–2;

34:10. Many other scholars have identified the E passages here as coming from some other source, usually J, but no one to date has offered any refutation of Propp's or my identifications or reasoning. And the consistency of these identifications with all the other evidence here for the Levite connection may further support the identification. See note 83 below.

73. Later, in the book of Numbers, in the J spies story, Moses says to God, "And Egypt will hear it, for you brought this people up from among them with your power." Moses never refers to slavery, Pharaoh, or plagues, but only to the fact that they *left*. The closest it comes is when God says, "all of these people, who have seen my glory and my signs that I did in Egypt and in the wilderness." But that is nonspecific about the signs and whether they occurred in Egypt proper or on the journey and in the wilderness, and it does not mention the exodus itself.

74. The identifications of the Bible's sources that I (and others) had made in the past now came to fit with the identification of the Levites as the people of the exodus. And this, in return, confirmed those identifications of the sources as correct. This is not circular reasoning. It is a puzzle coming together. It is two mysteries pointing to a mutual solution.

75. In the law of the goring ox, the penalty is different if the victim was a slave than if the victim was a free person (Exodus 21:28–32).

76. Exodus 21:26–27.

77. Exodus 21:20–21. See the comment on this avenging of a slave's death in R. E. Friedman, *Commentary on the Torah*, comment on Leviticus 19:18, p. 381.

78. Deuteronomy 21:10.

79. Exodus 20:2; Deuteronomy 5:6.

80. Exodus 20:10; Deuteronomy 5:14.

81. Exodus 34:21. On Exodus 34:14–26 containing the J text of the Ten Commandments, see Friedman, *The Bible with Sources Revealed*, p. 179. Cross too attributes the core of this passage to J, *Canaanite Myth and Hebrew Epic*, pp. 85–86. Likewise Martin Noth, *A History of Pentateuchal Traditions*, trans. B. Anderson (Englewood Cliffs, NJ: Prentice-Hall, 1972; original German edition *Überlieferungsgeschichte des Pentateuch*, Stuttgart: Kohlhammer, 1948), pp. 31, 271; Carpenter and Harford-Battersby, *The Hexateuch*, p. 135; Ronald E. Clements, *Exodus* (Cambridge: Cambridge University Press, 1972), pp. 220–21; Baruch Halpern, *From Gods to God* (Tübingen: Mohr Siebeck, 2009), p. 30; Alan W. Jenks, *The Elohist and North Israelite Traditions* (Missoula, MT: Scholars Press, 1977), p. 39; Propp, *Exodus 19–40*, p. 150; Georg Fohrer, *Introduction to the Old Testament* (Nashville: Abingdon, 1968; German edition, 1965), p. 69. Joel Baden, in *J, E, and the Redaction of the Pentateuch* (Tübingen: Mohr Siebeck, 2009), p. 169, argues against the identification of this passage as a J Ten Commandments. Whether he is right or wrong (in my view, the latter), he still acknowledges that these verses are part of J, whether they were written on Decalogue tablets or not. So the point here, that J does not include slaves in a Sabbath command, remains in his reading as well. In a later book, Baden changed the J attribution of these verses and said rather that they were the work of a later compiler (Baden, *The Composition of the Pentateuch* [New Haven: Yale, 2012], pp. 224, 276n., 126). Again I think that he is mistaken, but in any case, for the present issue, this still leaves J with no concern for slaves by any reckoning of this passage. The same goes for Albrecht Alt (*Essays on Old Testament History and Religion* [Garden City, NY: Doubleday, 1967], p. 151n.), and all others

who regarded the passage in Exodus 34 as a later compilation, still leaving J with no concern for slaves.

82. Exodus 22:20; 23:9 (E); Leviticus 19:33–34 (P); Deuteronomy 10:19 (D). Commandments to love the alien and to treat an alien the same as one's own people also occur in Exodus 12:49; 20:10; 23:12; Leviticus 16:29; 17:8, 10, 12, 13, 15; 18:26; 19:10; 20:2; 22:18; 23:22; 24:16, 22; 25:35; Numbers 9:14; 15:14, 15, 16, 26, 29, 30; 19:10; 35:15; Deuteronomy 1:16; 5:14; 10:18, 19; 14:21.

83. Propp, Exodus 1–18, p. 128. Most blatantly, Isaiah 14:1 says, "and the alien will be joined to them." The Hebrew word that is commonly translated there as "will be joined" is *nilwāh,* which is cognate to the word *levi* (*lwy*). And the very name Levi is explicitly connected to this verb meaning to be joined or attached in the naming of Levi (*yillāweh*) in Genesis 29:34 (J) and in the attachment of the Levites (*yillāwû*) to the Priests in Numbers 18:2 (P). See the entry on the root *lwh* in Francis Brown, S. R. Driver, Charles Briggs (BDB), *A Hebrew and English Lexicon of the Old Testament,* p. 530.

84. Review by Glen A. Taylor of Jack Lundbom's *Deuteronomy: A Commentary* (Grand Rapids: Eerdmans, 2013), http://www.bookreviews.org/pdf/9357_10328.pdf.

85. English translation by John Wilson, *ANET,* pp. 376–78; see Avi Faust, "The Emergence of Iron Age Israel: On Origins and Habitus," *IETP,* p. 469. The situation is further complicated by the (controversial) fact that the name is given the Egyptian determinative for a people rather than a (settled) land. The debate on this is summarized, with references, by Faust, *IETP,* pp. 478–79.

86. Halpern has 1207, Malamat 1208.

87. Malamat, *The History of Biblical Israel* (Leiden: Brill, 2001), p. 60.

88. Finkelstein and Silberman, *The Bible Unearthed,* p. 60.

89. Most recently Manfred Bietak of the University of Vienna expressed this view in "Exodus Evidence: An Egyptologist Looks at Biblical History," *Biblical Archaeology Review* 42:3 (May/June, 2016): 37.

90. Shishak (corresponding to Pharaoh Sheshonk I) in 2 Chronicles 12:2–9; 1 Kings 11:40; 14:25. Necho (corresponding to Pharaoh Necho II) in 2 Kings 23:29.

91. Finkelstein and Silberman, *The Bible Unearthed,* p. 65.

92. Carol Meyers, *Exodus,* New Cambridge Bible Commentary (Cambridge: Cambridge University Press, 2005), pp. 33–34.

93. "Whoever supplied the geographical information that now adorns the story had no information earlier than the Saite period (seventh to sixth centuries B.C.)." Redford, *Egypt, Canaan, and Israel in Ancient Times,* p. 409.

94. Finkelstein and Silberman, *The Bible Unearthed,* p. 68.

95. Finkelstein and Silberman, *The Bible Unearthed,* pp. 65–71.

96. Friedman, *WWTB,* pp. 61–79; and *The Bible with Sources Revealed,* pp. 18–21.

97. So when Redford and others say that our lengthy and detailed account of Moses, in all his roles, is late, either exilic or post-exilic, meaning sixth century or later (Redford, *Egypt, Canaan, and Israel in Ancient Times,* p. 418), they likewise have to at least mention the fact that those accounts are in sources written in classical, PRE-exilic Hebrew. See Robert Polzin, *Late Biblical Hebrew: Toward an Historical Typology of Biblical Hebrew Prose* (Atlanta: Scholars Press, 1976); Gary Rendsburg, "Late Biblical Hebrew and the Date of P," *Journal of the Ancient Near Eastern Society* 12 (1980): 65–80; Ziony Zevit, "Converging Lines of Evidence Bearing on the

Date of P," *Zeitschrift für die Alttestamentliche Wissenschaft* 94 (1982): 502–9; Jacob Milgrom, *Leviticus 1–16,* The Anchor Bible (New York: Doubleday, 1991), pp. 3–13; "Numbers, Book of," *ABD,* vol. 4, pp. 1148–49; Avi Hurvitz, "The Evidence of Language in Dating the Priestly Code," *Revue Biblique* 81 (1974): 24–56; *A Linguistic Study of the Relationship Between the Priestly Source and the Book of Ezekiel* (Cahiers de la Revue Biblique; Paris: Gabalda, 1982); "Continuity and Innovation in Biblical Hebrew—The Case of 'Semantic Change' in Post-exilic Writings," *Abr-Naharaim* Supp. 4 (1995): 1–10; "The Usage of שש and בוץ in the Bible and Its Implication for the Date of P," *Harvard Theological Review* 60 (1967): 117–21; Ronald Hendel, "'Begetting' and 'Being Born' in the Pentateuch: Notes on Historical Linguistics and Source Criticism," *Vetus Testamentum* 50 (2000): 38–46; Jan Joosten, "The Distinction Between Classical and Late Biblical Hebrew as Reflected in Syntax," *Hebrew Studies* 46 (2005): 327–39. A recent attempt to challenge the work on linguistic dating was Ian Young, Robert Rezetko, with the assistance of M. Ehrensvärd, *Linguistic Dating of Biblical Texts: An Introduction to Approaches and Problems,* 2 vols. (London–Oakville: Equinox, 2008); it was thoroughly rejected in the review by Jan Joosten, Regius Professor of Hebrew at the University of Oxford in *Babel und Bibel* (2011); and by Professor Ronald Hendel of UC Berkeley in "Unhistorical Hebrew Linguistics: A Cautionary Tale," http://www.bibleinterp .com/opeds/hen358022.shtml. Essays that address their claims critically appear in Cynthia Miller-Naudé and Ziony Zevit, eds., *Diachrony in Biblical Hebrew* (Winona Lake, IN: Eisenbrauns, 2012).

98. Amos 9:7.

99. James Hoffmeier wrote in "'These Things Happened'—Why a Historical Exodus Is Essential for Theology," in J. Hoffmeier and D. Magary, eds., *Do Historical Matters Matter to Faith?* (Wheaton, IL: Crossway, 2012).

100. Joel Baden, "The Violent Origins of the Levites: Texts and Tradition," in Mark Leuchter and Jeremy Hutton, eds., *Levites and Priests in Biblical History and Tradition* (Atlanta: Society of Biblical Literature, 2011), pp. 103–16. I have even heard it suggested that the Levites might be a remnant of the warlike Hyksos dynasty that had once ruled Egypt. This would require a substantial amount of proof, to establish that these people survived the expulsion of the Hyksos from Egypt, remained for some three hundred years, and then, for an unknown reason, made an exodus, became known as Levites, and then immigrated to Israel.

101. Numbers 18:21–24. "And to the children of Levi, here, I've given every tithe in Israel as a legacy in exchange for their work that they're doing. . . . It is an eternal law through your generations. And they shall not have a legacy among the children of Israel, because I've given to the Levites as a legacy the tithe of the children of Israel that they will give to Yahweh as a donation. On account of this I've said to them: they shall not have a legacy among the children of Israel."

Deuteronomy 14:28f. "At the end of three years you shall bring out all the tithe of your produce in that year and leave it within your gates, and the Levite will come, because he doesn't have a portion and legacy with you . . . and they shall eat and be full."

102. Judges 17:7–13.

103. Deuteronomy 33:10. The song identifies the Levites as both priests and teachers (33:8–10).

104. Leviticus 10:11.

105. On the antiquity of this credo, see Gerhard von Rad, *The Problem of the Hexateuch* (New York: McGraw-Hill, 1966; original German edition Gesammelte Studien zum Alten Testament, Munich: Kaiser Verlag, 1958), pp. 3–5.

106. B. C. Benz is an example of scholars coming from a variety of positions who still recognize this essential point. Writing about Israel's origins, he says: "While some may have been geographical outsiders who participated in an exodus from Egypt, and others may have been economic and/or political outsiders, some were geographical, economic, and political insiders. In each case, as these groups were identified as "Israelite," so too were their historical memories and the traditions that developed around them. As this identity took shape and solidified over time, some of these traditions, including those revolving around an exodus from Egypt and life in the land before the monarchy, were retained, reworked, and applied to the people as a whole." Benz, "In Search of Israel's Insider Status: A Reevaluation of Israel's Origins," in *IETP*, p. 464.

107. Genesis 15:13; Exodus 12:40.

108. Ronald Hendel, "The Exodus in Biblical Memory," *Journal of Biblical Literature* 120 (2001): 601–22. I believe it was Hendel from whom I first heard the analogy to Thanksgiving many years ago. Since then, a number of colleagues have joined in making that comparison.

109. Nadav Na'aman, "The Exodus Story: Between Historical Memory and Historiographical Composition," *Journal of Ancient Near Eastern Religions* 11 (2011): 39–69. Gottwald makes a similar connection in *The Hebrew Bible*, p. 225.

110. Sperling, *The Original Torah*; and "Were the Jews Slaves in Egypt?" in *Reform Judaism* (Spring 2013): 56–57, 64.

111. Hosea 2:17; 11:1; 12:10, 14; 13:4; Amos 2:10; 3:1; 9:7; Micah 6:4; 7:15; Isaiah 11:16; 19:20–22; Jeremiah 2:6; 7:22, 25; 11:4, 7; 16:14; 23:7; 31:32; 32:20, 21; 34:13; Ezekiel 20:5–10, 36; Haggai 2:5.

112. Psalm 78:12, 43; 81:11; 105:23–38; 106:7; 114 (the entire psalm).

113. Deuteronomy, which is presented as a retrospective reflection on the events, has the most references to the enslavement, but even in Deuteronomy there are references to the exodus in forty-eight verses but mentions of the "house of slaves" in eleven.

114. This development is traced through the book *Exodus in the Jewish Experience: Echoes and Reverberations* (Lexington/Rowman & Littlefield, 2015), edited by Pamela Barmash of Washington University. Professor Barmash's own contribution in the book's opening chapter cites and affirms Hendel's point. She writes, "The theme of Egyptian oppression and bondage and the tales, reports, and rumors of runaway slaves returning to their homeland must have resonated throughout Canaan, a land under the specter of Pharaonic control for centuries." And so, "In ancient Israel, what might have been the story of one segment becomes the foundational story of the whole. The memories of a single component of ancient Israel became the memories of the whole" (p. 5).

115. Joshua 5:2–9.

116. Amnon Ben-Tor, "Who Destroyed Canaanite Hazor?" *Biblical Archaeology Review* 39 (2013): 26–36; Amihai Mazar, "Archaeology and the Bible: Reflections on Historical Memory in the Deuteronomistic History," in Christal M. Maier, *Congress*

Volume Munich 2013, International Organization for the Study of the Old Testament (Leiden: Brill, 2014), p. 349. Volkmar Fritz, *The Emergence of Israel in the Twelfth and Eleventh Centuries* BCE (Atlanta: Society of Biblical Literature, 2011), pp. 74–75.

117. Joseph Calloway and Hershel Shanks, "The Settlement in Canaan: The Period of the Judges," in Shanks, ed., *Ancient Israel* (Washington, DC: Biblical Archaeological Society and Prentice-Hall, 2011), p. 62: "Careful examination of the archaeological evidence has almost thoroughly destroyed the Conquest Model." William Dever, *Who Were the Early Israelites and Where Did They Come From?* (Grand Rapids, MI: Eerdmans, 2003); Halpern, *The Emergence of Israel in Canaan,* p. 249; Amihai Mazar, *Archaeology of the Land of the Bible 10,000–586 BCE* (New York: Doubleday, 1990), p. 334.

118. William Dever, "The Western Cultural Tradition Is at Risk," *Biblical Archaeology Review* 32/2 (March/April 2006): 76; cf. Dever, "Is There Any Archaeological Evidence for the Exodus?," in Ernest Frerichs and Leonard Lesko, eds., *Exodus: The Egyptian Evidence* (Winona Lake, IN: Eisenbrauns, 1997), pp. 67–86; Fritz, *The Emergence of Israel,* pp. 74–76.

119. Baruch Halpern, "The Exodus from Egypt: Myth or Reality?," in Hershel Shanks, William Dever, Baruch Halpern, and P. Kyle McCarter, *The Rise of Ancient Israel: Lectures Presented at a Symposium Sponsored by the Smithsonian Institution* (Washington, DC: Biblical Archaeology Society, 1992); Kindle edition location 1761.

CHAPTER THREE

The Mystery of Israel

1. There is a debate about whether to distinguish between the terms Jew and Judean. Some would use the term Jew just starting in a particular period: the Persian period or the Roman period. Some would use the term Jew just as a religious identification and use the term Judean as an ethnic identification. I do not agree with those who make these distinctions. Both English terms translate the same Hebrew word. For a recent treatment, see Daniel R. Schwartz, *Judeans and Jews: Four Faces of Dichotomy in Ancient Jewish History* (Toronto: University of Toronto Press, 2014).

2. "Impression of King Hezekiah's Royal Seal Discovered in Ophel Excavations South of Temple Mount in Jerusalem," http://new.huji.ac.il/en/article/28173; "Hezekiah Seal Proves Ancient Jerusalem Was a Major Judahite Capital," http://www.haaretz.com/jewish/archaeology/1.695308.

3. 2 Kings 14:22. G. E. Wright, *Biblical Archaeology,* rev. ed. (Philadelphia: Westminster, 1962), p. 102; Amihai Mazar, *Archaeology of the Land of the Bible,* 10,000–586 BCE, The Anchor Bible Reference Library (New York: Doubleday, 1990), pp. 449–50.

4. Ruth Hestrin and Michal Dayagi-Mendels, *Inscribed Seals: First Temple Period Hebrew, Ammonite, Moabite, Phoenician and Aramaic from the Collections of the Israel Museum and the Israel Department of Antiquities and Museums* (Jerusalem: Israel Museum, 1979), p. 18; Ruth Hestrin et al., *Inscriptions Reveal: Documents from the Time of the Bible, the Mishna and the Talmud* (Hebrew kĕtûbôt mĕsappĕrôt; Jerusalem: Israel Museum, 1972), p. 30; see also pp. 95ff. Jeroboam is actually the name of two of Israel's kings.

5. Philip King and Lawrence Stager, *Life in Biblical Israel* (Louisville, KY: Westminster John Knox, 2001), p. 312. Baruch Halpern has noted that "the lmlk jars are distributed abundantly, in forts large and small, in the north, on the border between Judah and the Assyrian province of Samaria, and in the west, between the Judahite hills and the Philistine coast" (*Law and Ideology in Monarchic Israel* [Sheffield: JSOT Press, 1991]: 24–25; see also pp. 35–40 for more examples). See also H. Eshel, "A lmlk Stamp from Bethel," *Israel Exploration Journal* 39 (1989): 60–62.

6. Ephraim Stern, *Archaeology of the Land of the Bible,* vol. 2, The Anchor Bible Reference Library (New York: Doubleday, 2001), pp. 172–73.

7. Jeremiah 36:10–12.

8. Gabriel Barkay, *A Treasure Facing Jerusalem's Walls* (Jerusalem: Israel Museum, 1986); Ada Yardeni, "Remarks on the Priestly Blessing on Two Ancient Amulets from Jerusalem," *Vetus Testamentum* 41 (1991): 176–85.

9. These Samaria ostraca are mainly letters and records of shipments of items such as wine, oil, and grain. They include Hebrew names and dates related to the regnal years of a king. (In the Bible, Samaria was the capital of Israel.) George Andrew Reisner, Clarence Stanley Fisher, and David Gordon Lyon, *Harvard Excavations at Samaria, 1908–1910* (Cambridge, MA: Harvard University Press, 1924); see also the website: http://ocp.hul.harvard.edu/expeditions/reisner.html; King and Stager, *Life in Biblical Israel,* p. 312; W. F. Albright, "The Ostraca of Samaria," in *Ancient Near Eastern Texts* (hereafter: *ANET*), Princeton, NJ: Princeton University Press, 1969), p. 321; G. E. Wright, *Biblical Archaeology,* pp. 100–102.

10. The letters include appeals to Yahweh, and they give names of people that include forms of Yahweh's name. As summarized in the *Oxford Bible Atlas:* "These unique documents not only reveal the authentic style and language in which men of Judah thought, wrote, and spelt in the days of Jeremiah, but also throw independent and parallel light on events recorded in the pre-exilic chapters of the Old Testament—a contemporary commentary many centuries older than the earliest existing manuscripts of the Bible" (Adrian Curtis, ed. [Oxford: Oxford University Press, 1984], p. 114). See translations and bibliography in *ANET,* pp. 321–22.

11. Oded Lipschitz, *The Fall and Rise of Jerusalem: Judah under Babylonian Rule* (Winona Lake, IN: Eisenbrauns, 2005), p. 225.

12. *Highlights of Archaeology* (Jerusalem: Israel Museum, 1984), pp. 82–83.

13. "Sons of Korah" (*běnê qōraḥ*): Psalms 42; 44–49; 84; 85; 87; 88.

14. Exodus 6:21, 24; Numbers 16:1–32; 17:5, 14; 26:9–11; 27:3; 1 Chronicles 6:7, 22; 9:19.

15. It is a place in the eastern Negev. It had twenty-eight Hebrew octraca, one in Edomite (Edom was just across the border from there), and one in Aramaic.

16. The Hebrew inscription from Yabneh-yam, a city located about ten miles south of modern Tel Aviv, is on an ostracon from the late seventh century BCE. It is addressed to someone named Hoshaiah (again, a name with a theophoric element of the name YHWH). It is a legal document, apparently a petition. Frank Moore Cross, *Bulletin of the American Schools of Oriental Research* 165 (1962): 34–36; King and Stager, *Life in Biblical Israel,* p. 315; R. Westbrook, *Studies in Biblical and Cuneiform Law,* Cahiers de la Revue Biblique 26 (Paris, 1988): 30–35; F. W. Dobbs-Allsopp, "The Genre of the Mesad Hashavyahu Ostracon," *Bulletin of the American Schools of Oriental Research* 295 (1994): 49–55; Shmuel Ahituv, *Handbook of Ancient Hebrew*

Inscriptions from the Period of the First Commonwealth and the Beginning of the Second Commonwealth (Hebrew, Philistine, Edomite, Moabite, Ammonite and the Bileam Inscriptions) (Jerusalem, 1992), pp. 97–99; Anson Rainey, "Syntax and Rhetorical Analysis in the Hashavyahu Ostracon," *Journal of the Ancient Near Eastern Society* 27 (2000): 75–79.

On the inscriptions from Tel 'Ira, see Graham I. Davies, Markus N. A. Bockmuehl, Douglas R. De Lacey, and Andrew J. Poulter, *Ancient Hebrew Inscriptions: Corpus and Concordance,* vol. 2 (Cambridge: Cambridge University Press, 2004), p. 870; Aaron Demsky, "The MPQD Ostracon from Tel 'Ira: A New Reading," *Bulletin of the American Schools of Oriental Research* 345 (2007): 33–38.

Eighth-century BCE inscriptions from Beer Sheba with photographs appear in Hestrin et al., *Inscriptions Reveal,* p. 81.

17. Jeffrey Tigay, *You Shall Have No Other Gods,* Harvard Semitic Studies (Atlanta: Scholars Press, 1986), pp. 9, 12. Thirty-five have names of other deities. Some are the lesser deities whom the Israelites may have included in their beliefs alongside their chief God. Others are Egyptian, not local. See Tigay's comments, and Ziony Zevit, *The Religions of Ancient Israel* (London: Continuum, 2001), p. 649.

18. Alan Millard, "The New Jerusalem Inscription—So What?" *Biblical Archaeology Review* 40 (May/June, 2014); Christopher A. Rollston, "What's the Oldest Hebrew Inscription?" *Biblical Archaeology Review* 38 (May/June, 2012); Aaron Demsky, "What's the Oldest Hebrew Inscription?–A Reply to Christopher Rollston," *Biblical Archaeology Review,* August 22, 2012, http://www.biblicalarchaeology.org/daily/biblical-artifacts/inscriptions/what's-the-oldest-hebrew-inscription/; Aaron Demsky and Moshe Kochavi, "An Alphabet from the Days of the Judges," *Biblical Archaeology Review* (September/October 1978); Yosef Garfinkel, "Christopher Rollston's Methodology of Caution," *Biblical Archaeology Review* (September/October 2012). Further on literacy, see Christopher Rollston, *Writing and Literacy in the World of Ancient Israel* (Atlanta: Society of Biblical Literature, 2010). See also Alan Millard, review of Rollston, *Writing and Literacy,* June 14, 2012, http://www.biblicalarchaeology.org/reviews/writing-and-literacy-in-the-world-of-ancient-israel/.

19. William Dever, *Who Were the Early Israelites, and Where Did They Come From?* (Grand Rapids, MI: Eerdmans, 2003), p. 83; Aaron Demsky, "A Proto-Canaanite Abecedary Dating from the Period of the Judges and Its Implications for the History of the Alphabet," *Tel Aviv* 4 (1977): 14–27; Volkmar Fritz, *The Emergence of Israel in the Twelfth and Eleventh Centuries BCE* (Atlanta: Society of Biblical Literature, 2011), pp. 115–17.

20. Ron E. Tappy, P. Kyle McCarter, Marilyn J. Lundberg, and Bruce Zuckerman, "An Abecedary of the Mid-Tenth Century BCE from the Judaean Shephelah," *Bulletin of the American Schools of Oriental Research* 344 (November 2006): 5–46; Ron E. Tappy and P. Kyle McCarter Jr., eds., *Literate Culture and Tenth-Century Canaan: The Tel Zayit Abecedary in Context* (Winona Lake, IN: Eisenbrauns, 2008).

21. Michael Homan, "Tel Zayit Inscription: My Account of the Discovery," November 20, 2005, http://michaelhoman.blogspot.com/2005/11/tel-zayit-inscription-my-account-of.html.

22. Shira Faigenbaum-Golovina, Arie Shausa, Barak Sobera, David Levin, Nadav Na'aman, Benjamin Sass, Eli Turkel, Eli Piasetzky, and Israel Finkelstein, "Algorithmic Handwriting Analysis of Judah's Military Correspondence Sheds

Light on Composition of Biblical Texts," *Proceedings of the National Academy of Sciences* (April 2016); see also Isabel Kershner, "New Evidence on When the Bible Was Written," *New York Times*, April 11, 2016. And see note 16 above. Alan Millard concluded: "In light of the evidence from all sources it appears that literacy reached beyond the palaces and temples of Israel and Judah to quite small settlements" ("Literacy [Israel]," *ABD*, vol. 4, p. 340). See also Brian Schmidt, ed., *Contextualizing Israel's Sacred Writings* (Atlanta: SBL Press, 2015).

23. Mordechai Cogan, *The Raging Torrent: Historical Inscriptions from Assyria and Babylonia Relating to Ancient Israel* (Jerusalem: Carta, 2008); James Pritchard, ed., *ANET*; Michael D. Coogan, *A Reader of Ancient Near Eastern Texts; Sources for the Study of the Old Testament* (New York: Oxford University Press, 2013); Victor Matthews and Don Benjamin, *Old Testament Parallels: Laws and Stories from the Ancient Near East* (New York: Paulist Press, 2006).

24. Amihai Mazar, *Archaeology of the Land of the Bible,* Anchor Bible Reference Library (New York: Doubleday, 1990), p. 234; Abraham Malamat, *The History of Biblical Israel* (Leiden: Brill, 2001), p. 7; *ANET*, pp. 375–78; Elizabeth Bloch-Smith, "Israelite Ethnicity in Iron I: Archaeology Preserves What Is Remembered and What Is Forgotten in Israel's History," *Journal of Biblical Literature* 122 (2003): 420.

25. *ANET*, pp. 242–43.

26. *ANET*, pp. 279, 281.

27. See my translation of the Sennacherib prism inscription and discussion in *Who Wrote the Bible?*, 2nd ed. (San Francisco: HarperSanFrancisco, 1997), pp. 93–95.

28. Bezalel Porten et al., *The Elephantine Papyri in English: Three Millennia of Cross-Cultural Continuity and Change,* Documenta Et Monumenta Orientis Antiqui, vol. 22 (Leiden: Brill, 1996).

29. Andre Lemaire, "'House of David' Restored in Moabite Inscription," *Biblical Archaeology Review* 20/03 (May/June 1994): 30–37.

30. Avraham Biran and Joseph Naveh, "The Tel Dan Inscription A New Fragment," *Israel Exploration Journal* 45 (1995): 1–18; an attempt to discredit the inscription was refuted by David Noel Freedman and Jeffrey C. Geoghegan, "'House of David' Is There!" *Biblical Archaeology Review* (March/April 1995); William Schniedewind, "Tel Dan Stela: New Light on Aramaic and Jehu's Revolt," *Bulletin of the American Schools of Oriental Research* 302 (1996): 75–90; Baruch Halpern, "The Stela from Dan: Epigraphic and Historical Considerations," *Bulletin of the American Schools of Oriental Research* 296 (1994): 63–80.

31. 2 Kings 20:20; 2 Chronicles 32:30.

32. Eilat Mazar, "Did I Find King David's Palace?" *Biblical Archaeology Review* (January/February 2006); cf. Avraham Faust, "Did Eilat Mazar Find David's Palace?," *Biblical Archaeology Review* (September/October 2012).

33. Avraham Biran, "Dan," *ABD*, vol. 2, pp. 11–17; Amihai Mazar, *Archaeology of the Land of the Bible,* Anchor Bible Reference Library (New York: Doubleday, 1990), p. 412.

34. Amnon Ben-Tor, *Hazor: Canaanite Metropolis, Israelite City* (Washington, DC: Biblical Archaeology Society, 2016).

35. David Ussishkin, *Lachish I–V* (Tel Aviv: Institute of Archaeology, 2010).

36. 1 Kings 9:15.

37. Israel Finkelstein and Neil Asher Silberman, *The Bible Unearthed: Archaeol-*

ogy's New Vision of Ancient Israel and the Origin of Its Sacred Texts (New York: Free Press, 2001), pp. 209–11, 342–44.

38. Baruch Halpern, "The Gate of Megiddo and the Debate on the 10th Century," in A. Lemaire and M. Saebo, eds., *Congress Volume Oslo 1998, Supplements to Vetus Testamentum* (Leiden: Brill, 2000), pp. 79–121.

39. John S. Holladay, "The Kingdoms of Israel and Judah: Political and Economic Centralization in the Iron IIA–B (ca. 1000–750 BCE)," in Thomas E. Levy, ed., *The Archaeology of Society in the Holy Land* (New York: Facts on File, 1995), pp. 372–73.

40. Philip King and Lawrence Stager, *Life in Biblical Israel* (Louisville, KY: Westminster John Knox, 2001), p. 119; Brian Hesse and Paula Wapnish, "The Zooarchaeological Record: Pigs' Feet, Cattle Bones and Birds' Wings," *Biblical Archaeology Review* 22 (January/February 1996): 62; "Pig Use and Abuse in the Ancient Levant: Ethnoreligious Boundary-Building with Swine," in Sarah M. Nelson, ed., *Ancestors for the Pigs: Pigs in Prehistory* (Philadelphia: University of Pennsylvania Museum, 1998), pp. 123–35; Brian Hesse, "Husbandry, Dietary Taboos and the Bones of the Ancient Near East: Zooarchaeology in the Post-processual World," in David B. Small, ed., *Methods in the Mediterranean: Historical and Archaeological Views on Texts and Archaeology* (Leiden: Brill, 1995), pp. 198–232.

41. Elizabeth Bloch-Smith, "Israelite Ethnicity in Iron I: Archaeology Preserves What Is Remembered and What Is Forgotten in Israel's History," *Journal of Biblical Literature* 122 (2003): 411. Also weights have been found with (Egyptian hieratic) numbers incised in them. The primary weight is the *shekel*. They are consistent— the shekel weighed approximately 10 grams (.456 lb). That is, they were fixed by a central Judean administration, starting in the eighth century BCE. They have been found in over twenty cities in Judah. We also find standardized pottery starting in the eighth century BCE. This means that production is centralized. So it is both weights and measures that were being standardized. Ephraim Stern, *Archaeology of the Land of the Bible* (New York: Doubleday, 2001), p. 191; King and Stager, *Life in Biblical Israel,* p. 312.

42. For photographs of inscriptions from many centuries of the biblical world and a chart showing the development of each of the letters of the alphabet, see Ruth Hestrin et al., *Inscriptions Reveal: Documents from the Time of the Bible, the Mishna and the Talmud* (Hebrew *kĕtûbôt mĕsappĕrôt*; Jerusalem: Israel Museum, 1972). Photographs, drawings, and charts also appear in Shmuel Ahituv, *Echoes from the Past: Hebrew and Cognate Inscriptions from the Biblical Period* (Jerusalem: Carta, 2008).

43. Avi Hurvitz, "The Relevance of Biblical Linguistics for the Historical Study of Ancient Israel," *Proceedings of the Twelfth World Congress of Jewish Studies* (Jerusalem: World Union of Jewish Studies, 1999), pp. 21–33; "The Historical Quest for 'Ancient Israel' and the Linguistic Evidence of the Hebrew Bible: Some Methodological Observations," *Vetus Testamentum* 47 (1997): 301–15; "Continuity and Innovation in Biblical Hebrew—The Case of 'Semantic Change' in Post-exilic Writings," *Abr-Naharaim* Supp. 4 (1995): 1–10; *A Linguistic Study of the Relationship Between the Priestly Source and the Book of Ezekiel,* Cahiers de la Revue Biblique 20 (Paris: Gabalda, 1982); "The Evidence of Language in Dating the Priestly Code," *Revue Biblique* 81 (1974): 24–56; *Ben lashon le-lashon* (Jerusalem: Bialik Institute, 1972); "The Usage of שש and בוץ in the Bible and Its Implication for the Date of P," *Harvard Theological Review* 60

(1967): 117–21; Ronald S. Hendel, "'Begetting' and 'Being Born' in the Pentateuch: Notes on Historical Linguistics and Source Criticism," *Vetus Testamentum* 50 (2000): 38–46; R. M. Polzin, *Late Biblical Hebrew: Toward an Historical Typology of Biblical Hebrew Prose,* Harvard Semitic Monographs (Decatur, GA: Scholars Press, 1976); Gary Rendsburg, "Late Biblical Hebrew and the Date of P," *Journal of the Ancient Near Eastern Society* 12 (1980): 65–80; Ziony Zevit, "Converging Lines of Evidence Bearing on the Date of P," *Zeitschrift für die alttestamentliche Wissenschaft* 94 (1982): 502–9; Jacob Milgrom, *Leviticus 1–16,* The Anchor Bible (New York: Doubleday, 1991), 3:3–13; "Numbers, Book of," in *ABD,* vol. 4, pp. 1148–49; R. E. Friedman, "Solomon and the Great Histories," in Ann Killebrew and Andrew Vaughn, eds., *Jerusalem in Bible and Archaeology: The First Temple Period* (Atlanta: Society of Biblical Literature, 2003), pp. 171–80; *The Hidden Book in the Bible* (San Francisco: HarperCollins, 1998), p. 62; Steven E. Fassberg, Moshe Bar-Asher, and Ruth A. Clements, eds., *Hebrew in the Second Temple Period: The Hebrew of the Dead Sea Scrolls and of Other Contemporary Sources,* Studies on the Texts of the Desert of Judah 108 (Leiden: Brill, 2013); and see the review of this work by Gary Rendsburg, "Review of Fassberg, Bar-Asher, and Clements, eds., *Hebrew in the Second Temple Period*," *Journal of Semitic Studies* 61 (2016): 278–81; Jan Joosten, "Pseudo-Classicisms in Late Biblical Hebrew," *Zeitschrift für die Alttestamentliche Wissenschaft* 128 (2016): 16–29.

44. The Bible's stories say that these nations were descended from a family of immigrants who came from Mesopotamia: Abraham and Sarah, Isaac and Rebekah, Jacob and Leah and Rachel. The family went to Egypt, became a nation there, and returned and conquered the land after an exodus. We have looked at the Egypt and conquest stories in Chapter 2. For excellent treatments of the variety of alternative hypotheses about the origins of Israel, see William Dever, *Who Were the Early Israelites and Where Did They Come From?* (Grand Rapids, MI: Eerdmans, 2003); and Baruch Halpern, *The Emergence of Israel in Canaan* (Chico, CA: Society of Biblical Literature, 1983). Note Halpern's caution there: "Any explanation of Israel's origins will be an exercise in speculation" (p. 81).

45. Genesis 49:5–7; Deuteronomy 33:8–11. Frank Cross and David Noel Freedman wrote: "No serious question has been raised by scholars as to the premonarchic date of the majority of the individual blessings in Gen. 49. The only exception worthy of comment is the blessing of Judah" (*Studies in Ancient Yahwistic Poetry,* 2nd ed. [Grand Rapids, MI: Eerdmans, 1997], p. 46). In the case of the Blessing of Moses, on the basis of several considerations they conclude, "We hold that this Blessing, like the Blessing of Jacob, was composed, most probably, in the eleventh century B.C." (p. 64).

46. Numbers 18. This is discussed in *WWTB,* pp. 210–13.

47. Exodus 6:20.

48. Mark G. Thomas, Karl Skorecki, Haim Ben-Ami, Tudor Parfitt, Neil Bradman, David B. Goldstein, "Origins of Old Testament Priests," *Nature* 394 (1998): 138–40.

49. Thomas et al., "Origins of Old Testament Priests," p. 139. See also Skorecki et al., "Y Chromosomes of Jewish Priests," *Nature* 385 (January 2, 1997): 32.

50. Thomas et al., "Origins of Old Testament Priests," p. 138.

51. David B. Goldstein, *Jacob's Legacy: A Genetic View of Jewish History* (New Haven, CT: Yale University Press, 2008), p. 65.

52. Siiri Rootsi, Doron M. Behar, et al., "Phylogenetic Applications of Whole Y-Chromosome Sequences and the Near Eastern Origin of Ashkenazi Levites," *Nature Communications* 4, Article number: 2928 (2013). They found: "In contrast to the previously suggested Eastern European origin for Ashkenazi Levites, the current data are indicative of a geographic source of the Levite founder lineage in the Near East and its likely presence among pre-Diaspora Hebrews."

53. Thomas et al., "Origins of Old Testament Priests," p. 139 (emphasis added).

54. Harry Ostrer, *Legacy: A Genetic History of the Jewish People* (New York: Oxford University Press, 2012), p. 100. Ostrer cites D. Behar et al., "Multiple Origins of Ashkenazi Levites: Y Chromosome Evidence for Both Near Eastern and European Ancestries," *American Journal of Human Genetics* 73 (2003): 768–79. See also Harry Ostrer and Karl Skorecki, "The Population Genetics of the Jewish People," *Human Genetics* 132 (2013): 119–27.

55. David Goldstein, *Jacob's Legacy* (New Haven, CT: Yale University Press, 2008), p. 69. John Bright, *A History of Israel,* 4th ed. (Lexington, KY: Westminster John Knox, 2000); Risto Nurmela, *The Levites* (Tampa: University of South Florida, 1998).

56. This is discussed in *WWTB,* pp. 48, 121.

57. Patrick D. Miller wrote on the story in Judges 17–18, it "raises the question of whether the term 'Levite' was originally a job title rather than a tribal name" (*The Religion of Ancient Israel* [Louisville, KY: Westminster John Knox, 2000], p. 172). Miller recognized that Levites may be a clergy professional group and not a tribe, as we have observed here, though he was unaware of the linguistic support that Propp showed from the meaning of the word *levi*. Miller noted that on the basis of this story Lawrence Stager suggested that perhaps originally the Levites were composed of men who were not firstborns (as in medieval Europe; "The Archaeology of the Family in Ancient Israel," *Bulletin of the American Schools of Oriental Research* 260 [1985]: 1–35, esp. 27–28). It is good that the distinguished biblical scholar Miller and the distinguished archaeologist Stager recognized this understanding of the Levites' status, but Stager's "non-firstborn" suggestion does not take account of all the other evidence we have observed that connects the Levites to Egypt (Egyptian names, etc.), not just to a social arrangement. Also, Richard Nelson points out that a man appoints his son as a priest of their family shrine in Judges 17:5, but the man unquestionably takes on a Levite as his priest as soon as one comes along (17:10–13; *Raising Up a Faithful Priest* [Louisville, KY: Westminster John Knox, 1993], p. 4). There is no issue of first- or second-born. The issue of who is a bona fide priest is Levite or non-Levite. And this story also confirms that a layman could become a priest, but a layman could not become a Levite. See Chapter 2, p. 74.

58. Other unsatisfactory explanations of the Levite gene result came when the researchers consulted with Orthodox rabbis. They started from acceptance of the biblical depiction of the Levites as being one of the tribes of Israel, descended from an individual named Levi. So they sought other explanations of when non-Levite males could have contributed to the Levite gene pool. These explanations involved readings of technical cases in the Talmud (e.g., the case of a daughter of a Levite in certain situations treated in the Babylonian Talmud, Tractate Bechorot 47a), which still would require statistically unrealistic scenarios of reaching such widespread diversity in the Levite population. By starting with that biblical depiction as a

matter of faith, unquestioned, they were unable to account for the genetic evidence satisfactorily.

59. G. Ernest Wright, *God Who Acts* (London: SCM, 1952); *The Old Testament Against Its Environment* (London: SCM, 1950); Henri Frankfort et al., *The Intellectual Adventure of Ancient Man* (University of Chicago, 1946); Yehezkel Kaufmann, *The Religion of Israel* (Chicago: University of Chicago Press, 1960), translated and abridged by Moshe Greenberg.

60. These include the Court History of David (2 Samuel), the Samuel A and the Samuel B sources in 1 Samuel, J, E, P, two prose sources in the book of Judges, a history of the kings of Judah from Solomon to Hezekiah (parts of which appear in the books of 1 and 2 Kings and parts in 1 and 2 Chronicles), and a history of the kings of Israel (parts of which appear in 1 and 2 Kings). Based on my arguments and evidence in various places, all of these were composed by 700 BCE. R. E. Friedman, "Solomon and the Great Histories"; "Late for a Very Important Date," in *Bible Review* 9:6 (1993): 12–16; *WWTB; The Hidden Book in the Bible* (San Francisco: HarperSanFrancisco, 1998); *The Bible with Sources Revealed* (San Francisco: HarperSanFrancisco, 2003). On the Solomon-to-Hezekiah source, see Baruch Halpern, "Sacred History and Ideology: Chronicles' Thematic Structure—Indications of an Earlier Source," in R. E. Friedman, ed., *The Creation of Sacred Literature* (Berkeley: University of California Press, 1981), pp. 35–54.

61. In the stage of Biblical Hebrew at the time of this text's composition, the letter *yodh* (y) may not have been represented graphically, so the word *passim* would have appeared as *psm* rather than as *psym*. I think that the writer and his or her reading audience would still have perceived the pun on the name *ysp* on the written document.

62. Two of the best-known treatments of oral composition, those of Susan Niditch and David Carr, do not take this matter of puns (paronomasia) into account, and they misunderstand the manner of written composition and editing of the sources in the Pentateuch. See Susan Niditch, *Oral World and the Written Word: Ancient Israelite Literature* (Louisville, KY: Westminster John Knox, 1996); David Carr, *Writing on the Tablet of the Heart: Origins of Scripture and Literature* (New York: Oxford University Press, 2008); and my critique of Niditch in my Foreword to Jeffrey H. Tigay, ed., *Empirical Models for Biblical Criticism*, 2nd ed. (Dearborn, MI: Dove, 2005), pp. 4–5. Carr gives two examples of variants that "are particular to oral performance" to show that differences in two texts reflect the different ways that a word was *heard* rather than read. But both of the examples he gives could just as easily be visual divergences or errors by scribes and are in fact quite like ones that we find between the Masoretic Text and Qumran texts that are unquestionably scribal, not oral or aural (Carr, "Orality, Textuality, and Memory: The State of Biblical Studies," in Brian Schmidt, ed., *Contextualizing Israel's Sacred Writings*, p. 165).

63. D includes some much older texts. The historian who produced D, whom we call the Deuteronomistic historian, was a collector as well as a writer. He included old poetry: the Song of Moses in Deuteronomy 32 and the Blessing of Moses in Deuteronomy 33. And he included an old law code, which we call Dtn, in Deuteronomy 12–26. This is discussed in *WWTB*, pp. 117–20.

64. See Baruch Halpern, *The First Historians* (Harper & Row, 1988).

CHAPTER FOUR
The Mystery of Midian

1. Frank Moore Cross reviews the formulators of the "Midianite Hypothesis" and comes to accept and argue for a form of it himself in *From Epic to Canon* (Baltimore: Johns Hopkins University Press, 1998), pp. 66–67.

2. Thomas Römer, "The Revelation of the Divine Name to Moses and the Construction of a Memory About the Origins of the Encounter Between Yhwh and Israel," *IETP*, pp. 313–14; Andre Lemaire, *The Birth of Monotheism: The Rise and Disappearance of Yahwism* (Washington, DC: Biblical Archaeology Society, 2007), p. 23; William Propp, "The Exodus in History," *IETP*, p. 432.

3. William Propp, *Exodus 19–40*, p. 790.

4. Donald Redford, *Egypt, Canaan, and Israel in Ancient Times* (Princeton, NJ: Princeton University Press, 1992), p. 273.

5. Redford, *Egypt, Canaan, and Israel in Ancient Times*, p. 273.

6. Genesis 25:1. 1 Chronicles 1:32 identifies her as Abraham's concubine. Post-biblical rabbinic commentary sometimes asserts that Keturah and Hagar are the same person. See Rashi on this verse, citing Genesis Rabbah. This has no basis whatever. Ibn Ezra rejects it on textual grounds.

7. Genesis 25:2–4.

8. Genesis 37:28a, 36. In the J source, meanwhile, it is Ishmaelites who convey Joseph to Egypt; Genesis 37:25b–27, 28b; 39:1.

9. Appendix A, pp. 217–23.

10. Exodus 4:18.

11. Exodus 18:3. (The J text, in a doublet, gives the same explanation of the naming of Gershom in Exodus 2:22.)

12. Cross, *From Epic to Canon*, p. 61. A number of scholars have denied even the existence of E as a source. All of the evidence that I have listed that connects E with the Northern Kingdom of Israel and J with the Southern Kingdom of Judah argues plainly against this denial, as do the visible doublets between J and E (and between P and E) as well as the consistent matter of the revelation of the divine name. See Friedman, *WWTB*, pp. 61–88; *The Bible with Sources Revealed*, pp. 18–21, 29–30. Besides by Cross and by me, the verses I am discussing here are identified as E by J. E. Carpenter and G. Harford Battersby, p. 83; S. R. Driver, *An Introduction to the Literature of the Old Testament* (Gloucester: Peter Smith, 1972; original edition, 1891), p. 27; Martin Noth, *A History of Pentateuchal Traditions*, p. 36; R. Coote, *In Defense of Revolution: The Elohist History* (Minneapolis: Augsburg Fortress Press, 1991), p. 141; Propp, *Exodus 1–18*, p. 192; and J. Baden, *J, E, and the Redaction of the Pentateuch*, p. 234, n. 78.

13. Exodus 4:10.

14. Ezekiel 3:5–7.

15. Exodus 3:16.

16. Exodus 4:16.

17. Carol Meyers, *Exodus*, New Cambridge Bible Commentary (Cambridge: Cambridge University Press, 2005), p. 12.

18. R. E. Friedman, *WWTB*, pp. 85–86; *The Hidden Book in the Bible* (San Francisco: HarperSanFrancisco, 1998), pp. 51–52.

19. This is confirmed in the book of Ezekiel, the prophet who is also a priest from the same priestly house as the author of the Priestly source. See Ezekiel 20:5 (Römer, *IETP*, p. 312). On the relationship between P and Ezekiel, see *WWTB*, pp. 166–71; *The Bible with Sources Revealed*, pp. 15–17.

20. Regarding the plague, see *The Bible with Sources Revealed*, p. 288n., and *Commentary on the Torah*, comments on Numbers 8:19 and 25:8.

21. Baruch Halpern adds, "P's polemic against Midian can have had no relevance whatsoever in P's own time: the Midianite league disappeared at the end of the 12th century. . . . The only Midianites of which P could have known in Iron II were those in the background of the Mushite priesthoods" ("Kenites," *ABD*, vol. 4, p. 21).

22. This is treated in *WWTB*, especially pp. 188–204. See also above, Chapter 2, note 39. Many scholars do not accept the "Mushite" designation. For our present purposes, it is enough to recognize at minimum that, whether we call them Mushite, Shilonite, or just plain Levite, they are definitely not Aaronid. They are some other Levite group, and they look mainly to Moses, not Aaron, as their central figure.

23. Deuteronomy 1:2.

24. G. E. Mendenhall, "Midian," *ABD*, vol. 4, p. 816.

25. Graham Davies, "Was There an Exodus?" in John Day, ed., *In Search of Pre-exilic Israel* (London: Clark, 2004), p. 30.

26. Thomas Römer, *The Invention of God* (Cambridge, MA: Harvard University Press, 2015), pp. 69–70.

27. It is also known as the Kenite hypothesis. The Midianite-Kenite combination (or distinction) is extraordinarily complex. Numbers 10:29 identifies Hobab son of Reuel the Midianite as either Moses' father-in-law or brother-in-law. Judges 4:11 refers to Hobab, Moses' in-law, as a Kenite rather than as a Midianite, and Judges 1:16 also refers to Moses' in-law as a Kenite. For a thorough introduction to the arguments and alternatives, plus bibliography, see Baruch Halpern, "Kenites," *ABD*, vol. 4, pp. 20–22. See recently Joseph Blenkinsopp, "The Midianite-Kenite Hypothesis Revisited and the Origins of Judah," *Journal for the Study of the Old Testament* 33/2 (2008): 131–53. And see note 1 above.

28. See Habakkuk 3:3, 7; Psalm 68:7–8.

29. Lemaire, *The Birth of Monotheism*, pp. 21–23.

30. Sigmund Freud, *Moses and Monotheism*, trans. and ed. James Strachey (London: Hogarth Press, 1974); original German edition: *Der Mann Moses und die monotheistische Religion* (Amsterdam: Verlag Allert deLange, 1939).

31. William F. Albright, *From the Stone Age to Christianity*, 2nd ed. (Garden City, NY: Doubleday, 1957), p. 112. More recently, Aren Maeir wrote, "Even if Freud's *Moses and Monotheism* is a simplistic (and largely incorrect) interpretation of the el Amarna origins of Israelite monotheism . . ." (*IETP*, p. 415); and Brian Fagan wrote that the book "had no basis in historical fact" ("Did Akhenaten's Monotheism Influence Moses?," *Biblical Archaeology Review* [July/August 2015]: 49).

32. Propp adds another irony: "Ironically, compared to most biblical scholarship, Albright's position approaches Freud's relatively closely" (*Exodus 19–40*, p. 764, n. 7).

33. Freud, *Moses and Monotheism*, p. 9.

34. Freud listed many more. He credited Otto Rank for doing key research on this. *Moses and Monotheism*, pp. 10–12.

35. Jan Assman, *Moses the Egyptian* (Cambridge, MA: Harvard University Press, 1997), p. 150.

36. See Propp for a splendid summary of the possibilities on Aten and Israel's monotheism, *Exodus 19–40*, pp. 762–84, 793. For the letters themselves, see William L. Moran, *The Amarna Letters* (Baltimore: Johns Hopkins University Press, 1992). For helpful bibliography, see Donald Redford. "Akhenaten," *ABD*, vol. I, pp. 136–37.

37. Jan Assman, *Moses the Egyptian*, p. 148.

38. Donald Redford writes, "The parallels are to be taken seriously. There is, however, no literary influence here, but rather a survival in the tradition of the northern centers of Egypt's once-great empire of the *themes* of that magnificent poetic creation" (*Akhenaten the Heretic King* [Princeton, NJ: Princeton University Press, 1984], pp. 232–33). Miriam Lichtheim of the Hebrew University writes: "The resemblances are, however, more likely to be the result of the generic similarity between Egyptian hymns and biblical psalms. A specific literary interdependence is not probable" (*Ancient Egyptian Literature,* vol. 2, *The New Kingdom* [Berkeley: University of California Press, 2006], p. 100). Sirje Reichmann, *Bei Übernahme Korrektur? Aufnahme und Wandlung ägyptischer Tradition im Alten Testament anhand der Beispiele Proverbia 22–24 und Psalm 104*, Alter Orient und Altes Testament 428 (Münster: Ugarit-Verlag, 2016). James K. Hoffmeier gives all the verses from both texts that are thought to be parallel. He concludes, "Problems on the connection between the two pieces abound" (*Akhenaten and the Origins of Monotheism* [New York: Oxford University Press, 2015], pp. 247–48). Mark Smith gives a fair and thorough discussion of the scholarly treatment of the Hymn and Psalm 104 in *God in Translation: Deities in Cross-Cultural Discourse in the Biblical World* (Grand Rapids, MI: Eerdmans, 2010), pp. 69–76.

39. "The Hymn to the Aton," translated by John A. Wilson, appears in *ANET,* pp. 369–71; and in Victor Matthews and Don Benjamin, *Old Testament Parallels* (Mahwah, NJ: Paulist Press, 2006), pp. 275–79.

40. See Hoffmeier's discussion in "Is Atenism Monotheism?" in *Akhenaten and the Origins of Monotheism,* pp. 193–210.

41. Baruch Halpern writes, "Monotheism, in short, as the modern monotheist imagines it, was neither original to nor practiced in the historical Israel of the Bible," *From Gods to God* (Tübingen: Mohr Siebeck, 2009), p. 117.

42. Hoffmeier, *Akhenaten and the Origins of Monotheism,* pp. 245–46.

43. A recent example is Eckart Frahm, a professor of Assyriology at Yale. Frahm uncritically accepts an assumption by unnamed Bible scholars that the Joseph story was written later than Esarhaddon (who reigned from 681 to 669 BCE), and then he writes, "Even though there is no proof, these parallels suggest that the author(s) of the Joseph story borrowed a number of key motifs from the story of Esarhaddon's rise to power" ("'And His Brothers Were Jealous of Him': Surprising Parallels Between Joseph and King Esarhaddon," *Biblical Archaeology Review* 42/3 [May/June 2016]: 45). He does not address or even show awareness of all the evidence that both the J and the E versions of the Joseph story had to have been written before 722 BCE, when Judah and Israel were two separate kingdoms, long *before* Esarhaddon. And so he arrives at the unjustified conclusion that the Bible's authors "borrowed" from Assyria.

44. Henri Frankfort et al., *The Intellectual Adventure of Ancient Man* (Chicago:

University of Chicago Press, 1946); Yehezkel Kaufmann, *The Religion of Israel,* translated and abridged by Moshe Greenberg (Chicago: University of Chicago Press, 1960); G. Ernest Wright, *The Old Testament Against Its Environment* (London: SCM, 1950).

45. G. Ernest Wright, *God Who Acts* (London: SCM, 1952), p. 43.

46. Kaufmann, *The Religion of Israel,* p. 224.

47. See above, Chapter 2, note 48. The very name *yiśrā-'ēl* may mean "May El rule." The Genesis story understands it differently (something like "he struggles with El"), but whatever its precise meaning, "the name is clearly non-Yahwistic and presupposes a time when the population worshipped God as El." (R. A. Mullins, *IETP,* p. 523; see also Mark Smith, *The Early History of God,* 2nd ed. [Grand Rapids, MI: Eerdmans, 2002], p. 32).

CHAPTER FIVE

The Mysteries of Babylon

1. Exodus 15:11.

2. Genesis 1:26.

3. Job 1:6; 2:1.

4. Exodus 20:3; Deuteronomy 5:7.

5. "A text commonly dated to the pre-monarchic era." Baruch Halpern, *From Gods to God* (Tübingen: Mohr Siebeck, 2009), p. 26; Shalom Paul, *Studies in the Book of the Covenant in the Light of Cuneiform and Biblical Law* (Leiden: Brill, 1970).

6. The bibliography on First, Second, and a possible Third Isaiah is now vast. For an introduction and bibliography, the *Anchor Bible Dictionary* entry on Isaiah is divided into respective sections, each with bibliography, authored by Christopher Seitz, William Millar, and Richard Clifford (vol. 3, pp. 472–507). The most compelling treatment of the composition and redaction of Isaiah that I have seen is by H. G. M. Williamson, Regius Professor of Hebrew Emeritus at Oxford, *The Book Called Isaiah* (Oxford: Oxford University Press, 2005). The Anchor Bible commentary series includes both a *Second Isaiah* volume by John L. McKenzie (1969), and a three-volume treatment by Joseph Blenkinsopp: *Isaiah 1–39* (2000), *Isaiah 40–55* (2002), and *Isaiah 56–66* (2003). Other commentaries on Second Isaiah include Shalom Paul, *Isaiah 40–66: A Commentary* (Grand Rapids, MI: Eerdmans, 2012), which rejects the need for a Third Isaiah; and Walter Brueggemann, *Isaiah 40–66* (Lexington, KY: Westminster John Knox, 1998), who writes of both a Second and Third Isaiah. Paul Hanson, *Isaiah 40–66* (Lexington, KY: Westminster John Knox, 2012), explicitly divides his commentary between a Second and Third Isaiah.

7. Tryggve Mettinger, *In Search of God: The Meaning and Message of the Everlasting Names* (Philadelphia: Fortress, 1988; original Swedish edition, 1987), p. 42, cites this passage from Isaiah and quotes the equivalent passages in Deuteronomy 4:35 and 39 and 1 Kings 8:60 and says, "We later find the same idea in the writings of the exilic Prophet of Consolation (Isa 45:21–22)."

8. Paul Hanson writes, "With these magisterial words monotheism enters the disarray of a world long mired in the confusion of contentious gods" (*Isaiah 40–66,* p. 69).

9. John F. Kutsko, *Between Heaven and Earth: Divine Presence and Absence in the Book of Ezekiel* (Winona Lake, IN: Eisenbrauns, 2000), p. 37, affirms that scholars have most commonly identified Deutero-Isaiah as the first monotheistic voice; Brent Strawn, "Commentary on Isaiah 44:6–8," https://www.workingpreacher.org /preaching.aspx?commentary_id=990https://www.workingpreacher.org/preaching .aspx?commentary_id=990. Cf. Mark Smith, *The Origins of Biblical Monotheism* (New York: Oxford University Press, 2001), p. 181.

10. Frank Cross and David Noel Freedman, *Studies in Ancient Yahwistic Poetry,* 2nd ed. (Grand Rapids, MI: Eerdmans, 1997), p. 85.

11. In this case, interestingly, Cross dated it later than the others, "not earlier than the ninth century" BCE. Cross, *Canaanite Myth and Hebrew Epic* (Cambridge, MA: Harvard University Press, 1973), p. 264n. Cross acknowledges strong arguments by Eissfeldt and Albright for the eleventh century BCE.

12. Freedman, *Pottery, Poetry, and Prophecy* (Winona Lake, IN: Eisenbrauns, 1980), pp. 100–101 and citations of other views on p. 123n. In my own work I observed that this Song of Moses was quoted and used by a writer whom we call the Deuteronomistic historian in an edition of his history that he composed in the very early years of the Babylonian exile—so the song had to be composed before that time. See R. E. Friedman, *The Bible with Sources Revealed* (San Francisco: HarperSanFrancisco, 2003), p. 360n.; "From Egypt to Egypt: Dtr1 and Dtr2," in B. Halpern and J. Levenson, eds., *Traditions in Transformation* (Winona Lake, IN: Eisenbrauns, 1981), pp. 178–79. See also Paul Sanders, *The Provenance of the Song in Deuteronomy 32* (Leiden: Brill, 1996); he provides a survey of scholarship on the provenance of the song; he concludes that a pre-exilic date is extremely likely for the song in its entirety. Likewise see George Ernest Wright, "The Lawsuit of God: A Form-Critical Study of Deuteronomy 32," in B. Anderson and W. Harrelson, eds., *Israel's Prophetic Heritage* (New York: Harper, 1962).

13. Matthew Thiessen, "The Form and Function of the Song of Moses (Deuteronomy 32:1–43)," *Journal of Biblical Literature* 123 (2004): 423; William Holladay, "Jeremiah and Moses: Further Observations," *Journal of Biblical Literature* 85 (1966): 17–27.

14. Much of the book of Deuteronomy has signs of coming from Judah in the reign of King Josiah (640–609 BCE). Following the terminology of Frank Cross, others and I use the term Dtr1 for the sections we trace to Josiah's reign. Other scholars have used other terms, and we have seen many different proposals and dating for the Deuteronomic text. I acknowledge that there are those among my colleagues who date it later. So I will just say here that at minimum, according to the Bible's own report, this text was found at the Jerusalem Temple during Josiah's reign, so this is a case where both pious and many critical readers of the Bible can agree on at least this much: the portions of the Bible under discussion here come from not later than King Josiah's time. For those who date them later, these portions do not apply one way or another to dating monotheism.

15. Martin Noth, *The Deuteronomistic History,* trans. J. Doull (Sheffield: JSOT, 1981); original German edition, *Überlieferungsgeschichtliche Studien* (Tubingen: Max Niemeyer, 1943); Frank Moore Cross, *Canaanite Myth and Hebrew Epic* (Cambridge, MA: Harvard University Press, 1973), pp. 274–89; Baruch Halpern, *The First Historians* (San Francisco: Harper & Row, 1988), especially pp. 114, 120 n. 19; R. E. Friedman, "The Deuteronomistic School," in Astrid Beck et al., eds., *Fortunate the*

Eyes That See; David Noel Freedman, *Festschrift* (Grand Rapids, MI: Eerdmans, 1995), pp. 70–80; Friedman, *The Exile and Biblical Narrative,* Harvard Semitic Monographs (Atlanta: Scholars Press, 1981); Richard Nelson, *The Double Redaction of the Deuteronomistic History* (Sheffield: JSOT Supplement Series, 1981); Moshe Weinfeld, *Deuteronomy and the Deuteronomic School* (Oxford: Clarendon, 1972); Hans Walter Wolff, "Das Kerygma des deuteronomistischen Geschichtswerks," *Zeitschrift für die alttestamentliche Wissenschaft* 73 (1961): 171–86; Iain Provan, *Hezekiah and the Books of Kings: A Contribution to the Debate About the Composition of the Deuteronomistic History,* Beihefte zur Zeitschrift für die alttestamentliche Wissenschaft 172 (Berlin: de Gruyter, 1988); David Noel Freedman, "The Deuteronomistic History," in Freedman, *Divine Commitment and Human Obligation* (Grand Rapids, MI: Eerdmans, 1997), vol. 1, pp. 279–85; Helga Weippert, "Die 'deuteronomistischen' Beurteilungen der Könige von Israel und Juda und das Problem der Redaktion der Königsbücher," *Biblica* 53 (1972): 301–9.

16. These words also appear in the source of the Chronicler in 1 Chronicles 17:20.

17. The story of Elijah at Carmel does not contain the many terms and phrases that are visibly characteristic of the Deuteronomist's own writing.

18. William Propp, *Exodus 19–40,* p. 777.

19. In J, E, P, and Dtr1 at the very least. See below.

20. Exodus 20:3; Deuteronomy 5:7.

21. Genesis 9:6; Numbers 35:33; 2 Kings 21:16; 24:4; Ezekiel 22:27.

22. 2 Kings 18:4; 23:8, 15, 19–20; 2 Chronicles 31:1; 34:3.

23. R. F. Friedman, "Late for a Very Important Date," *Bible Review* 9/6 (1993): 12–16; "Some Recent Non-arguments Concerning the Documentary Hypothesis," in Michael Fox et al., eds., *Texts, Temples, and Traditions,* Menahem Haran *Festschrift* (Winona Lake, IN: Eisenbrauns, 1996), pp. 87–101; *The Hidden Book in the Bible* (San Francisco: HarperSanFrancisco, 1998), pp. 361–78; "Solomon and the Great Histories," in Ann Killebrew and Andrew Vaughn, eds., *Jerusalem in Bible and Archaeology: The First Temple Period* (Atlanta: Society of Biblical Literature, 2003); "An Essay on Method," in Richard Elliott Friedman and William Henry Propp, eds., *Le-David Maskil,* Biblical and Judaic Studies from the University of California, San Diego (Winona Lake, IN: Eisenbrauns, 2003), pp. 7–8; "Response to Lemche's 'Writing Israel out of the History of Palestine,'" in *The Bible and Interpretation,* http://www.bibleinterp.com/articles/fri368024.shtml. And see the collection of essays in John Day, ed., *In Search of Pre-exilic Israel,* JSOT Supplement Series 406 (London: Clark, 2004).

24. See Chapter 2, note 97, and Chapter 3, note 43.

25. Ronald Hendel, review of D. Edelman and E. Ben Zvi, eds., *Memory and the City in Ancient Israel* (Winona Lake, IN: Eisenbrauns, 2014), *Review of Biblical Literature,* April 21, 2014, http://www.bookreviews.org.

26. Exodus 1:5.

27. So Rashi. See his comment on Deuteronomy 32:8.

28. Israel Knohl, "Nimrod Son of Cush, King of Mesopotamia, and the Dates of P and J," in Chaim Cohen, V. A. Hurowitz, et al., eds., *Birkat Shalom, Shalom Paul Jubilee Volume* (Winona Lake, IN: Eisenbrauns, 2008), pp. 45–52.

29. The Masoretic Text says seventy. The Septuagint and the Qumran (Dead Sea Scrolls) texts say seventy-five.

30. David Noel Freedman, "Introduction to the Leningrad Codex," in *The Leningrad Codex: A Facsimile Edition* (Grand Rapids, MI: Eerdmans; Leiden: Brill, 1998); Emanuel Tov, *Textual Criticism of the Hebrew Bible* (Minneapolis: Fortress, 1992).

31. Scroll 4QDeut^j.

32. Genesis 6:2, 4; Job 1:6; 2:1; 38:7. See also the variant *bĕnê 'ēlîm* in Psalms 29:1 and 89:7.

33. Thus Deuteronomy 29:25 (Dtr2) says, "They went and served other gods and bowed to them, gods whom they had not known *and He had not allocated to them*." This, too, is consistent with Deuteronomy 32 ("When the Highest gave nations legacies . . .").

34. On the methods and standards of doing responsible textual criticism of the Hebrew Bible, especially in poetry, see Emanuel Tov, *Textual Criticism of the Hebrew Bible*; P. Kyle McCarter, *Textual Criticism* (Guides to Biblical Scholarship Old Testament Series) (Minneapolis: Augsburg Fortress, 2001); Frank Moore Cross, *The Ancient Library of Qumran and Modern Biblical Studies* (Westport, CT: Greenwood, 1976); Theodore Lewis, "The Textual History of the Song of Hannah: 1 Samuel II 1–10," *Vetus Testamentum* 44 (1994): 18–46; and the important collection of essays in Frank Moore Cross and Shemaryahu Talmon, eds., *Qumran and the History of the Biblical Text* (Cambridge, MA: Harvard University Press, 1975). For a good demonstration of the practice of textual criticism plus a helpful bibliography of works, see Ronald Hendel, *The Text of Genesis 1–11: Textual Studies and Critical Edition* (New York: Oxford University Press, 1998).

35. The full verse says: "And the sons of the gods came to stand before Yahweh, and the *satan* also came among them." That can mean that the *satan* is one of the gods or that the *satan* is not a god itself but it comes and is present with the gods on this occasion. It is hard, perhaps impossible, to say. It makes quite a difference. If the *satan* is a god, then we should understand it, in Israel's theology or mythology, to be dead, like all the other gods. But if the *satan* is not a god, then in that mythology it could still be alive.

The *satan* makes few appearances in the Hebrew Bible. Only later in Judaism and Christianity did people come to see it as a specific person, and the word *satan* became a proper name of that person, Satan. In the Hebrew Bible the word is preceded by the definite article *the,* like *the* Asherah and *the* Baal, except in 1 Chronicles 21:1; but there it can mean "a *satan*," not a proper name, and the picture is further muddied by the fact that the equivalent passage in 2 Samuel 24:1 says Yahweh instead of *satan*. The *satan* is not its name. The *satan* is what this being *is*. We commonly understand the term to mean "the adversary" or "the accuser." We derive this meaning from what the *satan* does in the few instances where it occurs. The most famous occurrence is here in the book of Job, where it accuses/criticizes/hurts Job.

We could compare the other, most similar, case where the satan figures, which is in Zechariah 3:1–2. We should be cautious because there it is in a vision that the prophet Zechariah has, while in Job it is pictured as an actually occurring event. But in any case, in Zechariah's vision Yahweh reprimands the satan. Again it is not clear what the satan is. At this late point in Israel's history (about five hundred years after the exodus), we would expect that all of the gods have already died, but we cannot be sure of that. And in any case, it is only a vision, so, as in a dream, persons and events from different times can be mixed. These cases are treated in Peggy Day,

An Adversary in Heaven: "Satan" in the Hebrew Bible, Harvard Semitic Monographs 43 (Atlanta: Scholars Press, 1988); and in Victor Hamilton, "Satan," *ABD,* vol. 5, pp. 985–89.

36. C. L. Seow's recent commentary on Job, which is well regarded, translated it as "divine beings" (*Job 1–21: Interpretation and Commentary* [Grand Rapids, MI: Eerdmans, 2013], pp. 249, 290).

37. Marvin Pope, *Job,* The Anchor Bible (New York: Doubleday, 1965), pp. 1, 9.

38. Deuteronomy 34:5. These texts are in the J source. In the P source and in the Book of Records, much longer lives are attributed to people in the early generations of humans.

39. See note 48 below.

40. A recent summary appears in John Day, *From Creation to Babel: Studies in Genesis 1–11* (Bloomsbury: T&T Clark, 2014), pp. 11–12.

41. Theodore Hiebert, "The Tower of Babel and the Origin of the World's Cultures," *Journal of Biblical Literature* 126 (2007): 29–58. Hiebert writes that in its context "it is a foundational part of the theme of cultural differentiation" (p. 53). In noting "God's call to the divine council to put an end to homogeneity," Hiebert brings together the deity's plural address and the dispersal of humankind (pp. 46–47).

42. The first text (Genesis 10:32) comes from the P source. The second (Genesis 11:9) comes from the J source. That is, two different authors both had the dispersal of humans take place at this point, and both never had God speak in the plural again after this point.

43. Gerhard Von Rad, *Genesis* (Philadelphia: Westminster, 1961), p. 145; original German edition, *Das erste Buch Mose, Genesis* (Göttingen: Vandenhoeck & Ruprecht, 1956).

44. William Propp makes this connection in his *Exodus 1–18,* p. 400.

45. And in my reckoning, J and P were both composed long before the exile, which provides us with two more major texts that are monotheistic before the Babylonian exile.

46. Ezekiel 14:14, 20.

47. Moshe Greenberg, *Ezekiel 1–20,* The Anchor Bible (Garden City, NY: Doubleday, 1983), pp. 257–58.

48. Peter Machinist, "How Gods Die, Biblically and Otherwise: A Problem of Cosmic Restructuring," in Beate Pongratz-Leisten, ed., *Reconsidering the Concept of Revolutionary Monotheism* (Winona Lake, IN: Eisenbrauns, 2011), p. 190.

49. Many books by competent, well-respected scholars treat Genesis 1–11 without making this connection. John Day, *Creation to Babel;* Gordon Wenham, *Rethinking Genesis 1–11: Gateway to the Bible* (Eugene, OR: Cascade, 2015); Joseph Blenkinsopp, *Creation, Un-creation, Re-creation: A Discursive Commentary on Genesis 1–11* (Bloomsbury: T&T Clark, 2011).

50. Machinist, "How Gods Die," p. 189.

51. Mark Smith, "The Death of 'Dying and Rising Gods' in the Biblical World: An Update, with Special Reference to Baal in the Baal Cycle," *Scandinavian Journal of the Old Testament* 12/2 (1998): 257–313.

52. The development of Akhenaten's monotheism includes a striking parallel. Donald Redford writes of an early speech "in which Akhenaten introduces his god to the court. Therein he describes his celestial deity in terms of uniqueness, transcendence, and permanence that were to become common throughout the reign,

while at the same time accusing the gods of having 'ceased one after the other'" ("Akhenaten," *ABD*, vol. 1, p. 135); "A Royal Speech from the Blocks of the 10th Pylon," *Bulletin of the Egyptological Seminar* 3 (1981): 87ff; *Akhenaten the Heretic King* (Princeton, NJ: Princeton University Press, 1984), p. 172.

53. As noted above, it is also called the tower of Babel. Babel and Babylon are the same word in Hebrew. It is only English translators who created a distinction between the two.

54. Some might ask here, but doesn't God speak to angels as well? The complex answer is that angels in the Hebrew Bible are not independent beings. They are manifestations (the technical term is hypostases) of God. This is treated in my *Disappearance of God* (published in paperback under the title *The Hidden Face of God* [San Francisco: HarperSanFrancisco, 1996]), pp. 9–13. The simpler answer is that God does not in fact ever speak to an angel in any of these texts. God rather speaks *through* angels sometimes.

55. Jeremiah 7:18.

56. William Dever, *Did God Have a Wife? Archaeology and Folk Religion in Ancient Israel* (Grand Rapids, MI: Eerdmans, 2005); Ze'ev Meshel, "Kuntillet 'Ajrud: An Israelite Religious Center in Northern Sinai" (Jerusalem: Israel Museum, 1978), http://www.penn.museum/documents/publications/expedition/pdfs/20-4/meshel.pdf.; Ziony Zevit, *The Religions of Ancient Israel*, p. 654.

57. Baruch Halpern, "The Baal (and the Asherah) in 7th-Century Judah: Yahweh's Retainers Retired," in Halpern, *From Gods to God*, pp. 57–97 (originally published in 1993). The term "Baal" is likewise a generic, normally preceded by the definite article, not the name of a particular male deity. John Day claims that the discovery of the Ugaritic texts, which have a divine consort named Athirat, lead us to understand Asherah to be a name, equivalent to Athirat (*Yahweh and the Gods and Goddesses of Canaan* [London: Sheffield Academic, 2000], pp. 42ff). He does not defend this connection, and he does not cite Halpern's solid case establishing the opposite, that Asherah is not a goddess's name, even though Halpern's treatment had first appeared in 1993. Day insists that "the fact that Asherah frequently has the definite article in Hebrew does not matter, since we likewise find Baal referred to regularly as 'the Baal' in the Old Testament." The definite article matters in the case of the Baal, and it definitely matters in the case of the Asherah. Even the cases where the word occurs in plural, "Asherot" (see Judges 3:7) do not dissuade Day, who says that the parallel with the plural of Baal there "makes it undeniable" that it refers to a divine name. The occurrences of the word Asherah with a definite article, in plurals, and with a pronominal suffix ("His Asherah") rather make the opposite conclusion undeniable. Also supporting this conclusion is the absence of Asherah in personal names as opposed to other names of goddesses. André Lemaire makes all of these points and firmly establishes that Asherah is a common noun, not the name of a goddess, in *The Birth of Monotheism: The Rise and Disappearance of Yahwism* (2007), pp. 57–62. I would list the many scholars who have treated Asherah as the name of a particular goddess, but I would have to include myself. I later became persuaded otherwise by the works of Lemaire and Halpern.

58. 1 Kings 18:19.

59. David Noel Freedman, "Yahweh of Samaria and His Asherah," *Biblical Archaeologist* (December 1987): 241–49; Ziony Zevit, *The Religions of Ancient Israel*, p. 652.

60. See, for example, the book of Hosea 2:21–22.

61. William Dever, *Did God Have a Wife? Archaeology and Folk Religion in Ancient Israel;* Saul M. Olyan, *Asherah and the Cult of Yahweh in Israel,* Society of Biblical Literature Monograph Series (Atlanta: Scholars Press, 1988); Judith M. Hadley, *The Cult of Asherah in Ancient Israel and Judah: Evidence for a Hebrew Goddess* (Cambridge: Cambridge University Press, 2000); Mark Smith, *Origins of Biblical Monotheism: Israel's Polytheistic Background and the Ugaritic Texts* (New York: Oxford University Press, 2001); Susan Ackerman, "Goddesses," in Suzanne Richard, ed., *Near Eastern Archaeology: A Reader* (Winona Lake, IN: Eisenbrauns, 2003), pp. 393–97.

62. 1 Kings 16:32–33; 2 Kings 13:6.

63. 1 Kings 15:13; 2 Chronicles 15:16.

64. 2 Kings 18:4.

65. 2 Kings 21:3, 7.

66. The Wadi Kidron. 2 Kings 23:6. Some of these reports sound similar to one another, and the matter of the Deuteronomistic historian's sources is a complex one. But at the least, the account of Josiah is likely to have been written very close to his reign (probably during it) since it appears to be part of the Josianic edition of the Deuteronomistic history (Dtr1). See this chapter, note 15.

67. Richard Dawkins, *The God Delusion* (New York: Houghton Mifflin, 2006); Christopher Hitchens, *God Is Not Great: How Religion Poisons Everything* (New York: Twelve, 2007).

CHAPTER SIX
The Mystery of Judah

1. Leviticus 19:18.

2. We differ on authorship as well. I trace this to the Priestly law code (P). Many scholars separate the Priestly text into a Priestly code and a Holiness code (H). This goes back to the nineteenth century CE and Wellhausen, but most prominent among recent Holiness code (or even Holiness School) scholars are Israel Knohl, *The Sanctuary of Silence: The Priestly Torah and the Holiness School* (Minneapolis: Fortress, 1995), and Jacob Milgrom, *Leviticus,* The Anchor Bible (New York: Doubleday, 1991–2001), 3 vols. I've said it before and I'll say it again: I see no evidence for the division into two sources, H and P. Friedman, *WWTB*, p. 172; *The Bible with Sources Revealed*, pp. 218, 296–97.

3. Mark 12:31.

4. Recall that we saw in Chapter 2 that the word for a sanctuary, *miqdash,* happens to occur fifty-two times as well, but that was in the entire Hebrew Bible. The treatment of aliens occurs fifty-two times in the Five Books of Moses alone! See Chapter 2, note 22.

5. See above, pp. 63–64. William Propp, *Exodus 1–18,* p. 128.

6. The italics are mine. Review by Glen A. Taylor of Jack Lundbom, *Deuteronomy: A Commentary* (Grand Rapids, MI: Eerdmans, 2013), http://www.bookreviews .org/pdf/9357_10328.pdf.

7. See the citation of Halpern above in Chapter 4, note 21.

8. Deuteronomy 20:10–15. Likewise, Israel is pictured as sending words of peace when asking to pass through King Sihon's land (Deuteronomy 2:26–29).

9. Deuteronomy 12:31; 18:9–14.

10. I understand this story to be part of a history of the Northern Kingdom of Israel, a text that was used as a source by the Deuteronomistic historian in composing his history.

11. That is the explanation of Rashi on Genesis 12:3 and 25:4.

12. It occurs in both the Niphal and Hithpael. Some people are taught that the Hithpael is reflexive and the Niphal passive. But that is a simplification that is sometimes made when one is first learning Biblical Hebrew, but one finds after reading enough texts that this dichotomy does not hold up. The two conjugations have an overlapping range of meaning. See Thomas O. Lambdin, *Introduction to Biblical Hebrew* (New York: Scribner, 1971), pp. 176–77.

13. Leviticus 19:18, 33–34.

14. Jacob Milgrom, *Leviticus 17–22*, The Anchor Bible 3A (New York: Doubleday, 2000), p. 1654; and see bibliography there.

15. Genesis 38:12, 20.

16. Exodus 11:2.

17. Exodus 2:13.

18. 2 Samuel 11–12.

19. Harry Orlinsky, *Essays in Biblical Culture and Bible Translation* (New York: Ktav, 1974), p. 83.

20. Wright, *The Evolution of God* (New York: Little, Brown, 2009), pp. 235–36.

21. Hector Avalos, *Fighting Words: The Origins of Religious Violence* (Amherst, NY: Prometheus, 2005), p. 140.

22. John Hartung, "Love Thy Neighbor: The Evolution of In-Group Morality," http://strugglesforexistence.com/?p=article_p&id=13. Likewise, most recently, Dan Barker makes this classic mistake in *God: The Most Unpleasant Character in All Fiction* (New York: Sterling, 2016), p. 300.

23. Dawkins, *The God Delusion*, p. 253.

APPENDIX A

From Egypt to Midian

1. The explanation of how I distinguish these source texts and determine that they are E, J, or P may be found in *WWTB;* in *The Bible with Sources Revealed,* pp. 119–26; and with especially detailed analysis in William Propp, *Exodus 1–18,* pp. 125–94. The distinction of the J text from E and P is particularly explained in my *Hidden Book in the Bible.* The most recent delineation of the sources is in two books by Joel Baden. On the positive side, Baden defends the existence of the E source against those who have denied it. On the negative side, Baden reverses much of the source identification of J and E in the section treated here and in the entire plagues text that follows. The evidence of language collected in *The Hidden Book in the Bible* is contrary to Baden's re-identification of E texts as J, but Baden does not cite or deal with this evidence. The E texts that he calls J are entirely lacking all fifty of the terms that are characteristic of the J source and its related texts (*The Hidden Book in the Bible,* pp. 379–87). The identification of those J texts is further confirmed by two studies that had come to the same conclusion about J and its related texts independently: Hannelis Schulte, *Die Entstehung der Gerschichtsschreibung*

im alten Israel, published in *Beihefte zur Zeitschrift für die alttestamentliche Wissenschaft* 128 (Berlin: De Gruyter, 1972); and Clarimond Mansfield, *The Book of Yahweh* (Boston: Cornhill, 1922). Both Friedman's and Schulte's work are discussed by John Barton, "Dating the 'Succession Narrative,'" in John Day, ed., *In Search of Pre-exilic Israel* (London: T&T Clark, 2004), pp. 100–104. It is also affirmed, with additional evidence brought, by David Noel Freedman, in "Dinah and Shechem, Amnon and Tamar," in Freedman, *Divine Commitment and Human Obligation* (Grand Rapids, MI: Eerdmans, 1997), pp. 485–95.

The distinctions between E and J are difficult in these early chapters of Exodus, and there have been many different proposals over the years. Though I am confident of my identifications, which are bolstered by Propp's, which are extremely similar though we arrived at them independently, I am obligated to inform the reader of this complex history.

At minimum, though, there is agreement on the crucial first verse of Exodus 3, in which the story of God's first revelation to Moses in Midian begins. Baden, like Propp and me, recognizes that this initiation of Moses must be from the source E. So do Carpenter and Harford-Battersby, pp. 82–83; S. R. Driver, p. 27; Robert Coote, *In Defense of Revolution: The Elohist History* (Minneapolis: Fortress, 1991), p. 141; Alan Jenks, "Elohist," *ABD,* vol. 2, p. 480; and Cross, *From Epic to Canon,* pp. 60–61. Of the standard scholarly works, only Martin Noth does not attribute this verse to E. Strangely, he recognizes the problem of the name Jethro, which is a well-known mark of E, in the verse (p. 183n.), and he attributes the last quarter of the verse to E (p. 203n.), but he still calls the verse part of "an addition in J" (p. 30n.).

❧ INDEX ❧

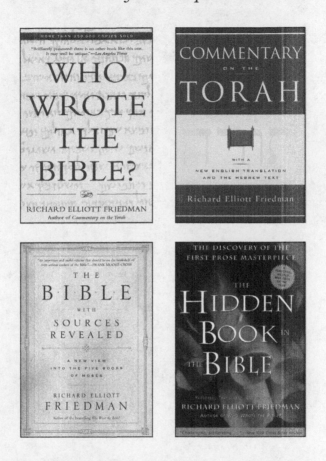